Confronting the Politics of Gridlock
Revisiting the Founding Visions in Search of Solutions

Books by Steven O. Ludd

Confronting the Politics of Gridlock
Revisiting the Founding Visions
in Search of Solutions

Reflections Off the Lake
Poems on Life, Love, and Democracy

Walking the Property Line
Messages from Nature's Sanctuary

Confronting the Politics of Gridlock
Revisiting the Founding Visions in Search of Solutions

2nd Edition

Steven O. Ludd

Distinction Press
Waitsfield, Vermont

Confronting the Politics of Gridlock: Revisiting the Founding Visions in Search of Solutions

Distinction Press
354 Hastings Rd
Waitsfield, Vermont 05673-7117

ISBN 978-1-937667-39-9 tradepaper
ISBN 978-1-937667-38-2 hardcover

Printed in the United States of America

Publisher's Cataloging-In-Publication Data
(Prepared by The Donohue Group, Inc.)

Ludd, Steven O.
   Confronting the politics of gridlock : revisiting the founding visions in search of solutions / Steven O. Ludd.

   pages : illustrations ; cm

   Issued also as an ebook.
   Includes bibliographical references and index.
   ISBN: 978-1-937667-38-2 (hardcover)
   ISBN: 978-1-937667-39-9 (paperback)

1. Political participation--United States. 2. United States--Politics and government--Philosophy. 3. United States--Politics and government--21st century. 4. Constitutional history--United States. 5. Founding Fathers of the United States. 6. Political leadership--United States. 7. Compromise (Ethics) I. Title.

JK1764 .L84 2014

323/.042/0973

To my Son

James Madison, President of the United States
engraving done between 1809 and 1817

"Justice is the end of government. It is the end of civil society. It ever has been and ever will be pursued until it is obtained, or until liberty be lost in the pursuit. In a society under the forms which the stronger faction can readily unite and oppress the weaker, anarchy may as truly be said to reign as in a state of nature, where the weaker individual is not secured against the violence of the stronger, and as, in the latter state, even the stronger individuals are prompted, by the uncertainty of their condition, to submit to a government which may protect the weak as well as themselves, so in the former state, will the more powerful faction or parties be gradually induced, by a like motive, to wish for a government which will protect *all* parties, the weaker as well as the more powerful…"

— *James Madison*, Federalist Papers, no. 51

Scene at the Signing of the Constitution of the United States
Painting by Howard Chandler Christy

Contents

Benjamin Franklin
Copy of painting by Joseph Duplessis, circa 1794–1802

Preface

WHILE OVER A DECADE HAS PASSED since the publication of this book, its central thesis and many of its recommendations remain essential if we are to overcome the chaos now being experienced by the country. As we approach the two-hundred-and-fifty-year anniversary of our Founding, nothing is more important for the protection of our democratic institutions than an understanding of both the fears and aspirations of those who risked their lives to provide generations of their countrymen and women with a future which would secure their liberties and yet provide for the public welfare.

It is not hyperbole to suggest that the Founders fear of concentrated power residing in the hands of a few and the destructive nature of "factions" manipulating our political process has now become a reality in American governance. We are at a tipping point in our history. If we are to preserve the liberties for which so many have made the ultimate sacrifice, we must heed the warnings of Madison, Hamilton, Jefferson, and Franklin. They, like us all, were imperfect human beings. Yet, their understanding of the human condition, led them to create a compact with each other which would minimize the potentiality of tyranny by constantly monitoring the excesses of governmental decision-making at the local, state, and federal levels. While the establishment of institutions of government, separating power between legislative, executive and judicial branches were established to assist in this oversight, the ultimate responsibility of oversight was left to the American people. The question remains—are we up to the task? Or, have we become so divided that we are incapable of finding common ground in an effort to preserve a future filled with possibilities for our children and tomorrow's children?

The Founders provided us with a compass by which to navigate the storm created by oligarchical rule. But, as this book has suggested, it requires us to call out government overreach instituted by the legislative, executive, or judicial branches of our government. Whether it is Executive Orders which trample on the fundamental rights of citizens and usurp the powers of the Legislative branch, or the Legislative branch instituting tax schemes which benefit only the top one percent of the country, or the Judicial branch overturning a half century of protections of personal autonomy privacy rights and providing what appears to be absolute immunity to the actions of Presidents placing them above the law, this book offers recommendations for future citizen involvement.

As suggested in the book, the Fourth Estate—the monopolistic mass media owned by a few oligarchs—has seemingly abdicated its responsibility to provide the public with investigative journalism and replaced it with pablum like "news", leaving the search for objective information so essential for citizen oversight to social media platforms sometimes funded by America's economic and political adversaries. Indeed, the search for profits throughout this essential guardrail of American democracy in the new digital information age may have rendered it more impotent than has been observed in over fifty years. Instead, too often the public is left with one-line sound bites concerning complex economic and political issues which drive the public to "entertainment journalism" for their news of the day. Our investigation of the mass media and the ownership conglomerates of 2014, inferred that political transparency offered by traditional sources of journalism protected by the First Amendment of our Bill of Rights was at risk of failing to fulfill their responsibilities to the American people. Thomas Jefferson recognized that Franklin's fear of our responsibility to protect our Republic would never be achieved if we did not establish an "enlightened citizenry". The call for a robust independent free press which was at risk and noted in 2014, remains one of the last guardrails of our democracy. The risk remains real in 2025.

The good news is that the importance of our Constitution and its Bill of Rights has taken on even more interest in American life. Regardless of one's political preferences it remains a guide post by which we can find resolution to some of our most divisive issues. But we need to understand the fears of the Founders and monitor those whom we have placed in positions of the public trust. The need to eradicate insider trading and reduce the impact of political lobbying by monied interests throughout our legislative process at both the state and federal levels and the necessity of overturning the disastrous impact of Citizens United by the Supreme Court are but two of the most important flash points to be addressed by We the People.

It may be that the following poem has relevancy as we continue to fight to preserve the Constitution and our Bill of Rights.

Saratoga Springs, New York
May 8, 2025

America

My sweet country where have you gone?
The drums roll, the bugle plays, the sunlight dims.
The whimpering sounds of your citizens fill the air.
Oh, Land of Liberty and Light
Beware the horses ride tonight.
In the distant horizon they can be seen –
Rising ever constantly coming to overtake Thee.

Rise up to meet them with the same defiance you displayed
At Bunker Hill and during the Battle of the Bulge.
Stand and be counted Brothers and Sisters.
This is the time.
Dig deep and resurrect the virtue
That you possessed throughout the years.
Set your sorrows aside and unite once again
As we become Children of Light.
Fight!!
Bring your sword and your shield.
But most of all, bring the Truth.
Confront the Darkness with compassion and empathy.
Expose the Oligarchs – the Puppeteers stoking fear
Amongst the citizenry with propaganda and hate.
Beware – the battlefield has changed.
No longer is the enemy only from without but
It is also from within.

Packaged now by faceless technocrats
Little men – behind computer screens
Constantly manipulating the unsuspecting masses
With beautiful images and promises of unsubstantiated claims.
Understand that the battle will not be won overnight.
It begins with the children who must be taught
That love will overcome hate.
And that generations of their countrymen and women
Have been left behind.
That much can be learned by listening
To their grievances and understand their pain.
Remain engaged. The task is clear.
Freedom will be won
When we overcome
Our fear.

Steven O. Ludd
From: IN BETWEEN YESTERDAY AND TOMORROW
A forthcoming book of poems
Saratoga Springs, New York
May 8, 2025

Author's Note

FOR THIRTY YEARS IT WAS MY privilege to challenge and be challenged by undergraduate and graduate students in the university classroom. Most frequently our interactions began there but often evolved into discussions outside of that setting where I was asked to assist them in finding methods by which to apply the theories underpinning our Constitution and American Government to the public policy issues impacting their lives. Regardless of the successes or failures of the innumerable projects instituted over three decades in response to their requests, one element was constantly present—their belief that they could "make a difference." Whether they chose to become lawyers, politicians, entrepreneurs, teachers, enter the armed forces, or serve as public administrators in a variety of local, state, and federal administrative agencies, their life choices were grounded to some degree in a commitment to the aspirational values reflected in the design and implementation of our system of rules. Their out of the classroom involvement in one public policy issue or another only served to remind them of the difficulty that the Founders confronted in finding political compromise and the necessity of balancing sometimes competing co-equal aspirational objectives. It was a rare occasion, however, when I would be informed that their participation in these activities was not worthwhile. They believed, as did I, that regardless of the challenges confronting the nation, that their futures were bright as was that of the country.

After the loss of millions of jobs from the flight of American corporations over the last two to three decades to low-paying labor pools across the planet, the impact of the recklessness which produced the "great recession" of 2007, and the emergence of political gridlock not observed in decades of American politics, the American Dream that appeared to be achievable now seems out of reach for all but a small segment of our society. This book is an attempt to rekindle the importance of citizen participation in our governmental process that was exhibited by my students. It is an effort to remind the general public and present students of our "least imperfect" experiment in government, of both the fears and aspirations of the Founders: they believed that without an engaged and "enlightened citizenry" our republic would be unsustainable.

Over a lifetime of teaching, researching and practicing the law, I have been continually amazed regarding the power of individual citizens to have a positive impact on the direction of our legal system and on public policy. As a mediator in the federal court in cases between disputing parties and as a dispute resolution facilitator in conflicts between different political subdivisions and interests groups, I have observed the strength of citizens who have come to recognize the legitimacy of good-faith negotiation and compromise. One theme which often encourages parties involved in public disputes to find common ground is the reminder of the sometimes forgotten irreparable harm that partisan political conflict inflicts on their families and their children's future.

While not every public policy issue confronting the nation can be "answered" by the insights of the Founders, the process that they established provides us with the opportunity to debate and find common ground with the leadership of, who James Madison described as, "those who hold the public trust"—our political representatives. I once swore an oath to the Constitution of the United States. So too did they. This book is my humble attempt to hold them to it.

Steven O. Ludd
Saratoga Springs, New York
March, 2014

Introduction

THE LAST SIX YEARS HAVE BEEN a remarkable time in the lives of Americans. With the crash of our economy and its devastating impact on millions of our citizenry, the fault lines of our social fabric have been exposed. Our political institutions, business communities, and private associational groups have retrenched into an understandable survivalist mentality. What became clear early in the process of "recovery" was the overwhelming lack of trust which had infected our body politic fueled to some degree by our collective amnesia of the origins of the Constitution. But this seeming void of memory regarding the creation of our collective covenant was quickly filled by those who continue to claim a "true" understanding of the objectives of our experiment in government. In the following pages we will journey back into our constitutional history and resurrect the observations of the Founders regarding their fears and aspirations in establishing a "More Perfect Union." What the reader will discover is that many of the problems of contemporary American life and politics were also confronted by the Founders. Their observations regarding human nature and the role of government in civil society compelled them to create a written document which they believed would provide a process by which to resolve the competing interests of a diverse society. We are at a time in our history when public policy "solutions" for the Nation's maladies are marketed as reflections of the Founding Visions. This investigation is an effort to resurrect the Framers' perspectives through their writings in support of the ratification of the Constitution. In so doing, it is hoped that the American public can evaluate the legitimacy of the claims by those who constantly defend their public policy recommendations as mandates from the Founders.

The first chapter of the book explores the political philosophical perspectives from which the Founders drew inspiration in legitimizing a revolution and ultimately crafting a written constitution of government. Particular attention is given to the meaning of "liberty" and its limitations derived from these philosophical origins and as understood by colonial Americans. Using the arguments presented in the *Federalist Papers* by James Madison, one of the most influential draftsmen of the Constitution, the investigation notes his vigorous defense of the proposed national government driven to a large degree by his overriding fear of "factions" and their impact on the "public good." The actual language of the Constitution which was crafted, debated, and ratified by the American people is also discussed in an effort to provide the reader with a snapshot of the structure and delegation of powers within the document.

Noting Madison's observations regarding the role of government in "regulating" the "mischiefs of factions," Chapter 2 describes the creation and activities of contemporary special interests groups and their role in the functioning of the Congress of the United States. Identifying the evolution and ideological claims of the Tea Party, the Tea Party Patriots, and Americans for Tax Reform, the book discusses their influence and asks whether Madison's formula for "controlling" factions has functioned as intended.

Because the role of our political representatives in the process of "recovery" has been at the center of debate within the country over the last six years, the investigation turns its attention in Chapter 3 to the Founders' view of political representation—the process of selection, the underlying presumptions which shaped the bicameral nature of the Congress of the United States, and Madison's observations regarding the "elected." With these observations as a constitutional backdrop, the analysis then provides a brief description of the demographics of our contemporary "political elite." Particular attention is given to the status of most Americans' income level and that of their representatives. The question is raised as to whether the significant difference in wealth acquisition of our "elected" has contributed to the failure of the legislative process to resolve lingering problems within our economy and other public policy issues before the nation.

Chapter 4 begins a discussion of the fundamental role that our "free press" was intended to play in the creation and protection of an "enlightened citizenry." After discussing the importance that the Framers attached to the functioning of the press and to the existence of a proliferation of independent newspapers and pamphlets throughout the colonies at the time of the Founding, the reader is asked to consider the present status of our mass communication industry. With particular attention placed on the concentration of power in contemporary mass media ownership produced by "deregulation" authorized by the Telecommunications Act of 1996, the investigation calls into question whether "a free marketplace of ideas" has been thwarted by the "industry's" emphasis on "political theatre" replacing objective investigative journalism as the basis for its programming. The discussion concludes by noting the industry's common practice of presenting what the study describes as "false equivalency" in its alleged "analysis" of the public policy issues presented to the American public. The reader is then asked whether the presentation of strident polar opposite political opinions provides the listener with objective information upon which to make a considered judgment or whether the practice only is a "pretense of objectivity."

Chapter 5 of the book returns to the observations of Thomas Jefferson, Benjamin Franklin, and Alexander Hamilton regarding the ultimate responsibility of each citizen in the preservation of our Republic. Reminding the reader of Jefferson's belief that "Self-government is not possible unless the citizens are educated sufficiently to enable them to exercise oversight," the investigation discusses the present status of our collective knowledge of the functioning of government. Noting the present seeming "illiteracy" of the general citizenry concerning the mandates of our Constitution and delegated responsibilities of those in government, the analysis turns its attention next to the "box makers"—the political marketers—who must take some responsibility for the general public's present "understanding" of our politics and institutions. After discussing the impact that relatively recent citizen participation has played in our politics—most notably the initial concerns of the Tea Party and the Occupy Wall Street movement—the remainder of the chapter offers recommendations to begin the process of revitalizing citizenship in the country. Beginning with the need to rekindle the use and importance of "critical thinking" in our public policy evaluation, the investigation explores the need for a reconsideration of citizenship education throughout the country if we are to follow the admonitions of the Founders to always be wary as Hamilton noted of "the snares of the ambitious" and to "prevent the perversion of power into tyranny" as Jefferson counseled.

Returning to what are described as the Founding First Principles, Chapter 6 identifies the need for a balancing of co-equal values reflected in the Constitution's design. Recognition of these First Principles and the acceptance of three important considerations necessary for political compromise are offered as the first step in ending the political gridlock in our governmental process. Using the attempt of creating legislation for "gun safety" as an example, the investigation notes both the successes and failures of utilizing this balancing process but offers hope for future political compromise on this and other public policy negotiations.

With the previous discussions of the Founders' fears and aspirations noted, Chapter 7 begins to confront some of the highly marketed claims of those most at the center of the gridlock in our politics and in contemporary American life. After a brief analysis of the "players" in this "conflict" between "rival parties" and a description of their techniques to engender the support of the public, the reader is asked to enter the world of Alice in Wonderland and to recall her experiences with a "beautifully labeled bottle" as they are encouraged to evaluate the "facts" presented by Freedom Works and their supporters. Throughout this journey "down the rabbit hole" the reader is reminded of the need to distinguish the "real" from the "imagined" in fulfillment of the late Senator Daniel Patrick Moynihan's observation that we are all entitled to our own set of opinions, not our own set of facts.

Chapter 8 provides a consolidation of the most important First Principles designed by the Founders and incorporated into the Constitution. This part of the study is offered as both a primer for the general public and students of public law and American government. It is suggested that contemporary public policy recommendations must reflect and be defended based upon these founding objectives.

Chapter 9 is an examination of the most often presented claims of who the investigation describes as contemporary Anti-Federalists. After an analysis of the arguments and "solutions" offered in the most recently published work of Mark R. Levin, *The Liberty Amendments: Restoring the American Republic*, the reader is asked to evaluate his commentary within the context of the First Principles noted by this study and the writings which produced these mandates.

The final segment of the investigation is presented in the form of Comments and Questions. A list of the short- and long-term public policy objectives are identified as potential subjects for future debate and resolution within the context of the founding First Principles. The subjects addressed include: the reinvigoration of citizenship; the need to monitor and protect "one person one vote"; the importance of confronting the issues associated with income inequality; the dangers associated with "Too Big to Fail Banks"; and the influence of money on our political process. The analyses and questions in this final portion of the investigation are offered in an effort to redirect the nation's public policy debates away from the ideological distortions of the founding values used to market highly suspect "solutions" to our contemporary economic and societal problems and, instead, offer recommendations grounded in the real "Contract with America"—the Constitution of the United States.

1 The Origins of the American Experiment in Governance

IT HAS BEEN ALMOST NINE YEARS of total frustration, anger and disappointment. Frustration regarding the political elite's unwillingness to put country first; anger concerning the total lack of leadership from our collective institutions (private sector, government, education and the media); disappointment in the citizenry's seeming ignorance of its government and the requisite balance necessary between government and private sector functioning in our so-called "free enterprise" economic system. America appears to be drowning in an ocean of uncertainty, distrust, and fear of the future.

At first glance, the situation seems dire—unemployment, unsustainable economic disparities between classes of our citizens, corporate unwillingness to invest in the country without governmental guarantees of short-term profit, an electoral process that is rampant with "big money" contributions often by a select few, and a political system seemingly incapable of responding to the short and long term needs of the country. Yet, there are solutions to these problems. But they will require Americans to take a deep breath; be willing to throw away the ideological boxes so often offered as a one size fits all solution to our fiscal, political, and social conflicts; and most importantly, reflect on our history and the original visions of our Founders. To move forward we must create a renewed consensus of what it means to be an American.

This book will examine some of the underlying problems which have created the current gridlock in American Government. An evaluation of the causes of these obstacles will be offered based upon an understanding of both the philosophical and constitutional principles underpinning our system of rules. Without such an understanding of these time-tested values, the current justifications for future public policy decisions become nothing more than polemical arguments grounded upon self-serving political ideologies which selectively "pick and choose" a single founding principle without placing it within the context of the myriad of principles that form what the Founders described as the American Experiment in governance. The ultimate objective of this book is to provide the reader with a renewed understanding of our governmental process and the constitutional first principles which underscore its functioning. This journey back into our constitutional history is offered as a snapshot of who we were, as we debate who we want to be.

In Search of Our Founding Values, the Overriding Principles

Somewhere hidden amongst the anger, the frustration, the collective sense of betrayal, and our fear of the future, exists a hard-fought history that provides a blueprint for a revival of the American spirit. Like a message scrawled across an ancient cavern wall intended to provide members of the tribe with images of past, present, and future realities, the Founders of the American Experiment have provided us with a compass with which to navigate the dangerous storm impacting the country. It is a compendium of experiences drawn from the ages—an amalgam of political philosophies shaped by the failures and successes of past communities in constructing governmental institutions. Nothing like it was ever created—a scheme to blend the need for security and order with an unyielding commitment to maximize individual liberty and promote the public welfare. Built upon their historical recognition of the tyranny of concentrated power, the Founders hammered out a governmental structure which would reduce its impact on "We the People."

Their vision would include a separation of governmental power, require political compromise, a politically insulated judicial body to act as a final arbiter of governmental conflicts, and a reliance upon an "enlightened citizenry." The covenant agreed upon by the Founders was a written document which they understood would be tested by the travails and triumphs of a young nation constantly in search for itself. This document was to provide the parameters by which we agreed to be governed. It enumerated the processes by which the will of the People, through their elected representatives, would be encapsulated into law, or amended, or even abolished. While the creation of the initial document reflected an overriding commitment to democratic institutions and the essentiality of majority rule, the Founders understood that if individual liberty was to be preserved, specific enumerations needed to be articulated and cautiously protected by a Bill of Rights. Ultimately, the drafters of our Constitution believed that without the consent of the governed their experiment in government would fail. The question, as we enter further into the twenty-first century, is whether the new challenges for our society and the world will be met with an understanding and commitment to the core values encapsulated within our Constitution or whether they will be abandoned to the exigencies of the moment.

The political philosophical roots of our constitutional republican government can be traced to the late seventeenth century writings of John Locke in *The Second Treatise of Civil Government*. His vision of the individual and his/her relationship to government or the collective society was subsequently encapsulated into a series of early eighteenth century popular and widely disseminated political pamphlets in colonial America entitled, *Cato's Letters*, written by John Trenchard and Thomas Gordon published in *The London Journal* in 1720. The importance of these writings to the development of the American Experiment in government and the legitimacy of contemporary political pundits and politicians' claims regarding the role of government and its relationship with individual citizens and corporations should not be underestimated. Indeed, from the beginning of the near collapse of many of our financial institutions and the onslaught of the "recession," much attention by our media has focused upon politicians representing special interests groups or newly minted political advocacy groups who claim a "true" understanding of our historical commitment to liberty. An analysis of the original visions of Locke and the Independent English Whig writers will provide a backdrop upon which to evaluate the legitimacy of contemporary claims to our constitutional understanding of liberty. While some may find that a revisitation of these treatises is an arcane academic exercise, it is hoped that such cynicism will be countered by Americans who believe that much can be learned from those who have come before concerning the human condition and the institutions that were ultimately crafted to help determine the balance between the individual and civil society.

Locke, not unlike other political philosophers who came before and after him, understood the importance of examining the human condition in an attempt to describe certain "givens" about the individual and his/her relationship to society. In one section of Locke's treatise on government entitled "Of the State of Nature," he discussed the inherent struggle between the need to maximize individual aspiration with the rewards that it can provide and the limits of such a quest.

> ...there cannot be supposed any such subordination among us that may authorize us to destroy one another, as if we were made for one another's uses, as the inferior ranks of creatures are for ours. Everyone, as he is bound to preserve himself, and to quit his station willfully, so by the like reason, when his own preservation comes not in competition, ought he, as much as he can, to preserve the rest of mankind, and may not, unless it be to do justice on an offender, take away, or impair the life, or what tends to the presentation of the life, the liberty, health, limb, or goods of another.[1]

He went on to write in the Treatise's section "On Property" that a person has the ultimate right to possess the "fruits of his labour" limited only to the degree that "there is enough, and as good, left in common for others." Locke then went on to explain that this natural right to possess property obtained through individual efforts was essential but that it was "useless, as well as dishonest, to carve himself too much, or take more than he needed."[2] While he was uncompromising regarding the paramount importance of reaping the rewards of one's labor and convinced that the freedom of the individual was at the core of this principle, he was resolute in conditioning his premise with what we will describe as the "harm qualifier." Locke's vision of the nature of man and his relationship to government was subsequently incorporated into the political philosophy of early eighteenth century English Whig writers. And, in turn, these writings were some of the most widely read pamphlets circulated in the American colonies prior to the revolution. Indeed, if there was one current of political thought which captured the hearts and minds of colonial Americans it was the writings of John Trenchard and Thomas Gordon published in the *London Journal* as *Cato's Letters*.[3] A brief sampling of their commentary regarding the legitimate aim of government will begin to reveal how a political philosophical treatise relatively quickly became a mechanism for a radical change in the relationship of the individual and government. And it is from these overriding presumptions that the parameters of our Constitution were debated and ultimately formed.

For the English libertarians and for many colonial Americans, government was not "to direct them in their own Affairs, in which no one is interested but themselves."[4] Indeed, they urged that government was a practical restraint and that the role of free government was to protect the people in their liberties. More specifically they wrote of liberty and government:

> And it is foolish to say, that Government is concerned to meddle with the private Thoughts and Actions of Men, while they injure neither the Society, nor any of its Members. Every Man is, in Nature and Reason, the Judge and Disposer of his own domestic Affairs: and, according to the Rules of Religion and Equity, every Man must carry his own Conscience. So that neither has the Magistrate…or anybody else, any manner of Power to model People's Speculations, no more than their Dreams. Government being intended to protect Men from the injuries of one and another, and not to direct them in their own Affairs, in which no one is interested but themselves; it is plain, that their Thoughts and domestic Concerns are exempted intirely from its Jurisdiction.[5]

Ultimately, Trenchard and Gordon concluded that "this Passion for Liberty in Men, and their Possession of it, is of that Efficacy and Importance that it seems the Parent of all Virtues."[6] They believed that the attainment and protection of liberty was at the core of any society which was committed to maximizing the potential of its citizens. Yet, neither the English libertarians nor the American colonialists believed that individual liberty was an absolute and unqualified right. As Locke argued before, they understood that the legitimate parameters of individual liberty and the corresponding obligation of government are shaped by a determination of whether the actions of an individual or groups of individuals harm "Society, or, any of its Members." There are, therefore, two implicit yet clear presumptions interwoven into these foundational principles of our republic. The first is that the autonomy of the individual is to be exalted as a first priority of government. The second is that before individual liberty can be limited government must demonstrate that harm has been or will be inflicted upon another citizen or the society as a whole. These principles then presuppose the essentiality of government and a system of rules which reflect these "givens" both in theory and action. It was understood that without government and a process by which to evaluate the impact of the action of the individual upon another or the collective as a whole, the fate of each citizen's liberty would be left to the most powerful members of society either defined by wealth or political majority.

The task then before the Founders was to shape institutions of government which reflected a strong commitment to liberty and yet guarded against abuse of power originating from individual citizens, groups of citizens or government itself. *No small task!* Yet, John Adams wrote that this vision of government and its importance to the attainment of individual liberty was not some abstract political philosophical thesis. Instead it was what he described as the "stamina vitae"—the life blood—for a constitution of government.[7]

Drafting a Constitution, A Review of the Foundational Principles

Just as Locke's understanding of the purpose of government and its relationship to the attainment of individual liberty was the product of evolving and sometimes competing social, political, and cultural experiences across time, so too was the establishment of our constitutional system. Our Constitution is the creature of revolution, experimentation, and vigorous debate. Its drafting was the by-product of contentious power struggles between numerous special interests all of which claimed superior importance over the others. Indeed, its design and ultimate adoption was achieved only after it became clear that our first attempt at governance through the Articles of Confederation was a failure. Similar to our brief overview of the political philosophical currents which provided much of the intellectual energy and popular support for dramatic change in colonial America, the following investigation of the writings of one of the most influential draftsman of the Constitution can provide us with some of the basic principles of our governmental system which are important for an analysis of contemporary public policy debates regarding the role of government as we move forward in the twenty-first century.

The negative experiences derived from the Articles of Confederation period in our early development as a nation were fresh in the minds of the Founders. A system of governance which created de-centralized power concentrated in state governments, placed supreme influence in state legislative bodies, elevated state citizenship over national citizenship, rendered the collective security of the country to individual state militias, and eventuated in a patchwork of differing financial and revenue creating systems throughout the country compelled a dramatically different vision of government. It was one in which compromise would be required to shape a system of rules for the competing interests of the sometimes widely disparate social, economic, and religious sectors of the emerging nation. It was to be a new covenant for power sharing between the states and a national government. It was to be a republican government committed to majoritarian rule but designed with structural safeguards to protect against abuses of power from whatever source. The Constitution and The Bill of Rights was to be a fulcrum upon which to balance the needs of the majority of the citizens with the protection of individual liberty. But how could such a balance be struck? What presumptions concerning human nature needed to be recognized and accounted for in the newly established contract with the People? What structural mechanisms would be necessary to guard against tyranny by the minority—or even, the majority?

James Madison, one the most influential draftsmen of the Constitution and a fervent supporter of majoritarian government, recognized that abuse of power can be created from a select few or from collective majorities. His insights remain powerful as we head into the second decade of the twenty-first century. He wrote:

> It has been said that all government is evil. It would be more proper to say that the necessity of any government is a misfortune. This necessity however exists; and the problem to be solved is, not what form of government is perfect, but which form is least imperfect; and here the general question must be between a republican government in which a lesser number or the least number rule the majority. If the republican form is, as all of us agree, to be preferred, the final question must be, what is the structure of it that will best guard against precipitate counsels and factious combinations for unjust purposes, without a sacrifice of the fundamental principles of

republicanism. Those who denounce majority governments altogether because they may have interest in abusing their power, denounce at the same time all republican government and must maintain that minority governments would feel less of the bias of interest or the seduction of power.[8]

Yet, Madison cautioned that abuse of power can sometimes originate from the collective People. He wrote:

> In our governments the real power lies in the majority of the community, and the invasion of private rights is chiefly to be apprehended, not from acts of government contrary to the sense of its constituents, but from acts in which the government is the mere instrument of the majority... [9]

As a staunch proponent of majoritarian government, Madison was not suggesting that government should be nonresponsive to the collective will—quite to the contrary. But his understanding of government was tempered by the experiences of tyrannical rule throughout history and particularly in the late eighteenth century. To protect the private rights of citizens who may not possess majoritarian political power, he warned that Americans must understand the important distinction between "popular" majoritarian and "constitutional" majoritarian government. He reminded his associates that "the majority, as formed by the Constitution, may be a minority when compared with the popular majority."[10] As long as the Constitution was operative, the only legitimate source of governmental action was derived from those citizens who accepted the values expressed by it—even if on occasion constitutional rule was not reflective of popular opinion. Madison understood that the protection of minority rights could not be totally dependent upon simple calculations of popular opinion.

The "popular majority" represented the collective opinions or interests of the largest numerical combination of Americans. In contemporary terminology, Madison's "popular majority" might be analogous to 51% of those citizens who responded similarly to a Harris or Gallup type poll. The "constitutional majority," while not mutually distinct from the "popular majority," was (is) limited in its composition to those individuals whose desires and interests generally reflect the expressed and implicit goals of the Constitution. It was this body of citizens which he argued would fulfill the purposes of democratic republican government. For inclusion in this group one needed more than simply an opinion. Instead, only those "opinions" which are grounded in a commitment to the values expressed in the Constitution would be legitimate directives from the People.

The American experiment in governance was a unique contract between the proposed government and its citizens. This new scheme of governance could not survive without a commitment by the People to the fundamental principle of majoritarian rule limited by a Bill of Rights designed to protect the rights of the minority not in political power, and ultimately each citizen. Additionally, there was to be a "fail-safe" mechanism which would be implanted into this new covenant. If, after the agreed upon processes of government—the Congress, Executive or Judicial branches—failed to reflect the desires of the citizens, the Constitution could be amended.

With an eye toward the dangers of legislative bodies simply carrying out the desires of popular whim, regardless of constitutional mandates, he urged vigilance. Majoritarian governance was to be preferred over any system based upon the minority ruling the majority. But if liberty was to be protected, a constant evaluation of the basis for majoritarian governmental action was essential. Concentrated power, whether held by a select few or legislative majorities, was to be monitored and evaluated based upon its conformity with the overriding first principle of maximizing human aspiration within the context of an ordered system of rules. But, what mechanisms could be created to minimize abuse of power in this proposed new more centralized governmental system? How could individual liberty be protected within the context of the broader needs of the collective community? A review of some of the most important structural mandates of the Constitution should provide a renewed understanding of why the Founders believed that this form of government, as Madison wrote, was the "least imperfect."

The draftsmen of our Constitution were revolutionaries. But they were at the same time practical men. They understood that they were creating a covenant that must withstand the currents of time. It was to be a document that began to define what it meant to be an American. Their emphasis then had to be to shape the broad parameters of a government which would underscore the preeminence of national citizenship without denying the need for state participation in lawmaking. It was to be a power sharing agreement between sometimes very diverse regional, social-economic, and political interests. It then had to be an agreement which could find support from sometimes widely divergent views. Indeed, many of the basic disagreements which were confronted by the Framers have found their way into our contemporary public discourse. Unfortunately, many of the discussions currently are without even a superficial understanding of the basic structure, specific enumerations or underlying presumptions of the agreement. Lost then within the contemporary morass of sometimes self-serving political commentary is an appreciation for the delicate balance and political compromise required under our Constitution. Therefore, a brief examination of the specific language of the Constitution and the corresponding presumptions which underscore its creation is in order.

The Constitutional Structure
The Creation of Blended Federalism

The design of the Constitution was a product of intense discussion across all sectors of the newly established country. It was not only the by-product of revolution and an initial failed attempt at a loosely configured governmental structure—The Articles of Confederation—but it was also the result of contentious political debate between advocates for the retention of power within state legislative assemblies and those who argued for a national government. Indeed, some of the same arguments that are being submitted by contemporary politicians and political operatives regarding the relationship of the state and federal government are very similar to those entered into by the Founders. Sadly, the contemporary political arguments rarely are presented within the context of the entire document. As tempting as it is to immediately call upon any one section of the Constitution to win some rhetorical argument for purposes of any current public policy issue, suffice to say at this point that an examination of the language of the document and the general intention of the Founders will guide us in determining whether recent public policy arguments regarding the role of government are constitutionally grounded or political hyperbole.

The Founders' commitment to minimize concentrated power in the newly established Constitution resulted in a unique division of responsibility among three branches of government. Each branch would possess power delegated by the American people to perform the necessary functions of government. This tri-parte separation of power mandated different responsibilities from the Legislative, Executive, and Judicial branches. It also "reserved" to the state governments, and to the "People," certain unenumerated powers. Because too often our contemporary discussions of the "failures" of government are sometimes based upon allegations of dysfunction by one of the coordinate branches or an overreach of power by the federal government upon the States, a closer examination of the language of the Constitution is imperative. Indeed, it is because so little attention has been paid to the real "Contract with America" that our ability as a public to objectively evaluate the constitutional legitimacy of the "solutions" offered by our political elite and various interests groups has seemingly vanished. This investigation categorically rejects the notion that Americans are incapable of understanding the core principles of their constitutional democracy and unable to appreciate the delicate balance that must be established between liberty and the promotion of the public welfare recognized by Locke, the English Whigs, and colonial Americans.

The language of any contract is theoretically open for interpretation and some-times honest disagreement occurs between the parties impacted by the document. Therefore, in an effort to produce fairness and compliance in the enforcement of contracts, our legal system has relied upon a methodology which examines both the "letter and the spirit" of the written document. Our analysis then will apply the same standard as we examine key provisions of the Constitution. The general objectives of the document are expressed in the "Preamble." It reads:

> We the People of the United States, in Order to form a more perfect Union, establish Justice, insure domestic Tranquility, provide for the common defence, promote the general Welfare, and secure the Blessings of Liberty to ourselves and our Posterity, do ordain and establish this Constitution for the United States of America.[11]

The language (letter) of the "Preamble" is relatively straightforward. The purpose of the Constitution is to remedy the problems created by our previous relationships in governance (to form a more perfect Union); create a system of rules that would provide fairness in the interactions of government with its citizens (establish Justice); maintain security and order in an effort to allow the mechanisms of government to function without violence or insurrection (insure domestic Tranquility); establish the power to create a military answerable to all citizens (provide for the common defence); recognize by its actions the needs of the entire country (promote the general Welfare); and finally, maintain and protect the importance of our collective and individual freedoms for generations of Americans (secure the Blessings of Liberty to ourselves and our Posterity). While each of these broad directives helped to shape the contours of the document, the most important overriding principle which we too often forget is the very first clause of the "Preamble"—"We the People." The Constitution is a contract by the American people which delegated power to its government to assist in the attainment of the broad objectives delineated in the "Preamble."

It was understood that the objectives could not be accomplished without a new scheme regarding the relationship of government with the American people. The contract was entered into without any illusions regarding the rights and responsibilities of the parties. The agreement would be enforceable to all citizens through the specific clauses and distribution of governmental responsibilities within the document. In other words, as long as the Constitution was operative, the terms of the agreement must be honored. But, the People retained the ultimate authority to amend the agreement through the constitutional amendment process and, if all else failed, could refuse to comply with the terms of the covenant. Inherent within the "Preamble" is a powerful presumption about the relationship between the "parties." No longer would legitimate power to govern be established by some "superior" monarchial source. Instead, the origin of all governmental authority emanated from the collective community—from the citizens of the United States. Some 225 years later it is important to remind ourselves that our federal system of governance was constructed on the principle of the supremacy of national citizenship. Because many of the current public policy issues before the country often include claims of unconstitutional manipulation of power by the federal government, it is essential that we examine the specific language of the Constitution which created the divisions of power delegated within the federal system.

In an effort to minimize concentrated power, the Constitutors created three co-ordinate branches of government at the national level and left unenumerated reserve powers within state governments. The distribution of federal power is provided in Article I, Article II, and Article III of the Constitution. The power to create all laws was delegated by the People to the Congress in Article I. While this section of the document provides specific guidance regarding the composition of the House of Representatives and the Senate and the responsibilities of each chamber, the language within Article I sec. 8 enumerates with relative specificity the power of Congress and its legislative function. Article I sec. 8 demonstrates the draftsmen's intention of providing the national legislative body the power to remedy the problems that were created by the Articles of Confederation. It reads in part:

> Article I section 8 cl. (1)—The Congress shall have Power to lay and collect Taxes, Duties, Imposts and Excises, to pay the Debts and provide for the common Defence and general Welfare of the United States; but all Duties, Imposts and Excises shall be uniform throughout the United States;
>
> (2) To borrow money on the credit of the United States;
>
> (3) To regulate Commerce with foreign Nations, and among the several States, and with the Indian Tribes;
>
> (4) To establish an uniform Rule of Naturalization, and uniform Laws on the subject of Bankruptcies throughout the United States;
>
> (5) To coin Money, regulate the Value thereof, and of foreign Coin, and fix current Coin of the United States:
>
> (11) To declare War, grant Letters of Marque, and Reprisal, and make Rules concerning Captures on Land and Water;

A wide variety of other enumerated powers of Congress are contained within Article I. But beyond those already cited, the most important provision in our

Constitution which delegates power to the Congress in its law-making function is Article I sec. 8 cl. (18). In this provision the Founders directed the Congress,

> To make all Laws which shall be necessary and proper for carrying into Execution the foregoing Powers, and all other Powers vested by the Constitution in the government of the United States, or in any Department or officer thereof.

This section of Article I was recognition that while the specific powers delegated to the Congress by the American people are to be regarded as particularly important legislative functions, not all law-making powers could be determined which will be required in the future to implement the mandates. Therefore, the People's representatives would be responsible to craft legislation over time to reflect the more specific directives listed above. It was to be and remains the Nation's legislative body—the Congress of the United States—which would be assigned the task to shape the laws impacting the American people. In both section 9 and section 10 of Article I, the power of state legislative bodies over most of the functions discussed above are sharply limited. For example, among numerous prohibitions, these provisions restricted the States from creating taxes on goods exported from their state; or, from providing some monetary benefit through the law of that state to any commercial enterprise originating from its state over commercial transaction from another state. Indeed, in Article I section 10 cl. (1)(2)(3), the limited role of state legislative bodies over most of the functions of lawmaking which could potentially conflict with the actions of the Congress were clearly identified. Just a snapshot of some of the language provides the unassailable intention by the Constitutors to remedy the problems experienced by the Articles of Confederation and the imperative of establishing the foundations of national citizenship. Article I section 10 cl. (1)(2)(3) reads in part:

> No State shall enter into any Treaty, Alliance, or Confederation...coin Money...pass any Bill of Attainder, ex post facto Law, or Law impairing the Obligation of Contracts...

> No State shall, without the Consent of Congress, lay any Imposts or Duties on Imports or Exports...

> No State shall, without the Consent of Congress,...keep Troops, or Ships of War in time of Peace...

While the powers provided to the Congress of the United States in Article I are significant regarding the relationship of the federal and state legislative functions, Article VI section (2) of the document provides even more clarity as to the intention of the Founders regarding the relationship of the national and state governments. It states:

> This Constitution, and the Laws of the United States which shall be made in Pursuance thereof; and all Treaties made; or which shall be made, under the Authority of the United States, shall be the Supreme Law of the Land; and the Judges in every State shall be bound thereby, any Thing in the Constitution or Laws of any State to the Contrary notwithstanding.

This section of the Constitution, which has come to be known as the "Supremacy Clause," when coupled with the other specifically delegated powers in Article I, leaves little debate as to the Founders' intention to dramatically shift the locus of concentrated power from state legislative bodies to the Congress of the United States. Of course, this redirection of law-making power, as with many of the other governmental structural changes we will discuss in a moment, did not occur with some magical swipe of a pen at the Constitutional Convention. The Founders understood that they must engender support from the People to institute this change. From 1787 until the eventual inclusion of the Bill of Rights in 1791, the ratification process was rife with public debate concerning the legitimacy of such a change. Indeed, powerful arguments to retain some form of the status quo with ultimate law-making authority in state legislative assemblies was offered by the Anti-Federalists while Alexander Hamilton, John Jay, and James Madison provided the reasons and a defense for the concept of a strong national government. Before we turn our attention to the language in Article II and Article III of the Constitution, a brief sampling of the Federalist positions and those of the Anti-Federalists will provide some insight into the "spirit" of the document we are reviewing. It will also provide a glimpse into the Founders recognition that only a structure of government which could diffuse the power of special interests and require compromise would be capable of forming a "more Perfect Union" and protect liberty.

Just as emerging democracies today are struggling with the most effective ways by which to channel the fervor of revolution into governmental structures, so too were the draftsmen of the Constitution. At the core of our debates was what one could describe as a seemingly irreconcilable contradiction within the Declaration of Independence. Professor Ralph Ketcham, one of this country's foremost scholars of American colonial history, has described the problem as a "tension built into the Declaration of Independence."[12] His analysis of the dilemma provides an excellent backdrop for our brief review of the differing positions on the proposed Constitution. The "tension" within the Declaration of Independence that Professor Ketcham identifies is between one clause which describes certain rights as "unalienable" and another which posits that "Governments …derive their just powers from the consent of the governed." He goes on to explain that the

Rights to life, liberty, and the pursuit of happiness were not to be submitted to a vote or to depend on the outcome of elections; that is, not even the consent of the governed could legitimately abridge them. But it was nonetheless possible that the people, through their elected representatives, might sanction laws violating "unalienable" rights. Suppose legislatures, state or national, passed laws abridging freedom of the press, or violating liberty of conscience, or permitting default on contracts, as happened in the 1780s. Which principle had priority, that of "consent" or that of "unalienable rights"?[13]

Professor Ketcham went on to suggest that the Constitution was "one effort to contain the tension, and the debate over its ratification often revolved around whether the framers had properly adjusted the balance of the two principles." He concluded that "...The key differences arose over which purpose to emphasize and what mechanisms of government best assured some fulfillment of each."[14] While it is certainly legitimate to question whether the motivations of the proponents of one position or the other were solely grounded in a concern over the supremacy of one principle or the other what is without debate was the necessity of balancing these important considerations through some ultimate compromise.

At the core of the Federalist position was that these two principles could be balanced by dividing power into differing governmental departments, limiting the ability of each department to function without the corresponding acceptance or acquiescence of the other legislative, executive or judicial branch, and ultimately securing approval from the American people through their compliance. Much of the focus of the Federalists arguments involved the necessity of controlling the impact of "factions" in the development of the Union. Madison, writing in *The Federalist Papers*, no. 10, discussed the dilemma and argued that the proposed Constitution was the best method by which to balance the need for a republican government with the protection of liberty. He observed,

Among the numerous advantages promised by a well-constructed Union none deserves to be more accurately developed than its tendency to break and control the violence of faction...Complaints are everywhere heard from our most considerate and virtuous citizens, equally the friends of public and private faith, and of public and personal liberty, that our governments are too unstable, that the public good is disregarded in the conflicts of rival parties, and that measures are too often decided, not according to the rules of justice and the rights of the minor party, but by the superior force of an interested and overbearing majority...By a faction, I understand a number of citizens, whether amounting to a majority or a minority of the whole, who are united and actuated by some common impulse of passion, or of interest, adverse to the rights of other citizens or to the permanent and aggregate interests of the community.[15]

Madison argued that there were two methods of "curing the mischiefs of faction." The first would be to "remove its causes; the other, by controlling its effects."[16] He believed that the "latent causes of faction are… sown in the nature of man…"[17] Indeed, if one attempted to abolish factions one would ultimately be destroying liberty. He therefore rejected the first option. Yet, he recognized that the damage that factions produce ultimately required regulation. His solution was to construct a legislative process which would minimize the power of a select few or a powerful faction which could control a state legislative body and require those interests to be placed in a larger body where that more regional or parochial faction would have to compete with others from across the Nation. This process would ultimately require all factions to compromise. The negative impact of factions then could be lessened by shifting power from the smaller and more easily manipulated state legislative assemblies to the larger and more diverse proposed Congress. He argued that the shift of law-making authority would reduce the power of "local prejudices and schemes of injustice"[18] and produce a process of interest-sharing compromise which would reduce the potential for oppression. Madison was convinced that the best protection from the negative consequences of factions was "…by a greater variety of parties, against the event of any one party being able to outnumber and oppress the rest."[19] He concluded:

> The influence of factious leaders may kindle a flame within their particular States, but will be unable to spread a general conflagration through the other States. A religious sect may degenerate into a political faction in a part of the Confederacy, but the variety of sects dispersed over the entire face of it must secure the national councils against any danger from that source. A rage for paper money, for an abolition of debts, for an equal division of property, or for any other improper or wicked project will be less apt to pervade the whole body of the Union than a particular member of it, in the same proportion as such a malady is more likely to taint a particular county or district than an entire State.[20]

While this argument would ultimately prove to be compelling throughout the ratification process, it did not go without challenge. In fact, some participants at the Constitutional Convention decried the Federalists positions as a power grab which would conclude in what one Anti-Federalist from Virginia, Colonel George Mason, predicted "would end either in monarchy, or tyrannical aristocracy."[21]

Instead of attempting to rebut the efficacy of Madison's argument, Mason challenged the entirety of the proposed document and its potential to destroy liberty. The proposed House of Representatives produced "the shadow only of representation." The Senate is delegated too much power. The length of the Senators terms coupled with their power to appoint all "public officers" and power of impeachment would produce a co-operation between them and the Executive branch that would "destroy any balance in the government, and enable them to accomplish what usurpations they please upon the rights and liberties of the People." Mason also attacked the proposed Constitution's delegation of power to the Executive and Judicial branches. Among a long list of criticisms, he warned that because the new plan does not provide the Presidency with a "constitutional council" which would provide "proper information and advice," the President would "generally be directed by minions and favorites; or he will become a tool to the Senate." The newly proposed Judiciary also created a serious problem. He claimed that the judiciary "is so constructed and extended, as to absorb and destroy the judiciaries of the several states; thereby rendering law as tedious, intricate and expensive, and justice as unattainable, by a great part of the community, as in England, and enabling the rich to oppress and ruin the poor."[22]

Throughout the ratification process attacks and defenses to the proposed Constitution were varied and robust. One of the most powerful Anti-Federalist arguments against acceptance of the document was delivered by Patrick Henry before the Virginia Ratifying Convention in 1788. Similar to his colleague Colonel Mason, Henry challenged the entirety of the proposed Constitution as a threat to liberty. At the core of his disagreement with the Federalists was his belief that, if state sovereignty was relinquished then the "rights and privileges" of its citizens would be "endangered." He began by challenging the notion within the Preamble of the proposed Constitution.

> The fate of ... America may depend on this: Have they said, we the States? Have they made a proposal of a compact between the States? If they had, this would be a confederation: It is otherwise most clearly a consolidated government. The question turns, Sir, on that poor little thing—the expression, We, the people, instead of the States of America. I need not take much pains to show, that the principles of this system, are extremely pernicious, impolitic, and dangerous. Is this a Monarchy, like England—a compact between Prince and people; with checks on the former, to secure the liberty of the latter? Is this Confederacy, like Holland—an association of a number of independent States, each of which retain its individual sovereignty? It is not a democracy, wherein the people retain all their rights securely.... We have

no detail of those great considerations which, in my opinion, ought to have abounded before we should recur to a government of this kind.[23]

Henry then argued that this shift of power from State governments to a proposed national Congress would put at risk the liberties already protected by State sovereignty. More specifically, he warned that "The rights of conscience, trial by jury, liberty of the press, all your immunities and franchises, all pretensions to human rights and privileges, are rendered insecure, if not lost…" For Henry, discussion by the Federalist as to the benefits of the proposed Constitution regarding commercial trade or the potential for the country to become a "great and powerful people" were simply wrong. The task of government was how best to secure liberty. At the core of Henry's rejection of the proposed governmental change was his disdain for what he saw as "ambiguity" throughout the document. He argued that the lack of specificity in the representation and amendment process was open to manipulation. As to representation, he foresaw the potential that with population shifts some states could have no representation. In regard to the amendment process, Henry noted that this check against tyranny could also be obstructed by "unworthy characters" either in the Senate or state legislatures. Clearly, what was most troubling to Henry was the lack of specific enumerations with the proposed Constitution as to the limits of government and the unalienable rights of the people. While his attacks on the proposed shift of power from the individual states to a national assembly ultimately failed to stop the ratification of the Constitution, his criticisms of the lack of specific guarantees of the rights of the American people were compelling and ultimately received support.

By 1789 James Madison introduced amendments to the Constitution to the Congress and by 1791 a Bill of Rights was established. The first eight amendments to the Constitution generally mirrored specific enumerations found in the existing Bill of Rights of some of the States. However, two unique provisions of the Bill of Rights reflected the Framers recognition of compromise regarding the balance necessary between the need for a national governmental structure, the retention of some power within each state, and the protection of individual liberty. The language in both the Ninth and Tenth Amendments of the Bill of Rights underscored the new power-sharing process.

Pursuant to the Tenth Amendment the States would possess what has come to be known as "reserved" powers. In succinct, but undeveloped language, the amendment reads:

> The powers not delegated to the United States by the Constitution, nor prohibited by it to the States, are reserved to the States respectively, or to the people.

In equally direct language in the Ninth Amendment of the Bill of Rights, the Framers expressed their commitment to the principle of ultimate power in the government vesting in the people of the United States of America. It reads:

> The enumeration in the Constitution, of certain rights, shall not be construed to deny or disparage others retained by the People.

Some of the initial Federalist resistance to a Bill of Rights came from their concern that if certain rights were articulated, others could be overlooked. Instead of only stating a few it would be better to not enter into the process at all. Madison ultimately rejected that argument. Instead he crafted language that not only reinforced the legitimacy of the enumerated rights in the First through the Eighth Amendments but also provided for future articulation of rights not mentioned. In these two provisions of the Bill of Rights, the Framers provided for the protection of liberty and the retention of some state legislative power. Our analysis will return to the Bill of Rights when we begin to analyze the public policy issues currently before the Nation.

At this point, it is important to acknowledge that while the compromise to establish a new structure of governance brought a process which could regulate factions, establish clarity over commercial transactions, and enumerate its commitment to the protection of individual liberty, it came at a price—a heavy one indeed. In an effort to create a representation process, which could accommodate the imbalance of population throughout the country, the Framers were confronted with another seeming irreconcilable dilemma—how could they achieve some level of equal representation when some states were proportionally smaller in population than other larger states? How could they encourage the smaller states to join a national government if they would have fewer representatives? Even more troublesome was the fact that the population of "freemen" in the Southern States was small in comparison to the Northern States.

A "solution" was offered by Governor Randolph of Virginia—for representation purposes, he suggested a plan that would calculate the total population of each state using a formula that would count slaves as three-fifth of a person. Such a formula would place the Southern States on an equal status with the Northern States. His recommendation ultimately was inserted into Article I. sec. 2. Cl. 3 of the Constitution. While this method for apportionment of representation in the proposed National government remedied the immediate problem of securing enough of a consensus for ratification of the Constitution, it only provided a relatively brief respite from the debate over slavery and its implications in establishing a "more perfect Union." After almost seven decades of public rancor, legislative action, and judicial decision-making regarding the legitimacy of treating human beings of color as less than a "person," the Union was torn apart by the horrors of a Civil War.

Whether the "compromise" struck by the Founders can be defended as one of necessity or condemned as a shocking example of hypocrisy, or some combination of both, remains an open-ended debate. What one can be certain of is that with the ratification of the Thirteenth, Fourteenth, and Fifteenth Amendments after the Civil War, many of the injustices of slavery began to be addressed. Yet the battle for a color-blind Constitution continues even today. Inherent within this epoch struggle for civil rights in America continues to be the dilemma confronted by the Founders in the design of their power-sharing contract with the People. Their task was to construct a government that would protect against the concentration of power which ultimately produces tyranny and destroys liberty, yet provide a system of governance which allowed for the evolution of conflicting societal norms to ultimately coalesce into a consensus for compliance with the rule of law. This structure of governance would require not only a constant balancing of competing interests both within the hearts and minds of the American People, but also in their newly designed institutions of government. The separation of powers implanted into the federal system would reduce the potential for abuse of power by any one department of government but it also could create constant conflict destroying efficient governmental functioning.

Part of the frustration by the American people today centers upon the appropriate balance between governmental "overreach" into their lives regarding health care, marriage, or any other personal liberty they hold dear and the absolute necessity of governmental leadership in fostering job creation, protection from terrorism, and creating social safety nets. Some contemporary social commentators have bemoaned the seeming futility of our present legislative process and have pointed to the "efficient" functioning of other governmental systems which seem to produce much more rapid responses to the needs of their people. Indeed, at times of national emergencies similar to our current financial and unemployment problems, it is to be expected that governmental action to remedy the issues would be immediate and decisive. But, putting aside the complexities of the issues surrounding our current problems, we have opted for a system of divided government, for a legislative process which requires compromise, for an Executive Branch with limited power and, for a Judicial branch which possesses "neither the power of the purse, nor the power of the sword, but merely the power of judgment." This system provides some protection against concentrated power but it also can produce political gridlock and governmental paralysis. It would appear that part of the current disappointment of the American people with their government is rooted, at least in part, in a misunderstanding of the limited powers delegated under the Constitution to the Executive and Judicial branches. Before we turn our attention to an analysis of some of the most important public policy questions facing the Nation, an examination of the language and general principles underpinning the responsibilities assigned to the Executive and Judicial branches is imperative. The limited delegated powers of the Executive and Judicial branches can be found in Article II and Article III of the Constitution.

Article II of the Constitution describes the requirements to become President of the United States, the process by which the President shall be elected and for their potential removal, and the powers generally delegated to the President to fulfill the responsibilities of the office. These duties are articulated in Article II section 2 cl. 1, cl.2 and Article II section3, they read in part:

> The President shall be Commander-in-Chief of the Army and Navy of the United States, and of the Militia of the several States, when called into the actual Service of the United States...and he shall have Power to grant Reprieves and Pardons for Offences against the United States, except in Cases of Impeachment. (Article II section 2 cl. 1)
>
> He shall have Power, by and with the Advice and Consent of the Senate, to make Treaties, provided two-thirds of the Senators present concur: and he shall nominate, and by and with the Advice and Consent of the Senate, shall appoint Ambassadors, other public Ministers and Consuls, Judges of the supreme Court, and all other Officers of the United States (Article II section 2 cl.2)
>
> ...he shall take Care that the Laws be faithfully executed (Article II section 3)

The President, then, has been delegated the power to be the Commander-in-Chief of all branches of our military, to make treaties with other countries with the advice and consent of the Senate, to nominate individuals to become a Justice of the Supreme Court, and to "faithfully execute" the laws of the United States. It is important to place these responsibilities in context with the powers delegated to the Congress of the United States in Article I of the Constitution. While the President has the responsibility to function as the Commander-in-Chief of the military, it is the Congress, the People's representatives, who possess the power to declare war. The President does hold the power to make treaties, nominate judges to the Supreme Court or appoint ambassadors, but only with the Advice and Consent of the Senate. And while the President has the duty to "faithfully execute the law," it is the Congress which possesses the constitutional power to make the law under our constitutional system.

The appropriate role of the Presidency has been the fodder for much debate over the last six years. While vigorous and thoughtful disagreements are a healthy sign that our republic is functioning, it behooves us to remember what the separation of powers are and why they were instituted. The fear of concentrated power can be seen throughout our Constitution. The language in Article II is reflective of that concern. No one, not even the President of the United States, will be allowed to make war—the People shall have the ultimate choice through their elected representatives in the Congress. The President can recommend legislation to remedy any particular economic or societal problem, but it is the Congress which must ultimately develop consensus to enact legislation which can gain the approval or override a Veto from the President. It is understandable that at times of national distress citizens will be susceptible to arguments which call for executive action when the legislative process appears to be ineffective or unwilling to provide leadership in the resolution of the country's maladies. Yet the observations of the Framers might once again offer some important guidance.

In a direct rebuttal to Anti-Federalist attacks on the proposed powers of the Executive Branch under Article II, Alexander Hamilton in the *Federalist Papers* no. 67, no.69, and no. 71, challenged Anti-Federalist claims that the President's powers would be akin to that of a monarch. In what could be described as one of the most scathing responses to his opponents, Hamilton, with sophisticated analytic clarity, identified the exact language, clause or provision of Article II that prevented any such concentration of power which could produce the establishment of a monarchy. He argued that the requirement to secure the "advice and consent" of the Senate on appointments and the creation of treaties; the term of office of the Presidency; the inability of the Executive Branch to ultimately prevent the passage of legislation; in addition to the limited powers assigned to the President as Commander-in-Chief without Congressional support; were powerful checks against any potential of the creation of a monarchy. Hamilton was so enraged by such a claim by the Anti-Federalists, some of whom resided in states where their governors possessed more power than that provided to the proposed Executive Branch, that he concluded in *Federalist Papers* no. 67:

> (It) proves that this supposition, destitute as it is even of the merit of plausibility, must have originated in an intention to deceive the people, too palpable to be obscured by sophistry, too atrocious to be palliated by hypocrisy.[24]

He went on in no. 69 and no. 71 to defend the limited powers placed in the Presidency and offered some observations regarding human nature and the impact of the checks placed in Article II both on the President, legislative assemblies and their role as representatives of the people in a republican government.

Hamilton noted that while the checks on the Executive Branch were essential to limit the concentration of power, the new Constitution also recognized the need for a counterbalance against the potential of prejudices produced through legislative action created by self-interested and manipulative factions. The Executive needed enough independent power to lead. His observations have particular significance today. He posited:

> The republican principle demands that the deliberate sense of the community should govern the conduct of those to whom they entrust the management of their affairs, but it does not require an unqualified complaisance to every sudden breeze of passion, or to every transient impulse which the people may receive from the arts of men who flatter their prejudices to betray their interests. It is a just observation that the people commonly intend the public good. This often applies to their very errors. But their good sense would despise the adulator who should pretend that they always reason right about the means of promoting it. They know from experience that they sometimes err: and the wonder is that they so seldom err as they do, beset, as they continually are, by the wiles of parasites and sycophants, by the snares of the ambitious, the avaricious, the desperate, by the artifices of men who possess their confidence more than they deserve it. When occasions present themselves in which the interests of the people are at variance with their inclinations, it is the duty of the persons whom they have appointed to be the guardians of those interests to withstand the temporary delusion in order to give them time and opportunity for more cool and sedate reflection…it is certainly desirable that the Executive should be in a situation to dare to act his own opinion with vigor and decision.[25]

In one of the most concise observations of why there must be a division of power in the new covenant, Hamilton explained:

> To what purpose separate the executive and the judiciary from the legislative if both the executive and the judiciary are so constituted as to be at the absolute devotion of the legislative? Such a separation must be merely nominal and incapable of producing the ends for which it was established. It is one thing to be subordinate to the laws, and another to be dependent on the legislative body…The representatives of the people, in a popular assembly, seem sometimes to fancy that they are the people themselves and betray strong symptoms of impatience and disgust at the least sign of opposition from any other quarter, as if the exercise of its rights, by either the executive or judiciary, were a breach of their privilege and an outrage to their dignity. They often appear disposed to exert an imperious control over the other departments; and as they commonly have the people on their side, they always

act with such momentum as to make it very difficult for the other members of the government to maintain the balance of the Constitution. [26]

Alexander Hamilton's defense for an Executive Branch with limited but independent power and his observations regarding legislative decision-making are important insights particularly today. Indeed, his understanding of the need to both guard against concentrated power and the dangers of public manipulation through the legislative process by the "wiles of parasites and sycophants, by the snares of the ambitious, the avaricious, the desperate, by the artifices of men who possess their confidence more than they deserve it..." are warnings for contemporary Americans as we attempt to evaluate the claims by special interest groups (factions), the political elite, and the mass media regarding the "correct" course for the country. But his support for the need for the separation of power in the newly formed government did not stop with the Executive Branch. Hamilton defended with equal vigor the proposed independent judiciary.

Article III of the Constitution describes the delegation of power from the American people to the Judicial Branch. While section I of Article III describes the distribution of judicial power into specified judicial departments, section II identifies the jurisdiction or types of disputes which will be addressed by the newly designed judicial bodies. For our purposes, the most important sections of Article III read as follows:

> The judicial Power of the United States, shall be vested in one supreme Court, and in such inferior Courts as the Congress may from time to time ordain and establish. The Judges, both of the supreme and inferior Courts, shall hold their Offices during good Behaviour, and shall, at stated Times, receive for their Services, a Compensation, which shall not be diminished during their Continuance in Office. (Article III, section I).
>
> The judicial Power shall extend to all Cases, in Law and Equity, arising under this Constitution, the Laws of the United States, and Treaties made, or which shall be made under their Authority; to all Cases affecting Ambassadors, other public Ministers and Consuls;...to Controversies to which the United States shall be a Party; to Controversies between two or more States;...between Citizens of different States, between Citizens of the same State claiming Lands under Grants of different States, and between a State, or the Citizens thereof, and foreign States, Citizens or Subjects. (Article III, section 2, cl. 1).
>
> In all Cases affecting Ambassadors, other public Ministers and Consuls, and those in which a State shall be a Party, the supreme Court shall have original Jurisdiction. In all the other Cases before mentioned, the supreme Court shall have appellate Jurisdiction, both as to Law and Fact, with such

Exceptions, and under such Regulations as the Congress shall make. (Article III, section2, cl.2).

While the meaning of the language of Article III has been the subject of literally hundreds of judicial decisions, legislative amendments, and constant debate, even to today, it is not beyond the understanding of most Americans that the above language empowers the federal judiciary—particularly the Supreme Court of the United States—to be the last branch of government to determine the constitutionality of laws enacted by both the Congress and state and local legislative bodies. Put in a short form, Article III declares that the Supreme Court of the United States shall possess the ultimate authority to hear "all cases and controversies...arising under" the Constitution. Additionally, that the Supreme Court Justices and judges in the lower courts shall be appointed for life terms, as long as they fulfill their responsibilities with "good Behaviour." And finally, that the jurisdiction or the obligation to hear certain types of cases, by examining both the legal principles and factual matters involved in each case, shall be divided by the type of case and whatever limitations the Congress places on the lower or "inferior" courts.

The newly constructed federal judiciary reflected the Framers' intention to establish a process for increased consistency and predictability in judicial decision-making across the nation and to provide for a level of finality to disputes regarding the meaning and application of the Constitution and its Bill of Rights. To accomplish these objectives the Founders believed it was crucial to empower the judicial branch with broad decision-making authority and protection from the political process. The key to the success or failure of their plan depended upon the degree to which the appointed Justices of the Supreme Court and the lower appellate courts could be insulated from the political process. Alexander Hamilton was called upon to defend the proposed independent judiciary. Knowing that the proposal would be attacked by the Anti-Federalists as the creation of the most undemocratic and unchecked branch of the national government, Hamilton addressed each argument raised against an independent judiciary. In the *Federalist Papers* no. 78, he argued that of all the branches of government established by the Constitution the judicial branch was the "least dangerous" and the "weakest of the three departments of power." Hamilton supported his conclusion based upon the following observation:

The Executive not only dispenses the honors, but holds the sword of the community. The legislature not only commands the purse, but prescribes the rules by which the duties and rights of every citizen are to be regulated. The judiciary, on the contrary, has no influence over either the sword or the purse, no direction either of the strength or of the wealth of the society, and can take no active resolution whatever. It may truly be said to have neither force nor will, but merely judgment, and must ultimately depend upon the aid of the executive arm even for the efficacy of its judgments. [27]

After over two centuries, Hamilton's analysis of the powers delegated by the American people to the three branches of the federal government is too often forgotten: Congress possesses the constitutional authority to coin money ("the power of the purse"); the Executive has the responsibility to function as the Commander-in-Chief ("the power of the sword"); and the Judicial branch has the task of determining the constitutional legitimacy of the actions of all the departments of government without the ability to enforce their decisions ("merely the power of judgment").

For this divided government to function, all the branches are obligated to respect and ultimately defer to the actions of each other. Constant gridlock was unacceptable. But, of course, Hamilton was not suggesting that a harmony of opinions and interests would somehow be produced by this new experiment in government. In fact, as has been pointed out throughout our investigation, the Founders planned for just the opposite result. Divided power will bring debate and vehement disagreement between the different departments of government and the factions within them and the American people. But, as Hamilton posited in *Federalist* no. 78, citing the French philosopher Montesquieu, "there is no liberty, if the power of judging be not separated from the legislative and executive powers." To overcome the potential governmental gridlock that can develop with divided government, there *must* be an independent judiciary whose task would be to shape decisions regarding the constitutional legitimacy of the actions of government. Only individuals who were insulated from political manipulation could be assigned the task to, on rare occasions, be asked to determine if the actions of government were contrary to the Constitution and therefore void.

Hamilton believed that life-appointment of judges based on "good Behavior," or permanent tenure of judicial offices, was required. He was confident that an independent judiciary would guard against "the effects of occasional ill humors in society" being reflected in legislative action. He reminded both supporters and opponents that life tenure was essential for the insulation of judicial decision-making from political manipulation emanating from either the Executive or the Congress. He stressed that "periodical appointments, however regulated, or by whomsoever made, would, in some way or other, be fatal to their necessary independence." He explained that if either the Executive Branch or the Congress possessed the authority to make these temporary appointments "there would be danger of an improper complaisance to the branch which possessed it." Those appointees would inevitably be beholden to either the President or whatever majority held sway in the Congress. Hamilton, and ultimately the American people through the ratification process, believed that justice and fairness was more likely to be established by the appointment of individuals for life terms based on "good Behavior" than by any other selection process.

Any objective reading of the Article III powers delegated to the Federal Judiciary must conclude that this branch of government is the least directly accountable department to the American people. Appointments for life terms, on first glance, strike against some of the very basic presumptions of republican government. Yet, with more careful examination, Hamilton's observations regarding the essentiality of an independent judiciary, only underscores the delicate balance that the Founders sought to achieve through the proposed national government.

While the Founders never wavered from the importance of majority rule and the supremacy of the desires of the greater number of the American people, they were constantly aware of the dangers of majoritarian tyranny. They believed that the need for some impartial "final arbiter" of disputes concerning the directives of the Constitution simply could not be achieved by electing federal judges to office or by temporary appointment. Once again the Founders offered a blended approach. While the appointment process would require participation through the political process, that is, that the President shall "nominate, and by and with the Advice and Consent of the Senate," life tenure would ultimately offer the best protection from the possibility of political influence impacting judicial decision-making. The Justices would not be beholding to any political party or faction for the continuance of their positions. Faced with the choice of designing a judicial branch which would be directly answerable to the other departments of government, the Framers constructed an independent judiciary which would be accountable to the American people through its commitment to an objective administration of justice based on past precedents and the directives of the Constitution and the Bill of Rights. Yet, while life tenure and the necessity of an independent judiciary were essential for the protection of individual liberty, the Framers once again placed a structural counterbalance within the proposed Constitution—the constitutional amendment process. This mechanism was designed as the ultimate "fail safe" against abuse of power originating from any department of government, including the judiciary. The availability of this constitutional option when coupled with the potential refusal of the Executive branch to implement the Court's decision(s) and the citizenry refusal to comply with its "judgment" were and remain to be powerful checks against judicial decisions contrary to the desires of the American people.

Whether the Supreme Court of the United States has always reflected the objectivity and commitment to its special role in the functioning of the American experiment in government has been the subject of innumerable jurisprudential treatises and popular commentaries. Such is the case in our current political debates regarding health care. At this point, it should be noted that the Founders understood that compliance with the decisions of the Court, by both the other co-ordinate branches of our federal system and ultimately the American people, would be dependent upon the perceived objectivity and balanced nature of its decision-making. To achieve this result some have argued that Supreme Court decision-making should be restricted to narrow application of past legal precedents while others have stressed that a broader interpretation of the Constitution's language is essential for the attainment of justice and fairness. Both positions have merit. To achieve the level of objectivity necessary to produce societal acceptance, Supreme Court decisions must produce consistency and predictability. If judicial decisions are not anchored in past precedent then they appear to be arbitrary or capricious. However, if the judgments of the Court are restricted to past decisions which are not reflective of the society's changing mores and values the potential for voluntary compliance with present and future decisions are at risk. The Founders left then the Supreme Court of the United States with the ultimate responsibility to carefully shape decisions which reflect a commitment to the rule of law through the application of past precedents but also to function as a cautious social barometer in an effort to achieve support for its decision-making.

As we have noted throughout our examination of the philosophical and political foundations of our governmental system, the ultimate task of the Founders was to design, as Madison noted, the "least imperfect" structure. The design of the Federal Judiciary and the Supreme Court in particular reflects a recognition of the constant struggle between the potential for tyranny from, in the case of the Court, a select few of appointed individuals acting upon their own bias or prejudices, and the necessity in our divided government for the calm wisdom and integrity of individuals who recognize their particularly unique responsibility in American government. Because of the important role assigned to it by the American people, the Supreme Court of the United States must maintain a status of legitimacy which will engender a willingness to comply with its judgments—even when there is significant societal disagreement with the Court's decisions. While the individuals who are appointed to the Court are often creatures of and vetted by the political process, they must be imbued with a respect for the rule of law and the objectivity necessary for its application. Over time if the Court is viewed by the American people as just another political institution, incapable of calm, objective, and deliberate reflection of both the letter and spirit of our Constitution, the Founders' quest for a mechanism to balance the competing interests inherent in a majoritarian republican government committed to the protection of individual liberty will have failed. With a few important exceptions, the Court has managed to produce decisions which have gleaned the support of the American people. One important reason for this may be that life tenure has helped to shape a commitment to the institution of the Court by the majority of the justices which surpassed their individual ideological preferences. Indeed, the legacy of each justice is and always will be directly connected to the People's respect for the institution of the Court and its unique responsibility in American government.

Our overview of some of the most fundamental theoretical principles which provide the rationales for the adoption of the Constitution and the development of our federal system is not intended as an exhaustive account of the multitude of checks against concentrated power inherent within the American experiment of governance. For example, whether it is the length of the term of office of members of the House of Representatives or the Senate mandated by Article I, the qualifications of individuals seeking the Presidency, as well as the limitation upon the term of office mandated by Article II, or the restrictions regarding the jurisdiction of "cases and controversies" which can be reviewed by the Supreme Court and the restrictions which Congress can place on the lower federal courts to hear certain cases in Article III, all can be identified as important limitations on the functioning of our elected and appointed public servants. The "reserved power" of the States pursuant to the Tenth Amendment, commonly described as concurrent governmental authority to "protect the health, safety, welfare, and morals" of its citizens, also has been and continues to be championed by some, as a limitation on the federal government. The list of intra-departmental and external checks on federal governmental entities does not end with these examples. Additionally, Congress can deny all or some of its "independent" administrative agencies (e.g., the Food and Drug Administration or the Federal Communications Commission) with funding as a method to restrain their regulatory rulemaking. Finally, the Supreme Court has established, through its decision-making, a variety of "self-restraining" theories to limit its judicial review powers under Article III. They include, but are not limited to, the Court refusing to review cases which the Justices have determined do not possess the requisite elements to have "standing," or cases which involve "political questions" which can be resolved in another co-ordinate branch of government.

Nevertheless, even with all the aforementioned checks on the potential for abuse of power in the newly designed Constitution, the Founders were not constructing a federal system of governance in an effort to create political gridlock as a method to protect unrestrained individual liberty. The amalgam of political theory which underscored their revolutionary experiment recognized that government was absolutely essential for the maximization of liberty in a community of individuals with potentially different aspirations. Wedded to their commitment to protect a maximization of individual liberty was also their acceptance of government's responsibility to "promote the general welfare" of the American people. In the middle of what has become a slow recovery from the worst economic collapse in decades of American life, the fundamental principles hammered out by the Founders have been forgotten, distorted, or selectively presented for short-term political gain. Concepts such as "liberty" and "We the People," are routinely used as rallying symbols of the legitimacy for a particular political cause by some of our elected representatives and political pundits without even a rudimentary understanding of the historical context and meaning of the terms. What we have discovered with our brief overview of the political philosophical and historical origins of the Constitution, its specific language, and the subsequent creation of our federal system, is that the Framers understood the importance of compromise for the successful attainment of governance. Without this principle as the core of our constitutional process, they understood that the meaning of the term "American" would be unattainable.

It will be remembered that while John Locke's treatises provided powerful philosophical arguments for the importance of individual liberty, he also recognized that liberty was not absolute. The English Whig Libertarians, John Trenchard and Thomas Gordon, in their provocative and popular pamphlets on liberty and government in *Cato's Letters*, also conceded that liberty can be constrained by government contingent upon the "harm" created through individual action. James Madison's observation that while the need for government was a "misfortune" yet a "necessity," also signaled a recognition by the Founders of the fundamental role of government in the protection of individual liberty and the advancement of the public welfare. For Madison and his colleagues at the Constitutional Convention the most dangerous counterforce against each citizen's acquisition of liberty was, in a republican government, the creation of "majoritarian tyranny" in the legislative process by the influence of factions. They understood that the need to balance the multitude of competing interests within the ever evolving citizenry would require a national forum in which compromises must be struck on behalf of the American people. It will be remembered that over the objections of Anti-Federalists like Patrick Henry, the Framers were adamant that the parties to their proposed contract were "We the People" not the "States of America" and the proposed national government.

However, it cannot, and should not, be overlooked that the meaning of "We the People" was restricted initially, almost exclusively, to white male property owners. With the aftermath of the Civil War and the enactment of amendments to the Constitution prohibiting slavery, establishing the right to possess property, to the equal protection of the law and to the right to vote, the concept of "We the People" did begin to slowly change through legislative action and judicial decision-making. By the 1920's, with the ratification of the 19th Amendment, "We the People" would finally include the fundamental right of women to vote.

It is undeniable that this expanding definition of who constitute "We the People" has been produced sometimes throughout our history through violence and societal unrest. But it is also important to remember that our ability as a nation to accommodate change has occurred, for the most part, within a governmental process that demands compromise and the balancing of competing interests. It was understood by the Founders that their vision of governance would endure only if it was malleable enough to conform to the evolving values of the American people. The document contains specific directives regarding the separation of powers and the delegation of responsibilities within each department of government. Yet, maybe, the true genius of the agreement between the People and their government is the elasticity of the language implanted in some sections of the Constitution. The directive to the Congress in Article I to "make all Laws which shall be necessary and proper for the carrying into Execution the foregoing powers....," or the responsibility of the Supreme Court under Article III powers to hear all "cases and controversies arising under the Constitution" or the Ninth Amendment mandate that the "enumeration...of certain rights, shall not be construed to deny or disparage others retained by the people," are examples of the Founders recognition of the need to leave for future generations the task of balancing the importance of individual liberty with the desires of the community.

What we have discovered is that the Founders believed that American government must be a process—one which is grounded in a commitment to maximize the aspirations of the individual citizen within the context of an ordered society. They believed to attain that objective, government was essential to act as a referee, a fulcrum, on which to balance the desires of the individual with the needs of the broader community. In an attempt to achieve some form of equilibrium between these two sometimes competing values our system requires constant vigilance of tyranny, from whatever source, political compromise, and an informed citizenry. In the next chapter we will explore the question of whether the contemporary political debates regarding the role of government in American life reflect a commitment to these Founding values.

2 "Curing the Mischiefs of Faction"

IT WILL BE REMEMBERED THAT THE Framers of the Constitution and the Bill of Rights feared the destructive impact that uncontrolled special interest groups (factions) could have on "...the rights of other citizens or to the permanent and aggregate interests of the community."[28] James Madison and other advocates for a national government identified uncontrolled factions as the most dangerous mechanism in the creation of abuse of power and tyranny from whatever source. As was noted earlier in our review of some of the arguments presented for the adoption of the proposed Constitution, Madison recognized that the "latent causes of faction...are sown in the nature of man"[29] and that any attempt to eliminate what we now commonly refer to as special interest groups would be to destroy liberty. Instead, he argued that the creation of a national forum, the Congress of the United States, would compel political compromise between competing interest groups and minimize the potential for abuse of power. He was convinced that this structure of lawmaking was the best protection to "control the violence of faction."[30] This process would create "...a greater variety of parties, against the event of any one party being able to outnumber and oppress the rest."[31] For the most part, Madison's fear of the influence of factions "...who are united and actuated by some common impulse of passion, or interest, adverse to the rights of other citizens or to the permanent and aggregate interests of the community,"[32] remains a powerful warning for contemporary Americans. At a time when the repercussions of the financial collapse still linger in the minds of many citizens, when the economic disparities of the last twenty, if not thirty years, have resulted in a collective fear that the American Dream of a prosperous future for our children is unattainable, and in a societal environment where information is too often presented with one-line sound bites, is there any question that special interest groups will become increasingly more visible in our political process? The problem is not the existence or even the proliferation of such "factions," but rather as Madison observed "... that the public good is disregarded in the conflicts of rival parties."[33]

What constitutes the "public good" must be determined through our political process and ultimately with the involvement of the American people. The Founders understood that our system of governance required both legislative and popular political compromise. But they were well aware that in a society which values and is committed to protect liberty, arriving at an understanding of the "public good" would require an open dialogue with and between sometimes widely divergent interests groups. The problem is not the existence of factions, but rather, as Madison argued, the ability or inability of government to control through compromise the impact of special interests on the broader electorate. Unfortunately, over the last six years, the Congress has been unable or unwilling, to reach beyond the inherent partisanship of our political process and find mechanisms for compromise on behalf of the American People. While there are many reasons for the current political stalemate in Congress, the influence of one faction has undeniably impacted the process and has made Madison's forewarnings even more relevant today.

The Tea Party

The near collapse of our financial system and its impact on all levels of society has produced a justified frustration by the American People regarding what appears to some as a failure of government to respond to the issues of unemployment and the level of deficit spending on the national, state, and local levels. One by-product of this anger has been the creation of one political action group which has grown from what appeared to be a spontaneous independent association of concerned citizens into a powerful wing of the Republican Party. Euphemistically described as "the Tea Party," this initial loosely configured collection of Americans has morphed into a powerful force in contemporary American politics. Because it represents both the positive and negative characteristics associated with the role of factions in the political process, a closer examination of its origins and principles within the context of the Founders vision of government is imperative.

Madison's insight regarding the causes of factions is once again relevant. He observed:

> A zeal for different opinions concerning religion, concerning government, and many other points, as well as speculation as of practice; an attachment to different leaders ambitiously contending for pre-eminence and power, or to persons of other descriptions whose fortunes have been interesting to the human passions, have, in turn, divided mankind into parties, inflamed them with mutual animosity, and rendered them much

more disposed to vex and oppress each other than to co-operate for their common good. So strong is this propensity of mankind to fall into mutual animosities that, where no substantial occasion presents itself, the most frivolous and fanciful distinctions excite their most violent conflicts. But the most common and durable source of factions has been the various and unequal distribution of property. Those who hold and those who are without property have ever formed distinct interests in society...The regulation of these various and interfering interests forms the principal task of modern legislation and involves the spirit of party and faction in the necessary and ordinary operations of the government. [34]

The collapse of one of the nation's largest "banks"—Lehman Brothers—and the subsequent response by other financial institutions as to their ability to withstand a potential "run on the banks" by frightened investors/depositors created a growing fear regarding the stability of our financial system. The Bush administration's call for Congressional approval of billions of dollars of governmental support in an effort to add necessary liquidity to the "banking" system added another layer of frustration by many Americans regarding the fairness of providing support for Wall Street while little or no support was being offered to "main-street." The insertion of billions of taxpayer dollars into the banking system appeared to stem the tide of a collapse of Wall Street, but the portfolios of most Americans stock market dependent retirement accounts were devastated. Additionally, the value of homes in the country plummeted resulting in millions of American homeowners being forced into foreclosure or their mortgages were significantly higher than the value of their home. While Congressional action produced an economic stimulus which would allow for the temporary retention of thousands of public servants, firemen, policemen, and teachers in public sector jobs, the absence of meaningful direct governmental assistance to protect citizens from corporate "down-sizing" in the private sector, created an environment ripe for political and personal scapegoating. With these and a multitude of other real and imagined grievances percolating within the country, ironically, it was a cable television bond market analyst/reporter, a once Chicago bond trader and an unabashed participant in the financial industry at the center of the so-called "great recession," who sparked the flame for the creation of the Tea Party.

More specifically, his on-camera rant against proposed Treasury department actions to assist some Americans facing mortgage foreclosures with the potential of securing government-backed mortgage modifications and his disgust of what he believed to be federal intervention into the financial markets with a stimulus plan, began a nationwide debate about the role of government in

American life. His commentary is worthy of examination not only because it allegedly sparked the Tea Party movement but also because it exposed some of its ideology. He castigated the proposed program as "promoting bad behavior" by "subsidizing the losers' mortgages." He suggested that such an action would be using taxpayer money to bailout "your neighbor's mortgage" which was obtained to put in "an extra bathroom" and now "can't pay the mortgage." He went on to rail against "governmental intervention" into the market and that "capitalists" should join in a Tea Party response to the proposed federal government actions. Asking if "President Obama—are you listening," he insisted that he and the market traders in the room, who chimed in enthusiastically with his analysis, represented a "silent majority" of Americans. He ended his commentary with what has become an oft-repeated defense by Tea Party supporters—he argued that governmental officials, and by inference anyone who disagreed with him, should read the writings of the "Founding Fathers"—Thomas Jefferson and Benjamin Franklin—because they would be "rolling over in their graves" with such governmental intrusion. With great applause from his colleagues anchoring the business cable television program and a guest billionaire bond investor discussing the impact of the potential government program, the stage was set. The ideological lines were drawn. Good and evil was now exposed. The "free markets" were at risk of being destroyed by governmental interlopers. In the name of the Founders, citizens who believed in private enterprise needed to rise up against this brazen attack on liberty. [35]

Subsequent support for this position was relatively swift and culminated in the creation of numerous so-called "political action" organizations, all in one fashion or another, describing themselves as "Tea Party" members. While the initial creation of numerous "Tea Party" groups appeared to be loosely configured and without a common political core other than a general disdain for "big government" and a commitment to "liberty," within a relatively short period of time, signs of more sophisticated political leadership began to emerge. Even the most uninitiated political observer detected the constant daily reiteration of the "Tea Party" evolution in the mainstream media or within the commentary offered most often by conservative political pundits and politicians. What might have been initially a spontaneous outcry of some citizens regarding the unfairness of governmental support for the very individuals and institutions at the center of the financial crash without a corresponding effort to provide direct assistance to "main street," now appeared to be a more politically co-ordinated attack on the federal government generally and the Obama administration specifically. After the passage of a stimulus plan by a predominately Democratic Congress and the constant castigation by self-described congressional "fiscal hawks," some of the mantra of the Tea Party advocates began to be espoused by Congressional Republicans most of whom, at the time, were in the minority in the House of Representatives and Senate. But what was not so clear in the genesis of the movement was the role of one powerful interest group—Freedom Works. The political sophistication and financial support of this "non-for-profit" lobbying organization helped to market through the mass media and within the halls of Congress a campaign for so-called "limited government," "fiscal responsibility," and "free market economics." The influence of this organization in funding and shaping the initial frustration of many of the original Tea Party supporters into a cohesive political machine cannot be understated.[36]

Freedom Works is the result of a merger in 2004 of two political action organizations—Citizens for a Sound Economy (CSE) and Empower America. The organization is funded by numerous "conservative" individuals and foundations, including but not limited to, David Koch and the Forbes Foundation.[37] Under the leadership of Dick Armey, an influential retired Republican Texas congressman, the once relatively amorphous Tea Party seemed to represent every right-wing political *cause célèbre* in the Congress of the United States. After the 2010 midterm election victories by Tea Party candidates running on the republican ballot in many states, evidence of this newly minted coalition's power within the Republican Party became even more evident with the creation by once Presidential-hopeful, Michelle Bachman of the Tea Party Caucus in the House of Representatives. Not surprisingly, many of the positions promoted by Freedom Works have found their way into legislative action or inaction through the efforts of Tea Party republicans. Since the arrival of the 2010, eighty-four republicans who won their seats in Congress by touting themselves as Tea Party members, the republican majority in the House of Representatives has voted for or offered legislation to reduce government spending, repeal the Affordable Care Act ("Obamacare") on enumerable occasions, voted against the increased regulation of Wall Street (Dodd-Frank legislation), rejected any legislation to raise revenue by taxing the income of the top one percent of Americans, and voted against legislation to require liability for oil spills.

It should be remembered that in the 1990's the American Petroleum Institute in conjunction with Citizens For a Sound Economy lobbied heavily against a proposed new energy tax and new EPA clean air standards as well as the Clinton health care proposals. And it also should not come as a surprise that major funders of both of these special interest groups (the oil, coal, gas industry billionaires Koch Brothers, and the country's foremost Flat Tax proponent multi-millionaire Steve Forbes) would be enthusiastic supporters of Freedom Works' "Key Issues" so readily adopted by Tea Party Republicans. Under the categories of Budget/Spending, Tax Reform, Workplace Freedom, Health Care Reform, Energy and the Environment, School Choice, Red Tape, Hidden Taxes, Regulations and Entitlement Reform, Medicare and Social Security, Freedom Works has offered Tea Party proponents a menu of public policy issues from which they can pick to attack "big government" intervention into their lives and into "free markets."

But Freedom Works is not the only player in the field of Tea Party activists. The Tea Party Patriots (TPP) have also played the role of "wing man" for some off-again-on-again Republicans drifting between the contemporary Libertarian movement and the broader political label of Tea Party supporters. Indeed, one of this special interest groups' core principles which appears to bind them with the positions of most self-described libertarians is their commitment to "constitutionally limited government." This principle coupled with their support for "fiscal responsibility" and "free-market economics" is strikingly similar to the rhetorical flourishes often espoused by Republican/Libertarian presidential candidate Representative Ron Paul and his son, Senator Rand Paul. A brief examination of the Tea Party Patriots' vision of what constitutes "constitutionally limited government" and the Republicans' seeming embrace of its legitimacy may provide a clearer understanding of the power of this faction in creating gridlock in the Congress of the United States.

The Tea Party Patriot's definition of constitutionally limited government is that:

> ...power resides with the people and not with the government. Governing should be done at the most local level possible where it can be held accountable. America's founders believed that government power should be limited, enumerated, and constrained by our Constitution. [38]

There are three claims within this "core principle" of the TPP. The first is that legitimate authority to govern is derived from the will of the people not with the institutions of government. The second is that governmental decision-making is constitutionally authorized only if it is instituted through the actions of local and or presumably state officials. The third posits that the "Founders' vision" of government was one grounded in "limited" and "enumerated" power. It should be noted that each of these claims often provide the centerpiece for harangues by right-wing politicians and some media political pundits who have made their careers touting governmental conspiracies to destroy the "founding values." Of course, it must be asked: from what historical source are these claims originating? Which Founder supported these principles? Have the proponents of these claims distorted the meaning of the terms "limited" and "enumerated" as understood and debated by the American people during the ratification process of the Constitution?

As we have discovered from our overview of the political philosophical origins of our Constitution and the intense debate regarding its ratification, an overriding first principle for our experiment in government was the supremacy of the People from which all legitimate governmental power derives. Indeed, it was because of that understanding that the Founders placed into the Constitution provisions which would reinforce both the rights of individual citizens and the collective people to have ultimate authority over the newly established departments of government at the national and state levels. The delegation of power from "We the People" to government was, as Madison noted, a "necessity." He believed that their task was to design the "least imperfect" process possible to protect liberty. Government was not by definition "evil" but rather a necessary tool to implement the desires of the People. As we have learned, the focus of the debate regarding the ratification of the Constitution was what was the best process of discerning the will of the People and correspondingly how best to secure liberty and act on behalf of the public welfare. The problem then with the first claim is not with the assertion regarding the supremacy of the will of the people, but rather with how the desires of the people would be discerned. The TPP's first claim, while on its face is consistent with the Founding vision, takes on meaning only within the context of the next two claims. Unlike the first broad claim, the next two are either historically incorrect or misleading.

The Tea Party Patriots' second claim that "governing should be done at the most local level possible," allegedly because it will engender accountability, is simply not supported by serious examination of the successful arguments presented during the debates prior to the adoption of the Constitution. While it may be a masterful marketing slogan for political campaigns or fundraising efforts to some on the political right in America, it cannot withstand historical scrutiny. It will be remembered that the Federalists successfully rebutted Anti-Federalists tirades against a national government by providing example after example of the failures caused by the Articles of Confederation and the concentration of power on the state and local level. The overriding task of the new Constitution was to create and preserve the importance of American citizenship—not state citizenship. As has been pointed out earlier in our investigation, the adoption of the Constitution did not vest power only in the national government. Some "concurrent powers" were retained by state governments through the Tenth Amendment. But no objective analysis of the ratification process, the language of the document, or subsequent decisions of the Supreme Court support the TPP's claim that state or local governing would best represent the will of the American people or protect against tyranny from legislative bodies. Our history prior to the adoption of the Constitution proved otherwise. Indeed, this claim and the last seemed to be reminiscent of Anti-Federalist objections to the proposed Constitution. It is then, indeed, ironic that the TPP, who project themselves as defenders of the Constitution, would promote a "core principle" based on claims rejected by the Founders. The last claim only serves to reinforce one's doubt as to the group's understanding of our history and values.

If we are to believe the TPP, the Founders' vision was one of "limited" government and was to be constrained by "enumerated" powers within the Constitution. This claim, on its face, is not necessarily inaccurate. The problem may be in its application. There can be little argument that the Founders designed a governmental structure which would "limit" the concentration of power. It is also true that the draftsmen of our governmental process were committed to a written document which would identify certain delegations of power to divided departments of government—none of which could act without the corresponding acceptance or acquiescence of the other branch(es). Additionally, the Founders were convinced that by "enumerating" the separation of powers, coupled with a declaration of certain fundamental rights which government could not usurp, that the "least imperfect" system of republican government would be achieved and liberty protected. But one is left with a sense that the TPP's third core principle is offered without a historical context of the meaning of the words so casually used to justify their particularly narrow definition of the role of government in contemporary American life. What was Madison's understanding of "limited government"? Did the Founders reliance upon "enumerated" powers always restrict governmental authority to act on behalf of the people? What does the TPP mean to suggest when it posits that governmental power is "constrained by the Constitution"?

Madison's observations regarding the meaning of "limited government" can be found in *Federalist* no. 39. He wrote:

> If we resort for a criterion to the different principles on which different forms of government are established, we may define a republic to be, or at least may bestow that name on, a government which derives all its powers directly or indirectly from the great body of the people and is administered by persons holding their offices during pleasure, for a limited period, or during good behavior. It is essential to such a government that it be derived from the great body of the society, not from an inconsiderable proportion or a favored class of it... [39]

He went on to describe the meaning of "limited government" under the proposed Constitution. Using both the proposed terms of office of members of the House of Representatives, the Senate, and the office of the President, Madison reiterated that the proposed restrictions on length of service were similar to those of the existing terms of office for State officials. He reminded the Anti-Federalists that, unlike many States, the proposed Constitution would provide for impeachment of appointed judges and most importantly prohibit the granting of titles of nobility either on the federal or state level. The new governmental structure was to be republican in form and process. Therefore, "limited government" for Madison and his supporters at the Constitutional Convention was to be obtained through restricted terms of political office, elections in which the "great body of the people" would participate, the creation of legal mechanisms by which public officials could be removed from office, and the "absolute prohibition of titles of nobility" granted at the federal or state level. One of the most important elements of the Founders' vision regarding the proposed Constitution was that "the great body of society"—the American people—would be the final arbiter of who would serve as their agent in the administration of government. They rejected any notion that local and state laws should supercede the authority of the American people as determined by their duly elected representatives. Madison wrote:

> The idea of a national government involves in it, not only an authority over the individual citizens, but an indefinite supremacy over all persons and things, so far as they are objects of lawful government. Among a people consolidated into one nation, this supremacy is completely vested in the national legislature... [40]

This understanding of the relationship of the American people to their government was powerfully articulated in Article VI of the Constitution. It states in part:

> ...the Laws of the United States...shall be the Supreme Law of the Land; and the Judges in every State shall be bound thereby, and any Thing in the Constitution or Laws of any State to the Contrary notwithstanding.

The unspecified concurrent powers were retained via the Tenth Amendment to the States. And it is accurate to suggest that our Constitution reflects what Madison described as a "composition" of both a national and federal system of governance. But the Founders left little doubt that the wishes of the American people reflected through their national representatives decision-making in the Congress of the United States, would be the law of the land. To infer then as does the TPP and many other contemporary "libertarian" special interest groups that the Founders believed that "limited government" meant state legislative supremacy or local government authority over issues which have implications regarding its constituent's rights as American citizens is simply unsupportable. Of course, what is accurate is that the Founders believed that government should be held accountable to the people. They understood that citizen oversight at every level of government—state, local, and national—was essential as a protection against any abuse of power. But their negative experiences with the Articles of Confederation and its reliance upon state and local governance processes, often controlled by small but powerful factions, convinced them that liberty could be better protected through the creation of a national government. "Limited government" then was understood to be accomplished not by transferring power to "the local level" as the TPP suggest, but rather by dividing power amongst the various branches of the national government, limiting terms of office, and the myriad of other restrictions implanted into the process of governing discussed in Chapter One.

One fears that the Congressional paralysis over the last few years has encouraged a historical revisionism that pines for simple solutions to complex national problems. Using the bromides that "all politics is local" or the need to return to "the laboratories of the States," the TPP and other loosely described Tea Party factions have found a marketing strategy to push their agendas. Indeed, these phrases were heard throughout the 2012 Presidential and Congressional elections by some Republican candidates. This "blending" of historical revisionism regarding the actual Founding vision with a neo-libertarian understanding of the role of governmental regulation of "Free markets" and "Fiscal Responsibility" has become the mantra of the present majority of republicans in the House of Representatives and most Republican Senators.

That said, there are those who suggest that what is meant by the use of the term "limited government" is that no government, national, state, or local has the authority to restrict the actions of individual citizens. They are comforted by the use of the term "enumerated" power, as if to suggest that the Constitution's language provides precise guidance on all matters of governance and the rights and responsibilities of citizenship. The powers of governance are limited only to the specific language found in the document so the argument goes. To these groups, now absorbed within the Tea Party movement, the Constitution is viewed as almost a codification system. This is something akin to an absolutist set of commandments fixed for all occasions and for all time. Of course, such an argument plays well to a large portion of self-described Tea Party supporters who have rallied around Republican-led efforts to appoint federal judges who will adhere to so-called "strict construction" of the Constitution and who, through their confirmation process, attest to their almost biblical faith to only "apply" and not interpret the language of the Constitution. Therefore, any decision originating from the Supreme Court of the United States which does not reflect a particular ideological litmus test is described as an example of "judicial legislating" and is a violation of the so-called "original intent" of the Constitution. Judicial decisions, then, which explore the historical and jurisprudential meaning of the Constitution and the Bill of Rights, are labeled as egregious examples of unconstrained governmental action reaching beyond its "enumerated" power. Our examination in Chapter One of the Founders' understanding of the role of the federal judiciary generally, and the Supreme Court specifically, does not support this strikingly narrow construction of judicial decision-making under the Constitution. Curiously, these same advocates for governmental non regulation of "free markets" often can be heard clamoring for legislation at the national and state level to restrict a woman's right to choose to only those occasions of "legitimate" rape or incest and to protect the life of the mother, to create an amendment to the Constitution which would define "life" to begin at conception, and to promote the "protection of marriage" by restricting the institution to heterosexual couples. It would appear, then, that the terms "limited government" and "enumerated" powers apply only to public policy issues which advance the Tea Party Patriots/Freedom Works supporters' agenda.

Notwithstanding what one may believe regarding the efficacy of the public policy positions advocated under the Tea Party label, what is so troubling is its leaders' willingness to defend them through a self-serving distortion of the Founding vision of government. Waving a copy of the Constitution, reciting the Declaration of Independence and uttering the patriotic words of "liberty" and "limited government" are certainly protected forms of symbolic and political speech under the Constitution. We can have a debate, indeed the Founders would have encouraged it—concerning the desires of the American people regarding the public policy issues cited and others proposed by Freedom Works and The Tea Party Patriots. But the misrepresentation or fabrication of the intention of the Founders and the system they designed is indefensible.

It would appear then that the "mischiefs of factions," as described by James Madison, is relevant in contemporary American governance. What may be different today is the seeming inability or unwillingness of the Congress to control the influence of this broadly structured faction. It may be that the Tea Party is not a faction. It may be that it has become an intractable and powerful part of the Republican Party. Certainly the Tea Party's influence within the Republican majority of the House of Representatives has successfully produced a gridlock in the legislative process not observed in decades of American politics. Proposed legislation offered by Democrats in the Congress, and the President, have been rejected at every level of the process. Indeed, the environment has become so toxic that the few moderates left within the Republican Party have chosen to leave office or have been defeated in recent primary elections by Tea Party candidates. Discussions of the "public welfare," the commitment to the Founding vision of political compromise, and bipartisan leadership that occasionally found its way into Congressional action at times of national distress is nowhere to be found.

Whether the reason for the lack of compromise is because of the complexity of the solutions necessary to resolve the economic maladies which face the country (by addressing the need for deficit reduction and revenue creation), the lack of leadership within both political parties to place the country first before short-term political gain, or the impact of one faction on the process, remains to be seen. The Presidential and Congressional elections of 2012 may have begun to provide solutions. But, unfortunately, recent Presidential elections have reflected a deep divide in the body politic. The recession has only served to expose this troubling fact of American life.

The impact of the financial collapse of 2007–2008 still resonates throughout the country. A slow but steady recovery has produced positive signs in some segments of the economy. Both the housing sector and consumer spending, two important economic indicators, have reflected a growing confidence for the future. Additionally, the devastating losses by millions of individuals and thousands of institutional investors in the stock market have begun to be replenished—at least for those individuals and institutions whose investments were not totally destroyed by the crash and remained in the stock market. And while there are reports of recent college graduates living in the basements of their parent's homes because of the lack of employment opportunities, the unemployment rate for this segment of the population remains relatively low—at 4%. This figure, of course, does not reflect the types of jobs available and whether they are commensurate with the personal and financial sacrifice associated with the cost of higher education. However, it should be noted that 93% of the "distributional effect" of the recovery has gone to only 1% of Americans. Indeed, vast disparities in the potential for educational attainment, wealth creation, and employment opportunity have become strikingly apparent. Pledges to resurrect and solidify the American middle class—the composition of which seems to be a continually moving political target—can be heard from our political elite across the ideological spectrum. Economic plans by both political parties at this stage to reinvigorate this essential stratum of American life, remain long on platitudes and short on specifics. Of course, political campaigns only serve to heighten the divisions within society and add to already festering animosities between different social, racial, and economic classes of citizens. If this by-product of American politics is coupled with the unwillingness of the current majority in the House of Representatives to participate in genuine compromise regarding the techniques for deficit reduction and revenue generation, then the likelihood of securing entry into and moving upward through the middle class is difficult to envision.

As has been noted, Tea Party members and their allies are a collection of factions which, depending upon the public policy issue, typically coalesce on one ideological mantra—government taxation is the anti-thesis of liberty. It stifles job creation, diminishes individual wealth creation, and provides a disincentive to work by redistributing wealth to unproductive members of society. In fact, almost every Republican member of the House of Representatives and Senate has pledged to never raise taxes. This extraordinary commitment has been the rationale or excuse for the rejection of numerous legislative proposals over the last four years offered to reduce the federal deficit. One special interest organization has been the major advocate for this response and can be viewed as either the stop-gap against big government intervention into the wealth creation of Americans or as a major threat to the process of political compromise that the Founders believed was so essential to control the impact of factions.

Americans for Tax Reform

Created in 1985, Americans for Tax Reform (ATR), a non-for-profit anti-taxation organization, has become an extraordinarily powerful force within the halls of the Congress of the United States. ATR "[o]pposes all tax increases as a matter of principle." And, in an effort to secure political support for this agenda, they have sponsored what they have described as the Taxpayer Protection Pledge. This document is a written promise by legislators and candidates for political office that allegedly commits them to oppose any effort to increase the federal income taxes on individuals and businesses. At last count, 237 members of the United States House of Representatives and 41 United States Senators have signed the pledge. It has also been signed by over 1,200 state legislators and 13 governors across the country. Almost all the legislators who signed the pledge are members of the Republican Party. At the core of the pledge and all of the ATR's lobbying activities is a political ideology which seems to view government as the reason for all of the problems of contemporary American life. Indeed, the ATR's founder, Grover Norquist, a well-known Washington lobbyist and co-author with Newt Gingrich of the Republican "Contract with America" of the 1990's, has been quoted as saying: "I am not in favor of abolishing government. I just want to shrink it down to the size where we can drown it in the bathtub." Using the "no new taxes" mantra, Mr. Norquist and his disciples envision an America free from governmental intervention into individual or corporate wealth creation. Apparently citing what he believed to be the golden age of American free enterprise, he has stated that his goal is to return the country back to the time "up until Teddy Roosevelt, when the Socialists took over—the income tax, the death tax, regulation, all that."[41] This perspective on the role of government does not stop with the solicitation of more no tax pledges, the monitoring of individual representatives, and senators' loyalty to their oath. The ATR, or Mr. Norquist, has placed its considerable influence in the halls of Congress behind numerous other well-healed lobby groups.

After founding the K-Street Project with once-house majority leader, Tom Delay, ATR has become a board member of the American Legislative Exchange Council. This consortium of corporate special interest groups creates "tasks forces" which shape and approve "model bills" for legislative approval. ALEC has supported: the Property Right Alliance, a "special project" to support legislation in opposition to the estate tax, environmental protection, licensing restrictions, federal purchase of land for national parks and wild life areas, and the seizure of land through eminent domain; the Alliance For Worker Freedom, a group which opposes collective bargaining by "educating movement conservatives on the threats to liberty posed by unions"; and the American Shareholder Project whose mission is to "provide a voice" for those opposed to estate taxes and support a "fairer," "simpler"—less progressive—tax rate.[42] One can only surmise the level of influence that the ATR possesses in the policy formation of this large consortium of special interests groups. But, as a member of the Board of this powerful lobbying conglomerate, it is not unreasonable to assume that Mr. Norquist's vision of government is shared by other members.

Very little criticism has been heard from the elected politicians who have signed the loyalty oath of "no new taxes" offered and monitored by ATR. There may be a myriad of rationales which explain this phenomenon ranging from a commitment to ideological purity to fear of losing the financial support of ATR and its numerous corporate supporters in the next election cycle. However, some criticism of the impact of the ATR's seemingly unyielding rigidity regarding revenue generation has been heard from a major figure in budget reduction formulation and a conservative/libertarian think tank. Alan Simpson, a retired Senator and conservative Republican fiscal hawk, who co-chaired a bi-partisan group of Congressional leaders asked by President Obama to offer a plan which would explore methods to reduce the federal deficit, has voiced his disgust with Grover Norquist's refusal to compromise on any form of revenue creation. Senator Simpson described Norquist's position as "no taxes, under any situation, even if your country goes to hell." [43] The Cato Institute, typically no ally of federal governmental policy making, has also criticized ATR's approach as one-dimensional.[44] But the motivations for the actions of ATR and its founder are extraordinarily difficult to describe and certainly beyond the scope of our investigation. It can be noted, however, that Mr. Norquist backed the "Romney-Ryan Plan" endorsed by the Republican Party in the 2012 Presidential election. He supported the plan because it "broadens the base, lowers rates, raises revenues through economic growth, and reduces the deficit."[45] Presuming that the Romney-Ryan Plan would have accomplished those goals—a number of public policy organizations which claim to be bi-partisan have disputed the conclusion—it is only fair to ask how expanding "the base" (adding more taxpayers to government rolls) or how revenue can be raised without taxation by "economic growth"? Both results would seem to directly contradict the unyielding pledge against "no new taxes." One conclusion, however, is indisputable. Mr. Norquist's Americans for Tax Reform has identified and deftly attacked his opponents with the seemingly unending irritant in the lives of humankind since we have emerged from the caves—*taxes!*

The payment of taxes strikes at the very core of our understanding of government and its purposes. It forces us to examine our commitment to liberty and the protection of the public welfare. It requires us to resurrect the insights of those enlightened souls from whom we have constructed our "least imperfect" system of governance. The Founders identified a process by which to debate and ultimately resolve the conflicts associated with citizenship in our Constitutional democracy—that is, through political compromise in the Congress of the United States. Once again Madison's understanding of the "most common and durable sources of factions..." is worthy of repeating:

> [They are derived from] the various and unequal distribution of property. Those who hold and those without property have ever formed distinct interests in society...the regulation of these various and interfering interests forms the principle task of modern legislation and involves the necessary and ordinary operations of government.[46]

What has been strikingly evident since the primary elections of 2010 and the successful efforts of the coalitions of Tea Party activists is that the process of regulating these "interfering interests" through the "necessary and ordinary operations of government" has failed. At the core of the contemporary political unwillingness to find compromise is, as Madison noted "the various and unequal distribution of property." If one is to believe the commentary of Mr. Norquist and his allies, hidden within the well-protected walls of anonymity provided by so-called "non-for-profit" lobbying and political action organizations, then their causes are mirror reflections of the will of the American people to be free from some Orwellian government bent on destroying liberty. Yet, closer examination of the individuals and corporate funding of these factions and their corresponding influence in the halls of Congress provides a much different motivation—the control of governmental decision-making via the influence of money flowing from the coffers of a very small percentage of Americans. Clearly, this is not a new phenomenon in American governance. This "unequal distribution of property" was present at the time of the debates for the ratification of the Constitution. Madison's objective was to "control" not eradicate the influence of the special interests in Congress. Presumably, compromise would be produced because of the power of other factions all vying for some form of governmental largesse.

While the action or inaction of the Congress from 2008 to 2014 would call into question this presumption, it may be too soon to evaluate the eventual success or failure of Madison's scheme for controlling factions through political compromise. With the recent re-election of Barack Obama in the 2012 Presidential election, the addition of a few new members of both the House of Representatives and Senate and the emergence of new demographic groups, namely Hispanic–Americans in future political campaigns, it may be that both political parties will find compromise positions for the American people. But there remain lingering questions concerning the health of our political process and its ability to provide solutions to the weak economic recovery, the growing income and wealth disparities within the country, and the reinvigoration of the American Dream.

It may be that the gridlock which has been observed in the Congress of the United States is the result of a "Perfect Storm" in American life—a financial collapse affecting millions of citizens, an insertion into the political process by a reactionary political ideology which disdains government, and a political party which was prepared to reject any attempt by their opposition to frame legislation which might bolster the re-election attempt by Barack Obama. However, the difficulties within the halls of Congress over the last few years may have even more disturbing causes. In the next chapter of our investigation, we will explore the nature of our "political elite" and their potential for leadership in finding compromise in American governance.

3 The People's Representatives
The Founding Vision and
Contemporary Political Demographics

AT THE CORE OF THE CONSTITUTOR'S understanding of republican government was a presumption that liberty would be best served by a representation process which reflected the desires of "the great body of the people." As has been noted throughout our investigation, this commitment to majority rule was tempered with a concern regarding the potential of "majoritarian tyranny." Consequently, numerous structural safeguards were designed to limit the concentration of power by any one group or faction. No better example of this recognition of the need to balance potentially competing interests can be seen than in the creation of the processes and qualifications for elected representatives to the Senate and House of Representatives in the Congress of the United States. Once again, the Founders' rationales for their proposed governmental system generally and the bi-cameral nature of the legislative branch are insightful as we explore the characteristics of our contemporary political representatives. In the *Federalists* no. 52, no. 53, and no. 57, James Madison discussed the nature of the legislative process, the arguments against and for the proposed system, and the political philosophical justification for the new scheme of representation. Discussing the proposed qualifications for election to the House of Representatives, Madison wrote in *Federalist* no. 52:

> ...the door of this part of the federal government is open to merit of every description, whether native or adoptive, whether young or old, and without regard to poverty or wealth, or to any particular profession of religious faith.[47]

He went on to observe that ".. it is essential to liberty that the government in general should have a common interest with the people..."[48] and that the legislative branch "...should have an immediate dependence on, and an intimate sympathy with, the people."[49] He concluded that ultimately the only way to maintain this relationship with the citizenry was to require "frequent elections."[50] After an analysis of the history of the English House of Commons and its tumultuous struggle in finding a lasting definition of what constituted a "frequent" electoral process, he concluded that if liberty was to be preserved our system must provide a relatively short period of time for members of the House to stand for re-election. Madison proposed a biennial election cycle. This time frame would, he believed, create a "requisite dependence of the House of Representatives on their constituents."[51] But even a two-year cycle of election was questioned. Addressing what he described as a "current observation" that "where annual elections end, tyranny begins,"[52] Madison once again drew upon his remarkable understanding of the human condition and its relationship to the protection of liberty. He suggested that the concern evinced by the proverb was not compelling as applied to the proposed electoral cycle. Madison responded in *Federalist* no. 53:

> No man will subject himself to the ridicule of pretending that any natural connection subsists between the sun and the seasons and the period within which human virtue can bear the temptations of power. Happily for mankind, liberty is not, in this respect, confined to any single point of time, but lies within extremes which afford sufficient latitude for all variations which may be required by the various situations and circumstances of civil society.[53]

The remedy to the concentration of power created by the electoral process Madison believed was the creation of the proposed Constitution. He argued:

> ...who will pretend that the liberties of the people of America will not be more secure under biennial elections, unalterably fixed by such a constitution, than those of any other nation would be where elections were annual or even more frequent but subject to alterations by the ordinary power of the government?[54]

Once again the issue before the country was not whether liberty was a paramount concern but rather how best it could be preserved. Madison also provided another reason for biennial elections—the importance of providing enough time for political representatives to acquire the "practical knowledge" necessary to perform their responsibilities. He noted that to fulfill the task of representation a "competent legislator" must possess not only an "upright intention and a sound judgment" but also a "certain degree of knowledge of the subjects on which he is to legislate."[55] While an individual could certainly bring their private experiences to their role as legislator, it was equally true that the representative must understand the process of "legislative service" which could only be gleaned through a two-year tenure in the House. Madison noted that, unlike political representation at the state level, representatives in the proposed national legislative body would require a much broader understanding of issues and laws affecting the entire country. He concluded that:

> ...the business of federal legislation must continue so far to exceed, both in novelty and difficulty, the legislative business of a single State as to justify the longer period of service assigned to those who are to transact it. [56]

Election to and membership within the House of Representatives for Madison and his supporters then was to mirror the importance of close citizen account-ability through a relatively short tenure process and yet allow enough time for individual representatives to acquire the requisite knowledge to serve both their constituents and the country.

While these arguments continue to resonate in contemporary discussions re-garding the need for legislative "term limits" as a method by which to control gridlock or concentrated political power across the federal system, Madison's commentary in *Federalist* no. 57 regarding the characteristics of political rep-resentatives and the oversight that the proposed process placed upon them, has particular significance as we explore later in this chapter the backgrounds of our current members of the Congress of the United States and the role of the American people in their selection. He wrote:

> The aim of every political constitution is or ought to be, first, to obtain for rulers men who possess most wisdom to discern, and most virtue to pursue, the common good of the society; and in the next place, to take the most effectual precautions for keeping them virtuous whilst they continue to hold their public trust. The elective mode of obtaining rulers is the char-acteristic policy of republican government. The means relied on in this form of government for preventing their degeneracy are numerous and various. The most effectual one is such a limitation of the term of appointments as will maintain a proper responsibility to the people.[57]

He went on to stress that ultimate control of those who would hold the public trust would be the "great body of the people of the United States." In the pro-posed representation system, he argued that the electors would be:

> Not the rich, more than the poor; not the learned, more than the igno-rant; not the haughty heirs of distinguished names, more than the humble sons of obscurity and unpropitious fortune...No qualification of wealth, of birth, of religious faith, or of civil profession is permitted to fetter the judg-ment or disappoint the inclination of the people.[58]

Yet, while the proposed electoral process would be open to all individuals who the people found to be the most meritorious to hold the public trust, the

Founders were ever conscious of the potential for the abuse of power. There-fore, regardless of the initial power that individual representatives possess, they would be always be:

> ...compelled to anticipate the moment when their power is to cease, when their exercise of it is to be reviewed, and when they must descend to the level from which they were raised—there forever to remain unless a faithful discharge of their trust shall have established their title to a renewal of it.[59]

At the core of Madison's defense of the proposed electoral process for the House of Representatives against claims that it would create "legal discrimina-tions" in favor of the elected representatives and "a particular class of society" was:

> ...the genius of the whole system, the nature of just and constitutional laws, and above all the vigilant and manly spirit which actuates the people of America—a spirit which nourishes freedom, and in return is nourished by it.[60]

Once again Madison and his colleagues were convinced that a system of governance with a multitude of separations of power, with checks and balances implanted within a written constitution, and electoral cycles which would place ultimate oversight on political representatives by the American people was the best process by which to "control the caprice and wickedness of man." Yet, they were not naïve men. They understood only too well that within the human condition power, and the quest for it, can compete with honor and trust for control. The only true check upon tyranny and the protection of liberty was the constant vigilance of the people. But while full and frequent citizen participation via the electoral process for members of the House of Representatives was proposed by Madison, selection and membership in the Senate of the United States required a different set of qualifications and defenses.

As we have discovered in our review of Article I, II, and III of the Constitu-tion, the Framers inserted numerous structural checks within the document in an effort to balance the differing delegations of powers within the national government. The justifications articulated by James Madison in *Federalist* no. 62 for the selection of Senators reflected their concern once again to provide a counterbalance to the electoral process established for the House of Representa-tives. Whether or not the more restrictive qualifications for membership in the Senate reflected a deep-seated distrust of republican values or a principled con-cern for moderation in legislative decision-making is a subject of debate even today. What can be said is that Madison and his colleagues believed that the Senate would serve a different role in the lawmaking function of the Congress of the United States as opposed to the House of Representatives.

With this in mind Madison proposed and then defended numerous differences in the qualifications of members of the Senate. The objectives were clear. The Senate must provide the American people with another legislative branch populated by individuals who were "more advanced in age" and who held "a longer period of citizenship" than members of the House. Each Senator must be at least thirty years of age and must be a citizen for nine years. While contemporary Americans might struggle to understand the significance of mandating an age requirement of five more years, as House members need to be only twenty-five, and a citizen for seven rather than nine years, it should be remembered that late eighteenth century America was populated by a wide variety of citizens. Indeed, memories of the Revolution and the divided loyalties concerning the Mother Country remained fresh in the minds of many Americans. Madison defended the citizenship requirement for Senate membership. He wrote in no. 62:

> The term of nine years appears to be a prudent mediocrity between a total exclusion of adopted citizens, whose merits and talents may claim a share in the public confidence, and an indiscriminate and hasty admission of them, which might create a channel for foreign influence on the national councils.[61]

Always aware of the potential for destructive discord between the various States regarding the methods of representation in the national government, the Framers once again recognized the futility of proposing either a purely proportional representation model based on population or one which was founded on equal representation. Instead, Madison proposed a representation process which was a mixture of both. He conceded that the proposed bi-cameral legislative process with proportional representation in the House, varied qualifications, and equal representation for Senatorial candidates from every State was the only course forward. In an observation relevant today, he wrote:

> …the advice of prudence must be to embrace the lesser evil and, instead of indulging a fruitless anticipation of the possible mischiefs which may ensue, to contemplate rather the advantageous consequences which may qualify the sacrifice.[62]

This mixture of proportional and equal representation was in his mind a compromise solution. It would provide the smaller states with an equal involvement in the Senate and a "constitutional recognition of the portion of sovereignty remaining in the individual States and an instrument for preserving that residuary sovereignty." As was noted in Chapter One, this compromise alone was not enough to garner the support of smaller Southern states. But when the "three-fifths" rule of the Randolph Plan was offered to provide more proportional representation in the House, the deal was struck. But these compromises resulting in a unique blend of proportional and equal representation in the Congress of the United States were more than practical necessities in achieving ratification of the proposed Constitution. Rather, they were a reflection of the Framers' constant recognition of the delicate balance necessary to maximize liberty within the context of majoritarian republican government. Equal representation within the Senate by each State in the Union would be an important check on the concentration of power from more populous States within the House of Representatives. Once again Madison reminded his countrymen of the "advantages" of creating "additional impediment(s)...against improper acts of legislation." While the House of Representatives would fulfill an important function of reflecting the popular desires of the People, the Senate, with its longer terms of office and blended representation process, would provide a structural safeguard against precipitous legislation. For centuries tyranny had been produced by the concentration of power under the rubric of the "divine right of kings." The rule of the minority over the majority was an anathema to liberty. Yet, as we discovered in Chapter One, the Founders understood that tyranny can be produced through majoritarian legislative bodies. Madison believed that one important check against this potentiality was the institution of the Senate. He admitted in *Federalist* no. 62:

> It is a misfortune incident to republican government, though in a less degree than to other governments, that those who administer it many forget their obligations to their constituents and prove unfaithful to their import-ant trust. In this point of view, a senate, as a second branch of the legislative assembly, distinct from, and dividing the power with, a first, must be in all cases a salutary check on the government. It doubles the security to the people by requiring the concurrence of two distinct bodies in schemes of usurpation or perfidy, where the ambition or corruption of one would oth-erwise be sufficient.[63]

The Founders were convinced that the addition of a second body, the Senate, with longer terms and different individual qualifications for office, would be less likely to, as Madison wrote, "...yield to the impulse of sudden and violent passions and to be seduced by factious leaders into intemperate and pernicious resolutions."[64] The final, yet equally compelling reason for the creation of a second legislative department, was that the proposed Senate, because of its longer term of office, would produce a level of "knowledge" regarding the means by which "good government" could be achieved. That is, that presumably a longer term of office allows each Senator more time for reflection and to acquire expertise on the complex matters associated with creating legislation impacting the Nation and the world than members selected to the House of Representatives.

With the advantage of historical hindsight, one can certainly question Madison's presumption regarding the level of expertise for lawmaking possessed by some individuals selected to the Senate of the United States. Indeed, some of the most revered public servants in American history have been members of the House of Representatives. But what cannot be disputed is that the creation of a bi-cameral legislature requiring different terms and qualifications for selection to office produced a legislative process that would require the balancing of the needs of various sectors of American life through political compromise. It is important to remember that Madison and his colleagues hoped that those who would be selected to serve in the public trust would be virtuous individuals who would act in the best interests of the American people. Yet, the Founders were certainly not altruists—quite to the contrary. As we have discovered throughout our investigation of the Constitution and its philosophical foundations, every delegation of power has a corresponding check. Every constitutional responsibility has a structural limitation. And, every political representative serves at the will of their constituents and must answer to them through a fixed electoral process. The Founders were wary of individuals or groups of individuals who held political power. Yet, they also understood that government was absolutely essential for both the protection of the public welfare and liberty. As we enter further into the twenty-first century, Americans have both the right and responsibility to ask just who are the individuals we have been offered by our political parties to represent us in the Congress of the United States?

The Congress of the United States
A Snapshot of the American Political Class

AS HAS BEEN NOTED THROUGHOUT OUR investigation, Americans have always possessed a healthy irreverence for government generally and specifically individuals who wield political power. Indeed, the sophisticated systems of checks and balances designed by the Founders attest to their commitment to restrain abuse of power. Nevertheless, as we have discovered from our examination of Madison's arguments for the electoral process and the qualifications for political representation, they also believed that the proposed

Constitution would produce individuals of quality to serve in the public trust. Their process can best be summed up as "hope for the best and plan for the worst." Theirs was to be the "least imperfect" government. Therefore, it should not come as a surprise that those who would be selected as the People's representatives would be simultaneously virtuous individuals acting solely on behalf of their electors and at the same time closely monitored for signs of corruption or personal ambition. Public opinion polls over the last six years have reflected this love/hate relationship that the American people have with their political representatives. Asked as to whether or not a particular representative has fulfilled their responsibilities to the satisfaction of the survey respondent, most constituents have a generally favorable opinion of their Representative or Senator. But when asked if the respondent had a favorable or unfavorable opinion of the Congress as a whole, Americans have overwhelmingly registered their dissatisfaction with the functioning of "Washington." Presently, only 9% of Americans have a positive opinion of Congress. The reasons for this seeming contradictory attitude are myriad and beyond the scope of this investigation. But what is clear is that the last two sessions of Congress possessed one of the lowest favorability ratings in memory. Its collective gridlock is certainly one, if not the most important factor, in its unpopularity with the public. As has been suggested in Chapter Two, ideological differences, raw political power grabs in a Presidential election cycle, and the influence of factious groups all played a part in creating the corrosive legislative paralysis which has existed over the last six years. Yet, the lack of leadership to shape political compromises at a time of devastating economic collapse may signal an even more troubling concern for the health of our democracy—that our collective representatives may be no longer representative of the vast majority of citizens.

The disparity in wealth between the average citizen and their representative in the Congress of the United States is striking. Data collected from the Congressional Research Service over the last few years regarding the income levels and net wealth of members of Congress may provide but one more reason, in addition to those already identified, for the seeming unwillingness of some members of Congress to understand the urgency to find compromise solutions to the Nation's economic maladies. While the data is relatively straightforward, what is open to debate is the impact of the wealth disparity between our political elite and individual Americans on what Madison described as Congress' responsibility to regulate the "various and unequal distributions of property."

The wealth gap between the top 1% and the other 99% of Americans is the largest in seventy years—since the latter half of the 1920s. The net worth of the average American household fell by 39% during the "recession." Since 1979 the national income going to the top 1% of Americans has doubled while it has risen only slightly for portions of the middle class and has sharply declined for the working poor and those in poverty. As of 2012 there were 46.2 million Americans in poverty.[65] It is within this broad economic context that the following data regarding our political representatives becomes disconcerting. While the median net worth of the average American fell by 39% during the 2008 recession, the current Congress median net worth rose by 5%. By 2012, the average estimated net worth for members of the House of Representatives was $896,000, while their colleagues in the Senate averaged $2,500,000 in net worth. It should be noted that there was virtually no difference between the wealth of Republicans and Democrats in 2010. Just six years earlier, the net worth of Republicans was reported as 44% higher than Democrats. The three sources of wealth reported by members of Congress were real estate, institutional funds, and wealth accumulated by and shared with their spouses. While three of the ten wealthiest members of Congress were Republicans, seven Democrats made the list. House of Representatives Republican Darrell Issa from California, held the top spot with a household wealth of $464,100,000. The runner-up was another Republican representative from Texas, Michael McCaul, $114,100,000. Following these two were seven Democrats and one Republican: Mark Warner, (D), Virginia, $96,310,000; Richard Blumenthal, (D), Conn., $85,320,000; Jay Rockefeller, (D), W. Va., $83,770,000; John Delaney, (D), Md., $68,350,000; Jared Polis, (D), Colo., $68,130,000; Scott Peters, (D), Calif., $44,740,000; Diane Feinstein, (D), Calif., $41,670,000; James Renacci, (R), Ohio, $35,900,000. The median for the members of the House of Representatives was: Democrats $896,000; Republicans $929,000. In the Senate the reported median was: Democrats $1.7 million; Republicans $2.4 million. It has been estimated that the "typical" member of Congress is worth more than nine times the average voter. The wealth creation of the current members of Congress, taken as an average, places most of our political elite within the top 1% of American households and some within the top .01%.[66]

In addition to the glaring disparities between the social-economic levels of the vast majority of Americans and their political representatives are other demographic variables which may play a role in the current governmental gridlock. Up until the national elections of 2012 only 16.6% of the members of the House of Representatives and 15% of the Senate were women. The 2012 elections increased Congressional membership to 20 women in the Senate. While African–Americans and Hispanic–Americans represent 12.6% and 16.3% of the population, they have only 1% and 2% representation in the Senate of the United States.[67] Vast income disparities between the elected and the electors and the under representation of women and minorities makes the task of determining and then balancing the needs of the American people an extraordinarily difficult task.

How one weighs the importance of any one element of the current political environment in the Congress can produce a completely different conclusions regarding the remedies necessary to resolve the gridlock and find political compromise. Indeed, arguments have been presented that the disparity in wealth between political representatives and their constituents is not an impediment to serving in the public interest. The thrust of this position is that personal wealth provides insulation from corruption. Some have suggested that conformity to political ideology (for example, the no taxation mantra of Grover Norquist and most Republicans) is merely a commitment to the will of the electors. Others would argue that while income inequality is present in American life that it is simply the natural and positive consequence of an economic system built on self-determination, personal responsibility, and "hard work." Countering these claims, of course, are a myriad of arguments which point to the growing inequality of wealth acquisition over the last thirty years produced by a tax code that favors the wealthy. They also cite the continued drastic under representation of major portions of the society in the Congress, and the collusion of both political parties to retain some form of the status quo through the gerrymandering of voting districts at the state level as egregious examples of an undemocratic political system. Ultimately, some critics conclude that our democracy has been hijacked by corporations and individuals using their special interest lobbying power to manipulate the legislative process in favor of the 1%.

Each of the aforementioned observations deserves examination and could be the focus of a totally separate investigation. For purposes of our analysis, it is sufficient to say that each argument or claim presents its own strengths and weaknesses. What we can note is that these claims are at the core of the dilemma that confronts our political system. While they present seeming irreconcilable perspectives, they are not novel claims in the evolution of our constitutional republican government. As has been noted throughout our investigation, many of these same issues existed at the time of our Revolution and the debates for a proposed Constitution. At the core of the rancor that has produced gridlock in our contemporary legislative process is the unwillingness of our political class to engage the country in an honest discussion of how best to strike the balance between the need to encourage individual citizens to aspire to economic self-sufficiency through wealth creation and yet recognize that that process cannot be a zero-sum game.

While the 2012 Presidential election provided an opportunity to address this question, the debates and media commentaries of political pundits provided mostly spin for their team. In fairness to both political parties, it may be that neither wanted to risk losing support from their alleged base by offering more nuanced approaches to resolving the problems associated with encouraging individual aspiration within a collective community. President Obama's commentary, sadly taken out of context, came close to raising the question to the level of a national discussion when, after praising the importance of private sector accomplishments, it noted that those individual accomplishments were often assisted by public support systems paid for by the American people. After thousands of news clips of his remarks were edited for the most newsworthy sound bite of the day, the importance of his observation was clouded by media political pundits whose two-minute analysis discussed the political consequences rather than the substance of his comment. Presumably, the President's political advisers suggested that the issue should be avoided in subsequent speeches because little was heard again directly on the topic.

It is unfortunate that political campaigns are not typically the best environment in which to confront social issues which require open-minded assessment and reflection. Ideological boxes are shaped with literally billions of dollars of one- dimensional advertising too often resulting in misrepresentation or fabrication of opposing views. Indeed, some responsibility for the paralysis in government today can be traced to the state of our mass communication industry. We will address the importance of our free press to our democracy in the next chapter. At this point, it can be suggested that, similar to the wealth disparity between our political representatives and Americans, legitimate questions can be also raised regarding the influence of money on the objectivity of the "news" provided to citizens.

But the ultimate responsibility under our Constitution to find common ground for compromise rests with the People's representatives. It should be remembered that the Founders believed that the ultimate enemy of the People was concentrated power. The economic status of the typical member of Congress (which places most of our representatives within the top 1% of the population), coupled with the constant barrage of money spent by corporate special interest groups in lobbying individual members of both houses, is worrisome. This is so, not only because it may create self-serving legislation, but even more importantly, it can create a myopic world view of American life. Even the most well-intended representative, constantly surrounded by the perks that political power can provide can be lulled into the delusion of self-importance and of the undeniable correctness of their position(s) on any subject impacting the country. Of all the potential negative consequences attributable to this eventuality, one in particular may be the most dangerous: they become susceptible to a world view that is totally non-reflective of the status of most citizens. Of course, there are currently, and throughout American history, individuals who have demonstrated the ability to break from the protective womb of ideological purity and challenged the powerful forces of factions to act on behalf of the country. In so doing, these individuals risk defeat in subsequent elections from political opponents both within and outside of their political party for supporting legislative measures which may have been contrary to the popular opinion of their constituents, or at least, the powerful faction controlling the purse strings necessary for their reelection campaign. While certainly maintaining a strong check by constituents on their elected representatives, ironically, Madison's powerful argument to establish fixed two-year election cycles for the House of Representatives also creates the constant need for contemporary politicians to almost immediately begin the process of soliciting campaign contributions for the next election. The influence of factions and their monetary support is then heightened to the degree to which acting on behalf of the American people is subsumed to the narrow interests of the well-financed factions. Presumably, Madison would respond that such an outcome will be inevitably balanced by differing factions and their impact on other representatives who will be brought to office and force compromise solutions for and among all the factions. The dilemma may be: what occurs when only a relatively few factions possess the overwhelming financial power to manipulate the legislative process? And, what effect, if any, does the socio-economic class of the political representatives offered by our political parties, have on the ultimate process of legislation?

Our recent Presidential election was the most expensive in the history of the country. Billions of dollars were expended by supporters of both political parties.[68] The Republican candidates received extraordinary amounts of financial support throughout both the primary and general elections from a relatively small group of sometimes undisclosed and occasionally disclosed donors who were able to shape the political messages both of their candidates and of their special interests. While the Democrats solicited financial support from allegedly a wider swath of the population, they also filled their campaign coffers with billions of dollars. Because President Obama was successful, one could surmise that the influence of special interest money provided by a much smaller yet extraordinarily wealthy group of individuals played a lesser role than expected in the outcome of the election. Instead, some would argue that the public policy issues presented by the President and the Democratic Party, plus their much more sophisticated "ground game" of bringing their supporters to the polls, were the central reasons for his reelection. There can be no doubt that both played a significant role in the success of the President and his party generally. But the influence of money on our political process is too important a subject to dismiss—particularly when the target of the special interest money is primary elections. It is here where election after election the narrowed interests of small but powerful factions aided by national lobbying interests influence the legislative process in the halls of Congress. No more recent example of this was the rise to power of the Tea Party Republicans in the primaries of 2010.

But the question is not whether politically right-wing or left-wing individuals are successful in our political process. Indeed, with a country as diverse in its regional, economic, religious, and racial/ethnic composition as America it is to be expected that our politics will reflect the wide spectrum of sometimes competing special interests. Nevertheless, it would seem that we are at particularly unique time in our history—a time when political leadership is crucial. It requires a leadership which directs the nation into a discussion of how we can maximize individual liberty within the context of the public welfare. Every contemporary political debate including the need to raise revenue by raising the rates of taxation of the top 2% of the country or by changing the tax code or both involve this question. Included within this debate is also the need to re-examine so-called "entitlement" spending usually identified as Social Security, Medicaid, and Medicare. The insights of Locke, Trenchard and Gordon, and the Founders are particularly compelling as we evaluate the legitimacy of the arguments proposed. No "solution" offered to fairly balance the importance of liberty with the need to protect the public good should be accepted by the American people without a demonstration of the impact that the proposed legislation will have on these two interrelated first principles.

This public discourse will require courage on the part of some politicians from all ideological preferences to suspend their short-term interests on behalf of the country. Some of the courage necessary will spring from what the Founders understood lies within the hearts of some citizens—to serve in the interest of their country. Others will find the strength to lead from the very citizens they have sworn an oath to serve. That is, contrary to some who would suggest that it is naïve to expect people to act against their own self-interest, examples of selfless acts occur every day in communities across the country.

Over the last six years, too few examples have been provided to the American people of small business owners who have struggled to keep as many of their employees on the job as possible, even when they spent sleepless nights worrying whether they could make the next payroll; of public servants, who through collective bargaining, have agreed to meager or no increases in salary to help keep their fellow teachers, fire fighters, or policemen on the job; or, of Americans of every race, religion, or political persuasion who run to the support of their fellow countrymen at times of national emergencies such hurricanes Katrina, Irene, or Sandy.

Our political elite bear a heavy responsibility. They must lead this country in a long overdue discussion about what it means to be an American. Can we be a nation of rugged individualists and at the same time commit ourselves to the public good? Can each citizen possess the "fruits" of his or her labor and yet recognize, as did Locke and the English Whig Libertarians, that such an objective was an inalienable right—as long as the acquisition and possession of those "fruits" did not harm another? What obligations, if any, do those citizens who have achieved success in wealth creation, have to the collective community? Does the community through government have an inalienable right to ask: how much is enough? And correspondingly, what are the minimum requirements of citizenship, regardless of socio-economic status? What expectations do we have of each citizen? What role, if any, should government play in facilitating the accomplishment of these goals? The presentation of objective factual information is absolutely essential regarding these and other questions surrounding the drafting of legislation which impacts contemporary American life. Alexander Hamilton's observation regarding his countrymen and the role of political leadership remains powerful and bears repeating. He wrote in *Federalist* no. 71:

> ...It is a just observation that the people commonly intend the public good. This often applies to their very errors. But their good sense would despise the adulator who should pretend that they always reason right about the means of promoting it. They know from experience that they sometimes err: and the wonder is that they so seldom err as they do, beset, as they continually are, by the wiles of parasites and sycophants, by the snares of the ambitious, the avaricious, the desperate, by the artifices of men who possess their confidence more than they deserve it... [69]

He understood that while Americans possess an inherent "other" regarding quality that they sometimes are led to support positions which are presented by politicians and factious leaders "who possess their confidence more than they deserve it." His defense against this occurrence, it will be remembered, was to argue for an additional counterbalance to the legislative process by delegating power to the Executive Branch. He argued, that to protect against the "wiles of parasites" and the "snares of the ambitious," the public good would be best served by "cool and sedate reflection" which could be offered by the Executive who must "dare to act his own opinion with vigor and decision." The responsibility of leadership must also fall upon the President of the United States.

Regardless of one's view concerning Hamilton's confidence in the Executive Branch as an interpreter of when "the interests of the people are at variance with their inclinations," his insistence that Presidential involvement with the shaping of legislation was and remains important. While ultimate constitutional authority to "make all laws" on behalf of the American people rests with the Congress, Executive leadership is essential. Whether Barack Obama received an overwhelming mandate from the country will be debated to serve who or whatever political point is under examination over the next four years. It is without debate, however, that his victory in the 2012 election was substantial. His use of the "bully pulpit" with Americans and members of Congress of both parties will be an important variable in shaping and entering into a national dialogue about the role of government and the balance necessary between the principles of liberty and the public welfare. Of course, how the positions of members of Congress and the President are presented to the American people is not solely within each individual political representative's purview. Instead, the delivery of information has been remarkably transformed over the last few decades.

Transcripts of Congressional debates and Presidential speeches can still be found deep within the bowels of public and university libraries. And a few national newspapers still remain on convenience and grocery store stacks to be purchased by fewer and fewer citizens. But more and more Americans are receiving their "news" via the Internet, text messages, or social media such as Facebook or Twitter. In fact, one line sound bites offered as "reporting" or information limited to 140 characters through Twitter communication is quickly becoming the rule not the exception to the process of information gathering on the part of large portions of the population. The technological revolution of the late twentieth century has provided access to information to millions, if not billions, of people across the planet. And while this bodes well for the shinning of light on government corruption across the world and a myriad of other positive benefits to human kind, there also may be unintended consequences which must be identified and remedied. One such potential problem which impacts directly on the functioning of our democracy is the creeping homogenizing of information through the mass media. The reasons for this and other potential negative impacts created by the rapidly changing mass communications industry on our democracy's need for a "Free Press" will be explored in the next chapter.

4 Freedom of the Press and the Shaping of an Enlightened Citizenry

AS WAS POINTED OUT IN CHAPTER One, the creation of a Bill of Rights was vigorously debated. Some States already had established their own declaration of inalienable rights during the Articles of Confederation period. Other state constitutions did not. While some, notably the Anti-Federalists, argued that the absence of such an enumeration of fundamental rights was reason enough to reject the proposed Constitution, Hamilton and some other Federalists defended the proposed Constitution as a better method by which to protect liberty by not specifying certain rights. In fact, Hamilton initially argued in *Federalist* no. 84, that a listing of rights was "not only unnecessary in the proposed Constitution but would even be dangerous."[70] He went on to ask "Why, for instance, should it be said that the liberty of press shall not be restrained when no power is given by which restrictions may be imposed?"[71] He argued that once such an enumeration of a right is established, it may allow "men disposed to usurp" that right to "prescribe proper regulations to be vested in the national government."[72] Why open Pandora's Box? He went on to make additional observations regarding the liberty of the press. He wrote:

> ...What is the liberty of press? Who can give it any definition which would not leave the utmost latitude for evasion? I hold it to be impracticable; and from this I infer that its security, whatever fine declarations may be inserted in any constitution respecting it, must altogether depend on public opinion and on the general spirit of the people and of the government. And here, after all, as is intimated upon another occasion, must we seek for the only solid basis of all our rights. [73]

Hamilton's specific observations concerning the protection of the press and his general disagreement with the enumeration of a Bill of Rights, of course, are to some degree reactions to what he believed were disingenuous objections to the proposed Constitution by some of the Anti-Federalists. In fact, some of the loudest voices decrying the absence of a protection for the press, were powerful political voices in States which did not have specific protection for the press in their own constitutions. While Hamilton lost the argument for the need for a Bill of Rights which would include a specific enumeration regarding a prohibition restricting "freedom of the Press," his insistence that the ultimate protection and importance of a free press to our democracy ultimately rests with the People and their continued support remains true even to today.

After over two hundred years of Supreme Court decision-making regarding the meaning and scope of the First Amendment's protection for freedom of the press, one thing remains constant—the centrality of a free press to the functioning of our democracy. It was no accident that in the First Amendment of the Bill of Rights the Founders underscored the protection of both freedom of speech and press. That these two fundamental freedoms were inextricably linked was self-evident to eighteenth-century Americans. A free press was the mechanism by which political speech in particular would be protected and nourished. While the Federalists and Anti-Federalists debated the best way by which to preserve these fundamental freedoms, there was no disagreement about its importance in exposing tyrannical rule. Indeed, it was described as "that scourge of tyrants, and the grand bulwark of every other liberty and privilege." It was understood that a free press would provide a forum for the competition of ideas. It did not matter that a large swath of the country was illiterate. They could, and did, listen to the Town Crier read the pamphlets and circulars on the community commons and often debated the issues of the day. The importance of the press in American life only continued to grow as the country expanded. In 1832 Alexis de Tocqueville wrote in his classic book, *Democracy in America*, that "there is scarcely a hamlet which has not its newspaper."[74] He observed:

> ...its influence in America is immense. It causes political life to circulate through all the parts of that vast territory. Its eye is constantly open to detect the secret springs of political designs, and to summon the leaders of all parties in turn to the bar of public opinion. It rallies the interests of the community round certain principles, and draws up the creed of every party; for it affords a means of intercourse between those who hear and address each other, without ever coming into immediate contact. When many organs of the press adopt the same line of conduct, their influence in the long run becomes irresistible; and public opinion, perpetually assailed from the same side, eventually yields to the attack. In the United States, each separate journal exercises but little authority; but the power of the periodical press is second only to the people...[75]

The role of the press to "detect the secret springs of political designs" and open the process of fact finding has been noted throughout our history. But no better description of the need for protection of freedom of political speech, and by inference the function of a free press, can be found than in Supreme Court Justice Oliver Wendell Holmes dissenting opinion in Abrams v. United States written in 1919. Arguing that we should be "eternally vigilant against attempts to check the expressions of opinions that we loathe," he went on to say "...that the best test of truth is the power of thought to get itself accepted in the competition of the market..."[76]—that is, an environment in which a multitude of opinions compete with each other in an effort to solicit support from the listener. Of course, Justice Holmes, like de Tocqueville before him, believed that the "press" provides a multiplicity of opinions which could and would be used by citizens to evaluate the "secret springs of political designs" and subject these ideas to the crucible of objective analysis. We will discuss the responsibility of the individual citizen in this essential function for the continuance of our democracy in the next chapter. But at this juncture, it is imperative to ask whether the contemporary functioning of our "free press" is fulfilling its responsibility to the democratic process by providing objective investigative reporting of the actions of American government. While there is no pretense that our inquiry can exhaust all the dimensions of what has come to be known as the mass communication industry in America, it is hoped that the identification of some of the more glaring examples of dysfunction in the press coverage of our political process will encourage future discussions of why the Founders believed that the "press" should receive its special status under our Constitution.

And the Truth Shall Set You Free
Fact Finding in Contemporary American Life

At a time in history when access to "information" is as simple as pressing a remote control button to activate our televisions, or access our computers, or "search" on our iPhones, it would appear nonsensical to suggest that our political institutions are at risk because of the unavailability of objective analysis regarding their functioning. After all, it is argued, all one needs to do is to "surf" the web or enter the "cloud" to observe the amazing proliferation of Internet sites which provide a vastly expanded "market place" for information gathering regarding our political institutions and political representatives. It is absolutely correct that the "blogosphere," to a large degree, has created a new forum in which to communicate individual or collective commentary regarding the politics of the day. And, it is also an accurate observation that more and more of the print media have adapted their enterprises to conform with the exploding technological devices and modes for communication now available to consumers.

Indeed, this expanding availability of collective information sharing has been correctly lauded as an important factor in exposing dictatorial regimes and advancing democratic political movements. The age-old tyrannical technique of censoring opposition critiques of governmental action is now being challenged by the availability of these new forms of technological communication. But technology alone is not enough to establish or preserve liberty and advance the public welfare. Thoughtful, objective, information gathering, the fundamental responsibility of the press in a free society, is also required.

One of the most vexing problems confronting citizens interested in obtaining objective information regarding the functioning of their government is the communication industry's seeming redefinition of what constitutes political reporting. Indeed, in the so-called "main-stream" media and across cable "news" programming, there appears to be a not so subtle blending of objective reporting with political demagoguery in a constant effort to retain or achieve market share for the particular program. This "reality," that our communication industry is a commercial enterprise, is at the core of any discussion regarding the Constitutional protection of a free press and its essentiality to our democratic process. While profit making and responsible journalism are by no means mutually exclusive, it is important to ask whether the special status that the press receives under our Constitution also requires higher journalistic standards than that which is being offered to the American public. Similar to the fundamental responsibility of our governmental institutions to constantly seek to find the correct balance between securing liberty and yet protect the public welfare, our communication industry is obligated to constantly evaluate the balance between its commercial objectives and its public responsibility. The present offerings of so-called "political analysis" too often degenerate into one-dimensional rants by highly compensated network "contributors" who predictably provide the viewer/listener with a daily dose of political opinion which reinforces their own political preferences. The by-product of this shift from traditional news gathering to more political ideological driven programming is the creation of what appears to be a growing mass media inspired separate reality of what constitutes "fact finding" regarding government and our political process. Or, more distressing, that such an enterprise is unnecessary.

The constant regurgitation of one-sided political dogma, while filling the coffers of news outlets and a few political pundits with millions of dollars from viewers or listeners who find comfort in having their world view re-enforced, has created a growing cynicism regarding the objectivity of the information being offered. This media-produced blurring of fact finding with political ideology/demagoguery has become so brazened that one high level adviser in our recent Presidential election process was quoted as saying that their campaign would not be driven by "fact checking." The absurdity of this comment, while reported for one or two news cycles by cable television political commentators often friendly to this political adviser's opponent, eventually faded into the oblivion of the next round of media produced "gotcha" reporting.

Two questions must be then raised: What are the major factors which contribute to this seeming race for the bottom regarding professional, objective investigative reporting by our "free press"? And what, if anything, should be demanded of those who we have cloaked with Constitutional protection to provide the American public with unbiased reporting of our political process and governmental functioning? There will be some who argue that any such inquiry is the beginning of a "slippery slope"—that is, that once a process of examination of the "free press" is instituted, or even suggested, government censorship is the ultimate result. Fear of control of objective information gathering and its dissemination regarding the operation of our institutions of government is an absolutely legitimate concern. It is because of that potential that a healthy skepticism must be applied to both those in the political process and those who try to shape public opinion in our mass media. One does not need to submit to far-fetched conspiratorial theories of collusion between government and corporate interests in the media to observe that self-interest between our political elite and media conglomerates do sometimes intersect. Therefore, it is because a "free press" is so fundamental to the protection of liberty and the public welfare that an examination of its contemporary functioning is required.

Concentrated Power in the Mass Communication Industry Time for a Reexamination

One possible reason for the present dirth of objective reporting of our political process, at least in the broadcast media, is that news gathering is, at its core, a business. It is a commercial enterprise which ultimately must succeed or fail based upon its ability to market its product to potential consumers. Therefore, a multitude of considerations ranging from corporate sponsorship to reader, viewer, listener, demographics are necessary in the production and delivery of the "news" through the "main stream" media and the more targeted cable television programming. And, with more and more competition for market share, it is only fair to recognize the enormous pressure on both network and cable outlets to produce programs which "sell" well to the consumer and therefore receive support from corporate sponsorship. Nothing can be more self-evident in our "free enterprise" system than its goal of increasing profit margins for investors. It is the engine that drives our economy. That being noted, private sector commercial enterprises did not receive the special status under our Constitution as did the press. Just as the Supreme Court of the United States has identified varying degrees of constitutional protection for political speech versus commercial speech, so should any serious inquiry of the functioning of the mass media. It should be remembered that the broadcast media is an industry which, at least theoretically, is permitted to function by licensure provided by the American people through their government. As shocking as it may sound to some, the air waves of this country are owned by its citizens and are regulated by the Federal Communications Commission. This administrative agency has been delegated the power by the Congress to, among a myriad of other rulemaking activities, grant or deny commercial media conglomerates with licenses to operate.[77] Unlike other corporate entities, those businesses which would participate in the media industry do so with the "privilege" granted to them via licensure. To secure and continue to receive the "privilege" to function in this unique public market place each licensee, at least hypothetically, accepts the standards established and monitored by the FCC.

Recognition then that the mass communication industry does not function solely as a private sector business venture which answers to its investors based upon quarterly profit reports alone, is central to any discussion of the responsibilities, as well as rights, of our "free press." Therefore, while government intervention into the "content" of the reporting of our political system must be carefully monitored by free speech and press advocates from across the ideological spectrum, it is also essential that the growing leviathan of multi-billion dollar media conglomerates are also reviewed and regulated. Indeed, at a time in our history when many citizens are clamoring for an exhaustive review and regulation of our financial industry with its "too big to fail" so-called "banks," it is not unreasonable to revisit the relatively recent explosion of media corporate mergers in the mass communication industry, their ownership, and the impact that these entities have on the delivery of information to the American people.

In fact, the recent controversy in England, concerning the activities of numerous "news" publications owned by Rupert Murdock regarding the wiretapping of citizens in search for titillating stories for its readership, and the alleged manipulation of some of the most influential members of Parliament, including the current Prime Minister, is a not so subtle reminder of the potential impact that concentrated power by media conglomerates can have on the political process and the lives of citizens. Mr. Murdock's, News Corporation (News Corp), is a global conglomerate. The creator of Fox Broadcasting, it now owns the *Wall Street Journal, New York Post,* Fox Television, Twentieth Century Fox Film, Harper Collins, and is a part owner of the Los Angeles Kings, Los Angeles

Lakers and the Staples Center.[78] With the guidance of Mr. Murdock, News Corp with its multidimensional involvement in both the print and broadcast media has become one of the most influential sources of "information" dissemination throughout America. Born, raised and educated in Australia, Mr. Murdock has recently received American citizenship. He is among some of the wealthiest individuals on the planet. Presently, his wealth is estimated at $6.2 billion. An unabashed critic of the Obama administration, his political ideological preferences could be observed throughout the recent Presidential election cycle through the "reporting" of Fox television, editorials in his daily newspapers, and occasionally via his Twitter commentary. That his and his employee's political opinions are absolutely protected by our Constitution is without question. The issue isn't whether the opinion(s) of extraordinarily successful news magnates should be available to the American public but rather whether the influence of a media behemoth similar to News Corp should be permitted to control such large swaths of information delivery systems in a society founded upon the importance of a robust "free press"?

It should be noted that there are other powerful broadcast and print media conglomerates which also control large segments of our information delivery systems. For example, Comcast Corporation, with thirty-three percent ownership by its founder's family, and directed by the founder's son Brian Roberts, is arguably the largest mass communication conglomerate in the country. Started as a regional cable television provider, through numerous corporate purchases and mergers it owns national and international cable television networks (regional sports and news networks), broadcast television companies including NBC, Telemundo, and numerous local television stations, and Universal Pictures just to name a few of its holdings.[79] Its CEO, Mr. Roberts, was the Chairman of the Board of the National Cable and Telecommunications Association, a powerful industry lobbying group, which pushed for the creation and passage of the Telecommunications Act in 1996 which deregulated the industry. In 2011, Mr. Roberts was a member of the Obama administration's Council on Jobs and Competitiveness. While Mr. Robert's net worth does not compare with Mr. Murdock's, his compensation as CEO of Comcast over the last decade has been estimated at $110,000,000.

Second only to Comcast Corporation in size and influence in the broadcast mass communication industry in the United States is the Time Warner Corporation. Its international holdings, however, make it the largest multinational media conglomerate. Time Warner owns Time Inc., HBO, the Turner Broadcast System, CW Television, Warner Bros., and CNN, among many other national and international broadcast entities.[80] Time Warner's present Chairman and CEO, Jeffrey L. Bewkes, has overseen the merging of various sectors of the mass communication industry into what is presently Time Warner. With ownership of Time Inc., the nation's largest magazine publishing company, and CNN, Turner Broadcasting System, Turner Network Television, and HBO, his influence over the functioning of these entities within the conglomerate is significant. Similar to other industry CEOs, Mr. Bewkes compensation was generous. In 2009 his total compensation was $19,560,000. While his "salary" was listed in Forbes Magazine as $2,000,000 his total compensation was $25,938,721 for the year 2011.

Regardless of how tempting it is to discuss the "compensation packages" provided by Boards of Directors often selected by the same corporate officers who will receive these benefits, what is of significance to our analysis is the impact that these media giants have over the quality and objective delivery of information concerning the political elite and the functioning of institutions of government. The political philosophical preferences of individual corporate leaders is no less a protected freedom than any other citizen's. But with the incredible power that the mass communication industry possesses over the dissemination of information transparency is imperative if Americans are to critically analyze the constant pablum too often offered as "news" by these media machines. Indeed, with the rapidly changing formats used by the print media in an effort to compete in the technologically driven new marketplace, the availability of local and regional newspapers is at risk. Given the present reality of broadcast media ownership with its concentrated power over the shaping of opinion on a multitude of public policy decisions, it is important to ask whether the commercial enterprise of the mass communication industry has replaced the very purpose of protecting a "free press" under our Constitution.

It is more than ironic that with all of the proclaimed platitudes offered by media lobbyists to the political elite and the American public about the generation of "more competition" by creation of the Telecommunications Act of 1996 that it has produced more and more mergers resulting in even more concentration of corporate and individual control. The same political mantra that created an environment for the deregulation of our financial industry by redefining what had traditionally constituted a "bank" and its functions during the second term of the Clinton Presidency also was used to pass the Telecommunications Act of 1996. The central thrust of the argument, presented with close to $400,000,000 of industry lobbying to the Congress, was that privatization of sectors of regulated industries would produce "free markets" which would create a proliferation of competition and in turn increase choices and lower costs for consumers. Similar to the regulatory reforms made to the functioning of our financial industry—gutting the restrictions instituted after the Depression through the Glass-Steagall Act which prohibited banks from participating in "proprietary trading," the Telecommunications Act of 1996 reduced governmental oversight by the FCC and allowed for more corporate ownership and mergers. Whether the framers of the legislation intended to create the contemporary media colossus, manipulate the American public, or naïvely believed that "deregulation" would produce more competition, has been the subject of discussion by numerous industry observers.[81] What is abundantly clear in 2014 is that the law is in need of comprehensive reexamination.

Monopolies are an anathema to a truly free enterprise system. Throughout our history we have confronted the problem of finding the correct balance between rewarding personal accomplishment in our private sector business environment and maintaining a fair or "level playing field" for competition. The role that government plays in providing that environment is too often forgotten or dismissed as unnecessary governmental intrusion into the "free markets." Indeed, it is truly remarkable that the loudest voices clamoring against "government regulations" are often those individual or corporate interests which once argued for "more competition" and now possess the largest share of the market. The enactment of legislation at the turn of the twentieth century to address the growth of monopolies in both the business and financial industries, for example, The Sherman Anti-Trust Act or the Glass-Steagall Act, have been dismissed as antiquated or have been rarely implemented over the last two decades. Whether the Telecommunications Act of 1996 was an intended retreat from these legislative techniques of providing a balance in the industry is a subject for another investigation. What is irrefutable is that this hybrid private/public sector business arena, which is so essential to the functioning of our democracy, is controlled by a select few.

The result of concentrated power without government oversight has been observed and felt directly by millions of Americans in the collapse of the "banks" in 2007(8) and continues to today. The loss of income or one's household wealth is visible and has immediate consequences. The creeping, intended or unintended, loss of objective information so essential for informed decision-making in our democracy is not as obvious. But it is equally devastating. An observation made by one of this country's most respected investors, Warren Buffett, concerning the use of mergers in the print media, may have similar relevance to our discussion of the concentration of power in the contemporary mass media. He noted that there are fewer better ways to make money than in a monopoly paper. That is, the tactic of buying all the newspapers in a particular market and then controlling the price of advertising by destroying competition through merger or outright purchase. Whether that practice when applied to the contemporary mass communications industry assists Americans in "detect(ing)the secret springs of political designs" as De Tocqueville observed is another question altogether. The tremendous concentration of both financial and political power in these gigantic media private sector enterprises runs contrary to our historical distrust of monopolies and may require serious legislative reexamination of the Telecommunications Act of 1996. There are, however, other "remedies" to the present problems surrounding the delivery of objective information within the broadcast media which would not require Congressional intervention.

The Use of "False Equivalency"
A Pretense of Objectivity

The question is whether the industry can provide leadership in establishing standards for the dissemination of the news which rewards objective journalistic fact-finding and in so doing begins to separate the entertainment value of the programing from informed political discourse. To accept this responsibility to the American public and to maintain the special status that our Constitution provides to the "press" will require industry recognition that brighter lines need to be drawn between the "reporting" of political "spin" as "breaking news" from objective political analysis derived from investigative fact finding. While the comments of political pundits or network political "contributors" regarding public policy issues of the day can add "entertainment value" to the programing, too often the viewer or listener is left with little or no analysis and much hyperbole. In an effort to market this so-called "news programing" as "balanced" the vast majority of both "main stream" and cable network news has intentionally or unthinkingly adopted the superficial technique of presenting "both sides" of a public policy issue. It is argued that objectivity is achieved by providing air time for often dramatically different opinions of whatever public policy issue(s) are "hot" during that news cycle. Over time this constant presentation of so-called "balanced" news reporting creates what can be described as a "false equivalency" to the information provided to the viewer or listener. Political spin or demagoguery then replaces a much needed nuance analysis of the public policy issues under consideration. Regardless of whether the source of the "analysis" is rooted in so-called "left" or "right" wing political ideology, too often easily discoverable "facts" are absent from the brief analysis presented as the news to the American public. The constant presentation of unyielding polar opposite political ideologies as fact-based news can create irreparable damage to our political process and to the necessary information gathering required for Americans to make an informed judgment regarding their institutions of government. This so-called "balanced programing" technique without thoughtful questioning creates a pretense of legitimacy for both the "news" outlet and the political positions espoused that should not go unchallenged.

The late Senator Daniel Patrick Moynihan is attributed as saying in paraphrase that everyone is entitled to their own set of opinions, but not their own set of facts.[82] There is, indeed, more than a grain of truth in that observation. Across the ages, human kind has recognized that the Sun rises in the East and sets in the West along with a multitude of other predictable phenomenon. With the assistance of scientific investigation and discovery more and more is being learned regarding the functioning of the universe and the minds and bodies of homo-sapiens. Yet still unresolved is our continuing struggle with determining what is real (factual) and what is imagined (opinion). In a society constructed on the concept of maximizing human aspiration in the context of promoting the public welfare, access to unbiased fact-finding is absolutely imperative. The appearance of objectivity, by providing "both sides" regarding complex societal issues, may be a remarkably effect marketing tool to create a sense of legitimacy for "news" programs more interested in market share than fact-finding. But the practice of presenting opposing views to subjects or public policy issues which are simply incapable of being analyzed through sometimes one-dimensional ideological boxes is a disservice to the public and leaves unfulfilled the special responsibility the Constitution places on the broadcast media.

The suggestion offered then is not that some governmental "Big Brother" should intercede into the sanctity of the "free press," but rather, that a serious soul searching, if you will, within the mass media should begin to re-access the correct balance between its quest for viewers and correspondingly corporate sponsorship and its responsibility to the American public. This self-regulation should include an honest examination of whether there should be a distinction between marketing for commercial products and news gathering. To be clear, "entertainment news" or programing which presents politically biased commentary or strident ideological interpretation of public policy issues should be explicitly marketed as entertainment for the ideological faithful not objective analysis. The implantation of boxes on the viewing screen with political contributors, sometimes with diametrically opposing views regarding easily discernible facts, and the program's host orchestrating the "discussion," or in some cases, manipulating the comments to enforce the host's political ideology cannot seriously be described as anything but political theater. Too often what is lost in this enterprise is that this façade of so-called news gathering plays to the lowest form of political persuasion and creates a separate reality of our society and our government.

At the minimum, industry program producers should consider providing the viewer with an objective biographical description of the "contributors" past and present political and professional associations in an effort to inform the audience of the not so obvious interests that may shape the "opinions" presented. Something as simple as making this information available via a script at the bottom of the screen while the individual is offering their insight would assist the viewer in evaluating the objectivity of the analysis being presented. There may be a place for this growing political theatre in our mass media. The venting of frustration with one political position or another can provide a healthy cleansing of our collective politics. And this mostly cable television market, with some more serious industry soul searching, can provide the body politic with its self-determined pound of flesh against whatever ideological position(s) it most despises. But what if this highly charged and too often error ridden "news" programming is offered in the so-called "main-stream" media? Political theatre is then offered as the news to millions of working Americans whose only source for information regarding the issues of the day is local network programming or a national nightly news offering.

It would appear that the traditional nightly news hour networks have chosen to provide this audience with more ideological neutral presentations. The by-product of this program packaging, while certainly filled with less obvious political commentary, constantly errs on the side of "soft" reporting which too often simply repeats the scripted one-line responses developed by the staffs of our political representatives without any serious analysis of the "facts" being provided or of the conclusions being presented. Indeed, this program methodology may be more damaging to the broad body politic than the political theatre which is presented as news programming. It can produce a predictable redundancy of current events and of our politics resulting in a mind numbing homogenizing of the news. That is, constant regurgitation of political spin, without objective investigative reporting, can easily lead the casual observer of American politics to accept the one-dimensional explanations too often repeated by our political and corporate leaders as "solutions" to our nation's maladies.

It does not come as a surprise that in a recent survey of television viewers a substantial majority of Americans "trusted" the information that they obtained from National Public Television and Radio over numerous other news outlets.[83] NPR has, since its inception, blended traditional techniques of news gathering with generally well-balanced and nuanced analyses of both domestic and world current affairs. Unlike the totally government-funded British Broadcast Corporation, while receiving some federal governmental support, NPR has managed to survive with increased aggressive private individual and corporate funding. But some have criticized NPR and its affiliates for its "liberal" bias. Predictably, calls for Congressional defunding of "Big Bird" became one of Republican Presidential candidate Mitt Romney's campaign's suggestions for reducing the federal deficit. This not so subtle threat to perceived "biased" reporting by a government-funded news-gathering entity does have theoretical justifications regarding government control of information dissemination. Government manipulation of the Nation's communication systems is unquestionably a threat to liberty. But so is the concentration of power held in the hands of a few mass media corporate magnates. Little was discussed by Mr. Romney of the constant access to air time he received from corporate media supporters to offer his solutions to the issues of the day. Presumably because the use of the airways was owned and controlled within the private sector little discussion was needed regarding the possible bias present in our contemporary mass media. The question is: Are our airways truly open to competition and the generation of a free "marketplace of ideas"?

Alexander Hamilton's observation concerning the ultimate protection of freedom of the press still has resonance today. He argued, it will be remembered, that its protection "...must altogether depend on public opinion and on the general spirit of the people and government." While the generalizability of the aforementioned survey is limited to the sophistication of the methodology used in deriving its ultimate findings, it would appear that at least those Americans responding to the questions regarding the current state of our news gathering industry "trust" the programming offered by NPR more than the other news outlets. However, NPR's continued solicitation of "private" sponsorship may erode this "trust" if it is not transparent in its funding sources and the impact which that may have on its historical image of objectivity. But, if the importance of objective journalism is at the core of this survey, and one suspects that it is, a powerful message is being sent to the broadcast media conglomerates. Objective news gathering sells. Don't dumb down your programming; don't present political theatre as news; and establish industry standards that justify your special status under the Constitution.

None of these findings will lessen industry profitability or reduce market share. There is still room for political theatre and "entertainment news" programming. What needs to be reexamined is whether the reason for less and less viewership in the "main stream" media is caused by the viewer's lack of interest in the public policy issues of the day and the role of government or whether the insertion of entertainment has so reduced the news gathering value of the programming that the American public is dissatisfied with the offerings. It may be that marketing a product has become a substitute for the quality of the product itself. Our democracy is dependent upon the process of informed debate and the formulation of public policy originating from the competition of a multiplicity of opinions. Essential to this process is the presentation of facts, as best that we can discern them Without objective fact-finding by a truly free press that process will fail.

Indeed, the current gridlock in the Congress of the United States in no small measure is being nurtured by the constant unthinking "reporting" by our mass media of the one-dimensional ideological "boxes" being presented to the American public by our political elite on a daily basis. Simplistic solutions to complex public policy issues are offered by both political parties and repeated by so-called network consultants. Deficit spending will spin our economy out of control—we will be the next Greece, bankrupt and on our knees to the rest of the world. So the Republican talking heads argue. Or, the devastating impact that any reformation of Social Security or Medicare will have on older Americans—heartless, truly mean-spirited. So the Democrat talking heads argue. A daily adventure in a seeming unending script presented to fill a two- to three-minute programming slot before the next commercial break.

The process works well for the participants in this modern day morality play. The political representative who is selected to provide the viewing public with the pablum of the day is placed in front of a majestic column in the halls of Congress seemingly dragged from some "investigative hearing" where the fate of the world is being determined. Then, with varying degrees of sophistication, provides his or her solution to the issues vexing the country. The news outlet fills the time slot of two to three minutes with a few "soft ball" questions and then thanks the interviewee for their predictable responses. With impressive music fading into the background commercial break ensues hawking the most recent pharmaceutical drug necessary for the targeted audience's pain free existence. Is it so difficult to understand why Americans of all backgrounds are dissatisfied with the process? All the participants in this grinding and mind numbing process have responsibility—the political elite, the mass media, and to some degree, the American public. In the next chapter, we will discuss the fundamental responsibility that we all share in the functioning of our government and its survival.

5 We the People
A Reinvigoration of Citizenship in America

AT THE CORE OF THE FOUNDERS vision of government was their understanding of the importance of citizen participation. They were convinced that liberty and the public welfare could not be maintained without the active involvement and ultimate oversight of the American people. Dr. James McHenry, one of Maryland's delegates to the Constitutional Convention, recorded in his notes that he overheard a conversation between a woman and Benjamin Franklin. She asked Franklin at the close of the Convention "What do we have—a republic or a monarchy?" Franklin replied, "A republic, if you can keep it."[84] While he was concerned that this new experiment with self-government would fall prey to the influence of a ruling class, he believed, along with Madison and others, that compromise or "joint wisdom" would reduce the mistakes which would ultimately come with this new "experiment in politics."[85] Similar to Madison, Franklin believed in human fallibility. The potential for abuse of power in the hands of a few, or the manipulation of the majority by, as Hamilton noted "...the wiles of parasites...or the snares of the ambitious..." was ever-present. While the structural safeguards placed in the Constitution were powerful methods by which to reduce the potential of concentrated power, the Founders knew that citizen oversight was essential to the preservation of the Republic. Thomas Jefferson noted that "An enlightened citizenry is indispensable for the proper functioning of a republic. Self-government is not possible unless the citizens are educated sufficiently to enable them to exercise oversight."[86] Jefferson's experiences and concerns emanated from an understanding of concentrated power used throughout the ages. He wrote,

> The most effectual means of preventing the perversion of power into tyranny are to illuminate, as far as practicable, the minds of the people at large, more especially to give them knowledge of those facts which history exhibits that possessed thereby of the experience of other ages and countries, that they may be enabled to know ambition under all its shapes, and prompt to exert their natural powers to defeat its purposes.[87]

The importance of an "enlightened citizenry" is now and always has been the ultimate check on the manipulation of our government from whatever source. This being said, some could suggest that America of the twenty-first century is vastly different than late eighteenth and early nineteenth century America. Americans, so the argument goes, are much more knowledgeable about the inter-workings of their government and the world in general. After all, it is insisted, the country has universal public education, some of the finest universities on the planet, and easier access to these institutions of higher education. These factors along with the technological advances offered by the Internet to the public for information gathering are reasons for confidence that the public at large is well-equipped to monitor what Franklin allegedly described as the "ambition and avarice of a ruling class." While these observations are generally accurate, it is also important to note that there is good reason to believe that these institutions and the availability of information provided by the technological advances of the last thirty years have failed miserably to provide the "enlightened citizenry" that Jefferson envisioned.

In survey after survey we are reminded of this fact. In 2009, the American Revolution Center surveyed citizens to determine their general understanding of the beliefs, freedoms, and liberties debated and established during the revolution. PRNewswire which published the survey's findings reported that 83% of survey respondents "failed" the test. When asked in what country the revolution took place more than one third incorrectly answered the question. Fifty percent believed that the Civil War (1861–1865), Emancipation Proclamation (1863), or the War of 1812 occurred before the American Revolution (1775–1783).[88] In March 2011 *Newsweek* magazine conducted another survey of the American people in an effort to determine their general understanding of our history, governmental structure, and contemporary politics. Twenty-nine percent of the respondents were unable to name the Vice President of the United States. Seventy-three percent could not say why we fought the Cold War. And, forty-four percent were unable to define the Bill of Rights. It was pointed out that this level of "enlightenment" regarding our history and governmental process has changed only slightly (1%) since the Truman Administration. In a recent national survey of Americans, partially funded by the American Bar Association and conducted by the Annenberg Public Policy Center in cooperation with retired Supreme Court Justice Sandra Day O'Conner's "Campaign for the Civic Mission of Schools," even more troubling findings were reported. The void of understanding of the basic configuration and functioning of our government reported in the findings of the study only reinforces the fear in Franklin's observation—"A republic—if you can keep it." Some of the findings deserve highlight:

- Only one-third of Americans could name all three branches of government: one-third could not name any.

- Just over a third thought that it was the intention of the Founding Fathers to have each branch hold a lot of power, but the President has the final say.

- Just under half of Americans (47%) knew that a 5–4 decision by the Supreme Court carries the same legal weight as a 9–0 ruling.

- Almost a third mistakenly believed that a United States Supreme Court ruling could be appealed.

- When the Supreme Court ruling is a 5–4 decision, roughly one in four (23%) believed the decision was referred to Congress for resolution: 16% thought it needed to be sent back to the lower courts.[89]

Our collective knowledge of world affairs has also been called into question. In the aforementioned *Newsweek* article discussing its 2011 survey, the publication also described the findings of a European Union study in 2009 which surveyed respondents from England, Denmark, and Finland regarding current events. According to *Newsweek*, the EU study asked survey participants to identify the Taliban. Sixty-eight percent of the Danes, 75% percent of the Brits, and 76% percent of the Finns correctly described the Afghan insurgent organization which America has been fighting for over ten years. It was reported that only 58% of Americans could do so.[90] Putting aside the methodological strengths and weaknesses of all social science surveys and their generalizability to entire national populations, the findings of these, and the multitude of other studies regarding the existence of an "enlightened citizenry," must not be dismissed as some crass manipulation of statistical information to support one self-interest or another. One does not need to accept the "sky is falling" scenario or to be so jingoistic as to reject these findings as a left-wing conspiracy to destroy American exceptionalism to conclude that we need to resurrect a national commitment to civic education. There is a vast difference between collective ignorance and collective illiteracy. The task then is to identify the myriad of causes for this dangerous lack of understanding of our institutions and governmental process and to recognize that the problem is, as James Fishkin, a Stanford University researcher of "deliberative democracy" has suggested, that we lack information not ability.[91]

Later in the chapter we will identify some important mechanisms which may assist in providing a more coordinated process of information delivery to the American people. But all the innovative techniques and institutional incentives to become an "enlightened citizen" will continue to fail until we first confront the underlying malady which seems to have crept into the collective psyche—an alienation from the functioning of our government—a sense of powerlessness to effect change through our institutions of government. The challenge then is to develop the consensus necessary to reinvigorate the latent spirit of the American people to be participants in their constitutional democracy not observers. The Founders understood that the task of consensus building for their revolutionary vision of government would require active citizen involvement. Franklin's observation, regarding the success or failure of the new government being in the hands of its citizens, remains true in contemporary American life. He and his compatriots knew that consensus for action required open informed debate. It presupposed both individual and institutional responsibility. That is, that each citizen is ultimately responsible for the actions of his or her government. Out of this responsibility it was expected that a "joint wisdom," forged through political compromise, would be reflected in the actions of our political representatives and our governmental institutions. The leadership to preserve this revolutionary compact must always fall on the People. It will be remembered that while Madison recognized the practical necessity of delegating power to elected representatives and hoped for their other-regarding commitment to their constituents and the country, he was unyielding regarding to whom the "elected" were responsible. He wrote in *Federalist* no. 57, that regardless of each representative's initial power, they would be always:

> ...compelled to anticipate the moment when their power is to cease, when their exercise of it is to be reviewed and when they must descend to the level from which they were raised—there forever to remain unless a faithful discharge of their trust shall have established their title to a renewal of it.[92]

The power to determine whether "a faithful discharge" of trust has been fulfilled still remains in the hands of each citizen. The question is whether we truly understand this or whether we have abdicated our responsibility in the process of oversight to those amongst us with the loudest but not necessarily the most informed voices. The Founders constructed a governmental structure that requires informed citizen input. Whether it is attending a "town meeting," or actively participating in support for one political party or another, volunteering one's time to causes impacting the public interest, or even participating in non-violent public protests of government action or inaction, each activity serves to directly or indirectly provide input to the "elected." There may be a contemporary notion that politicians are by definition leaders. That is, that at times of national distress they act on behalf of the entire country and accept the challenge of explaining to sometimes disgruntled constituents the reasons for their action. Unfortunately, too few examples of this form of political leadership by our political elite have been observed over the last six years. It certainly isn't the case that no opportunities have been presented to find true compromise on issues surrounding revenue creation, deficit spending, reformation of the tax code, unemployment, and a myriad of other public policy questions impacting the country.

Lost in the "divide and conquer" techniques often used by political party operatives to identify and market the most extreme views of some political ideologues, is that leadership in our constitutional democracy requires a constant reinforcement of the values that binds us together as Americans. Notions of fairness, respect for personal accomplishment, recognition of the importance of tolerance and the positive energy that ethnic, racial, and religious diversity has produced across our history as a people, are values which can be defended by our elected representatives of all political stripes. It is understandable that the importance of each of these uniquely American values ebb and flow with the currents of contemporary life. But a demand for an open dialogue, led by our political elite, as to where best to strike the balance between these values is the task of the "enlightened citizenry." It is a demand which must be made. Such a public discussion, as heated as it may be, is the very essence of the Founders recognition that consensus and subsequent political compromise can sometimes only be achieved through the competition of ideas closely monitored by the People. While these demands most often manifest themselves through the sometimes slow and grinding political process in the Congress of the United States, other forms of citizen oversight can and have encouraged the political elite to reexamine their public policy positions.

In Chapter Two we have discussed one recent example of how initial citizen participation in responding to a potential collapse of the financial industry morphed into a powerful force in the actions or inactions of the 112th Congress and now the 113th Congress. Public frustration with Congress' decision to "bailout" the banks without what was perceived to be corresponding support for "mainstreet" was relatively quickly used by one political party as a rallying cry for their return to power in the House of Representatives. Whether the initial public outrage was hijacked by special interests groups and evolved into anything but enlightened citizen participation remains to be seen. But the effect of coordinated citizen "oversight," as demonstrated by the creation of the Tea Party, remains to be a powerful example of the role that collective action can play in American politics. Another powerful, but much less coordinated public reaction to the financial collapse and Congress' seeming unwillingness to respond to the needs of the self-described ninety-nine percent, was the Occupy Wall Street movement.

Unlike the Tea Party with its well-financed marketing schemes, the Occupy Wall Street movement struggled to coordinate the fragmented groups which initially joined the effort to demand Congressional support for Americans devastated by the hubris of Wall Street. Similar to many of the peaceful protest movements of the 1960s and early 1970s concerned with issues of civil rights for African–Americans, the Vietnam War, and women rights, the initial public demonstrations of the Occupy Wall Street movement appeared to receive support from a potpourri of social protest organizations. Among these disparate groups were calls for Congressional action regarding homelessness, global warming, and an end to American military involvement in Afghanistan. One issue, however, appeared to rise above all others—the impact of income disparity over the last three decades and the subsequent concentration of wealth in the top 1% of citizens. This was an issue, which, on its face, theoretically should have produced support from a vast number of citizens regardless of their political affiliation. However, instead of generating an informed public dialogue, the subject was attacked through select mass-media outlets by the now well-entrenched Tea Party and their supporters as a call for a socialist income redistribution destroying the American value of personal responsibility and as a blow against individual liberty.

A recent 2013 demographic study of the initial Occupy Wall Street participants in New York City came to a significantly different conclusion. Colin Moynihan, of the *New York Times* reported that the study found that more than one-third of the protesters lived in households with annual incomes of $100,000 or more and more than two-thirds had professional jobs. In fact, eighty percent had a least a Bachelor's degree and one-half of these individuals had a graduate degree. Additionally the study found that one-third of the participants had been laid off or lost a job, twenty-five percent were under-employed and were working fewer than thirty-five hours a week, and one-third said they had acquired significant debt.[93] Professor Ruth Milkman, a co-author of the study, described the demonstrations as an important "major protest against the growth of inequality."[94]

Throughout the initial weeks of the "tent city" protest public opinion polls reflected a growing support for the protester's frustration with government's unwillingness or inability to address the impact of the "recession" and public policies which produced the drastic income inequality over the last thirty years. Unlike the relatively well coordinated and funded absorption of the movement which generated the creation of the Tea Party into the Republican Party and its political machine, the Occupy Wall Street movement received little structural support from the Democratic Party. However, a subsequent chain of events forced reluctant national Democratic leaders to reexamine their position.

Efforts by Republican governors and many state legislatures dominated by Republican majorities to overturn decades old collective bargaining laws both in the private and public sector, produced a "push back" response by organized labor not observed in years. Labor unions which provided seemingly only moral support for Occupy Wall Street began to institute similar public demonstrations in state capitals across the country. The citizen frustration reflected in the Occupy Wall Street demonstrations was now being channeled through more organized efforts of local, state, and national labor organizations. The Democratic Party, which was beginning to construct campaign strategies for its members up for election including the Presidency, began to respond. Indeed, the energy that produced the well-documented "ground game" of the Obama presidential campaign evolved, in part, from the protests in Wisconsin and Ohio and a resurgence of political participation on college campuses across the country.

Whether the money and effort of individual citizens produced the results it wanted in the Recall efforts in Wisconsin or the repeal efforts of state legislation regarding collective bargaining in Ohio is the subject for another investigation. What is relevant for our examination of citizen input and oversight of government is the impact that both the creation and marketing of the Tea Party and the use of public protest by Occupy Wall Street and its progenies have had on political decision-making. The Tea Party's influence on the functioning of the Congress, particularly the House of Representatives, has been significant and continues. While not as well co-ordinated and formalized as the Tea Party "first principles," the overarching issue of income inequality at the core of the Occupy Wall Street movement played an important role in the re-election of Barack Obama. Yet much more participation by an "enlightened citizenry" will be required as we review the actions of our "elected" to address what James Madison said was "the principal task of modern legislation." That obligation, it will be remembered, was to regulate the factions created by "the various and unequal distribution of property." To fulfill this mandate, a transparent, wide ranging, and fact based discussion monitored by an "enlightened citizenry" is imperative. Therefore, one line sound bites, political spin, or demagoguery presented as principled political philosophy cannot be the basis of legislation offered to address the staggering wealth disparity in the country, the sustained unemployment of large segments of the population, the reinvigoration of capital markets to support and grow small business, and the necessity of an objective review of the sustainability of our social network programs. Lasting compromises will be struck through our constitutional democratic processes only with the informed involvement of the American public. The Founders understood the risks of manipulation of the People, yet they understood also that ultimately the best protection against tyranny was from the People themselves—"A monarchy or a Republic?" The choice still remains with us.

The Box Makers

If our governmental system is to produce the "joint wisdom" so fundamental to our liberty and public welfare then we must begin to challenge those who would create and then market the "one size fits all" solution(s) to the Nation's maladies. These individuals are the modern day snake oil salesmen (women) of contemporary American life. Not unlike the horse drawn merchants of eighteenth and nineteenth century America who would market their bottled elixir claiming it would cure every medical problem from saddle sores to impotency, the hawkers of our consumer society have now found a fertile market in our politics. Instead of promoting the miraculous medicinal qualities of some concoction produced in the back of a covered wagon, the contemporary pitchmen (women) market one-dimensional political ideological "boxes" to citizens hungry for a simple "answer" to real or manufactured conflicts in American governance. The description of the "boxes" being marketed include, but are not limited to, such neatly phrased political ideologies as "Liberal," or when out of fashion, "Progressive," "Conservative," or when out of favor with certain demographic populations, "Libertarian," or the relatively new category, "Tea Party member." In case the "public relations" team hired to pitch the product wants to reach broader swaths of the consuming public then the tried and true method of political party identification, "Republican," "Democrat," or "Independent" may seal the sale. When none of the aforementioned "boxes" fit, simple, create one—"Soccer Moms," etc., etc., etc.

Billions of dollars were spent by both political parties in our last Presidential election in an effort to market in numerous and sometimes downright nefarious ways a very simplistic idea to the American public. Government is evil—Government is good. At the core of these "highly researched" marketing schemes was one insight into human nature recognized by medicine men of the past—fear sells. Americans are constantly bombarded through the mass media with images of random violence and the dangers associated with life on the planet Earth in the twenty-first century. Borrowing from their previous or on-going marketing schemes in our consumer-dominated society, our new-age political marketers operate with the presumption that the uncertainty of life, coupled with a healthy dose of fear, will influence citizens to choose the one "box" which will guarantee liberty and security wrapped in soothing images of one political leader or another. The "good life" will begin with the purchase of this survey tested political product (politician).

This political marketing will more than likely continue. As the Founders understood, humans are fallible. And, as Hamilton observed, we are susceptible to the "artifices of men who possess (our) confidence more than they deserve it." But he and his colleagues, nevertheless, were willing to challenge those who offered one-dimensional answers for the creation of a nation committed to the maximization of human aspiration in an ordered society. They were willing to stake their lives on a presumption that "joint wisdom," created out of a process of critical thinking based on the best knowledge available and constrained by the understanding that no one right is absolute, would produce a governmental process which would demand compromise and monitor abuse of power. With all their concerns about the susceptibility of the new government being manipulated by the ambition of a ruling class, they still believed that the tyranny which is created by concentrated power can be controlled by an "enlightened citizenry." It is important to remember that Franklin and his colleagues had faith in the wisdom of ordinary citizens. Human beings may be fallible and capable of being manipulated, but they are not stupid.

We all can point to a regretful decision we have made which with hindsight was based on our naiveté, bias, or fear. Our collective judgment(s) can produce similar results. Certainly our history as a nation has produced collective decisions on occasion which we now regret. The process of governing is a human enterprise. Sadly, mistakes will be made. The Founders understood that they were constructing the "least imperfect" form of governance which would reflect the diversity of values certain to exist in a society committed to individual liberty and the protection of the public welfare. Their legacy to contemporary Americans is a process of governing which demands objective critical thinking and an understanding that our collective decision-making must be grounded on the necessity of political compromise. Government is neither good nor evil—it is what we demand of it. Our first task then in our journey to maintain our constitutional democracy is to focus upon both traditional and innovative techniques to encourage informed citizen participation in the functioning of government. In the next segment of our investigation we will explore some of these methods and the role which our educational institutions must play in this process.

Nurturing an "Enlightened Citizenry"
The Importance of Critical Thinking

The use of the word "enlightened" in any discussion of citizenship can easily trigger reactions from ideological extremes both on the so-called political "Left" and "Right" in America. Clarion calls will rise from the "Left" warning of the creation of a Platonic Guardianship which will establish some prescribed set of "facts" and "truths" about our governmental process and history devoid of its weaknesses and injustices. They will also argue that the word is elitist and only serves to reinforce the legitimacy of a ruling class in the country. The "Right" will respond in kind. Their equally one-dimensional argument will defend the importance of certain precepts condensed into a few select readings of the "great thinkers" of western civilization. They will counter the "political correctness" of the "Left" with their own—without a commitment to attain the status of being one of the country's self-described "best and brightest"—the nation's business should be left to those select few who have graduated from our "elite" universities—defined by discussions in the country club, or by *US News and World Report's* yearly rankings. Of course, these views, while certainly providing fodder for lively discussions regarding the ultimate objectives of our educational system, may miss the Founders fundamental observation. That is, that abuse of power in a Republican form of government can be identified and checked only by a citizenry which is capable of critically examining the facts before them. How then can we nurture and reinforce the importance of its value to our governmental process? Our first task is to define what is meant by the term "critical thinking" and then we will focus on some of the institutional techniques which might enhance the reinvigoration of an "enlightened citizenry."

"Critical thinking," understood within the context of citizenship education, is the process of acquiring the best set of facts available from objective sources and then constructing general principles for future decision-making. Overtime, regardless of the specific subject matter under consideration, each citizen begins to build a compendium of knowledge which rises above mere opinion and empowers him or her to evaluate the public policy issues of the day. This process of analysis encourages the citizen to require those who would offer "solutions" to whatever problem is under consideration to bear the burden of clearly providing the facts upon which their "solution" is grounded. This process of critical analysis will also eventuate in the recognition that general rules or principles often, because of differing fact patterns, will require defensible "exceptions" to the general rule which he or she has developed. In legal education this process is often described as "treating like cases alike, and different cases differently." The importance of this thinking process to our constitutional democracy built upon principles of republican governance cannot be understated. As has been noted throughout our investigation, the Constitution is a reflection of the Founders recognition that their experiment in governance would succeed or fail based upon reciprocity between the rule and the ruled. That is, that while power had been delegated by the People to its government to balance the competing interests within a diverse population, government must constantly strive to receive the consent of the People through its words and actions.

The utilization of this "critical thinking" process across the various levels of American education serves to reinforce the central role that each citizen wields in the functioning of their government—that is, to maintain an informed and respectful irreverence to those in or out of government who offer public policy positions without factually defensible rationales. Moreover, this reasoning by analogy also begins to reinforce the legitimacy of thinking "outside of the box." Facts do matter. Similar facts can produce broad-shaped general principles. But different facts require exceptions to the general principles and can even create a set of new principles. As shocking as this may be for those who promote the aforementioned "boxes" of American politics, this fact-based process of problem solving in our legal system has helped in balancing the need for consistency and predictability in the application of past precedents with the necessity and fairness of rule modification. The renowned philosopher and observer of American life, Ralph Waldo Emerson, once noted that "A foolish (unthinking) consistency is the hobgoblin of little minds, adored by little statesmen, philosophers and divines."[95] Inflexible political positions non-reflective of the ever fluid contours of American life and defended as immutable principles of a political party or "philosophy" may serve as excellent examples of Emerson's satirical swipe at those who would continue to demand support from the People based upon a general principle long past its relevancy.

One important tool then in reinvigorating an "enlightened citizenry" and its capability to challenge the "foolish consistency" too often provided by the "box" makers is to reward those in our educational process who challenge their students with the empowerment that "critical thinking" can provide. It is important to note that this teaching methodology is adaptable to various subjects. Indeed, without venturing too deep into the contentious debates concerning "required curriculum," the idea of defining "citizenship education" as the rote memorization of historical "facts" in an attempt to answer a set of multiple choice questions on a standardized examination only serves to further the interest of the "box" makers and too often reduces student interest to explore the complexities of our government. That being noted, good instruction in citizenship necessitates both the utilization of innovative critical thinking opportunities with a full-blown study of substantive facts which will enable classroom dialogue and skill development. Unfortunately, discussions of what is required in citizenship education too often devolve into arguments regarding the superiority of methodology versus content. A reinvigoration of citizen participation in the necessary oversight of government will require both—"critical thinking" without historical content is as damaging as historical content without "critical thinking."

Of course, the key variable in the successful communication of any idea or set of ideas, including the study of government, lies with the sophistication of the communicator. For citizenship education to fill what appears to be an ever widening gap of substantive knowledge regarding our constitutional democracy, teacher preparation must be more than a course in "critical thinking" prior to so-called "certification." One wonders whether the teaching of method has become a substitute for the curricular exposure necessary to add substantive and inter-disciplinary depth for our newly minted educators. Indeed, in the rush to establish much needed common standards for teacher certification across the country, well-intended advocates may have produced through the use of required curriculum an unintended rigidity in course offerings in our schools of education.

The creation of "requirements" which superficially mandate student completion of a so-called liberal arts core without consideration of the content and the quality of the required class or classes, may have created a pathway to certification which on paper appears to provide depth of our intellectual traditions but in fact is a superficial response to the institutional need for state funding or external "reviews" of academic programs. Somewhere in our enthusiasm to establish common standards we may have forgotten that intellectual content is equally important with the need for exposure to the varying methods of instruction for our future educators. There should be no doubt that our schools of education across the country must provide guidance to future teachers in regard to the various methodologies available to construct writing assignments which allow for student critiques and the differing techniques which can be used for the creation of classroom environments encouraging extemporaneous discussions. But equally important is the depth of understanding that the educator brings to the subject matter and the importance that the institution attaches to the task of teaching citizenship.

Much is often heard from our political elite, the media, and some in our business community that the keys to a successful future for America lies with our ability to educate and train a new generation of students in the sciences, math, and the various vocational skills associated with computer-related technologies. No citizen interested in our collective capability to compete in world markets could disagree. Encouraging students to aspire to become scientists, engineers, or technicians in our emerging nanotech industries should receive support from both the public and private sector. One wonders, however, why a similar enthusiasm has not been forthcoming from the same groups for a national commitment to citizenship education as an integral part of any effort to compete in the new global economy. Indeed, our governmental process may be one of the most important considerations in a competition with other economic markets across the globe.

Even with the contemporary problems associated with the "great recession," capital has rushed to the safety of bonds issued by the United States Treasury. Without diminishing the monumental problems associated with the need for regulatory reform in our financial industry and the current political gridlock, governmental, institutional, and individual investors from across the world continue to flock to what they believe to be the safest place on the planet for investment despite the phenomenally low interest rates and return on their investment. Why do literally millions of people from across the globe continue to seek legal or illegal entry into the country? These individuals seek a secure future for themselves and their families. And there can be little debate that one reason for their desire to gain entry and ultimately secure citizenship is the potential of economic opportunity. But the story does not end there. Intermixed with the most fundamental need for economic security is the more ephemeral yet equally powerful human desire to live in a country which values and recognizes the inseparability of personal liberty and protection of the public welfare. This innate quest for liberty protected by a political system ultimately monitored by its citizens is at the core of the dream for American citizenship. In fact, at a time in world history where millions of people are challenging totalitarian political regimes and century's old social or economic caste systems, this is the moment when the Founders vision of government is equally important to our success in the global marketplace as the next version of the iPad.

We can, and should, promote the importance of the study of math and the natural sciences, and engineering and at the same time lauded the study of citizenship. For a multitude of reasons, our institutional "leaders" too often provide segmented choices. While this approach allows for a much needed targeted dialogue regarding one public policy issue or another, it also may produce unintended false choices. Americans can walk and chew gum at the same time. But they must be provided with objective information which allows for a critical analysis of the choices available to them in regard to whatever public policy issue is under review by our political elite. The presentation by our "elected" of all the differing facts that are relevant for an informed debate regarding gun safety, taxation, immigration reform, or a national educational commitment to emphasize the importance of the sciences and math in our schools and universities, requires a fundamental trust in the People and their capacity to critically and fairly balance the sometimes competing interests involved.

Clearly, our elementary and secondary educational institutions play a significant role in helping to set the priorities for academic achievement and the creation of rewards for student success. But identifying the study of citizenship as an equally important educational objective along with the natural sciences, math, and technology in elementary and secondary education is only the first step in reinvigorating the national consciousness concerning the importance of an "enlightened citizenry." Both higher education and professional education must also accept responsibility for the present information gap regarding the functioning of government and the role that each citizen must play in its functioning and oversight.

With the cost of higher education continuing to spiral and the fear of future unemployment or underemployment of those possessing a college degree still fresh in the minds of parents and students alike, the push for curricular choices which seem to lead directly to a "job" are becoming even more popular. While this movement toward vocational-oriented and so-called "pre-professional" education has been a part of the curricular options at many colleges and universities for at least two or three decades, it appears to be expanding to other institutions who believe they need to broaden their marketability in a very competitive cost-driven environment. The availability of curricular options for students is and should continue to be a trademark of institutions of higher learning. Yet, the proliferation of these programs with their emphasis on relatively inflexible "required" classes may have unintended consequences. Similar to the push to establish common standards for teacher certification, vocational and pre-professional curriculums narrow the course options available to students and often provide few "elective" opportunities outside of their programs.

With the constant pressure both within and outside of educational institutions to establish and continue "accredited" programs, checklists of courses necessary for graduation are provided to students from their first days on campus to their last. What once was an integral part of the academic experience—discussing with committed faculty all of the amazing "windows on the world" that a four-year undergraduate education can provide—now too often eventuates in a fifteen-minute "advising" session with faculty members and administratively selected students who hand out checklists of required classes. Once again in an effort to provide core classes which will provide the basic understanding necessary to become "X"—fill in the blank—we are, without question, reducing the potential for intellectual exploration which is the cornerstone of critical analysis. By noting this it should not be presumed that student exposure to the works, for example, of Friedrich Nietzsche, Lao Tzu, Edmund Burke, or, the Founders of the Republic or any other "great thinkers" will miraculously provide an automatic counterbalance to the box makers in higher education. What it may do, however, is provide the relatively small percentage of citizens who have the privilege of attending college or university and who more than likely will be in positions of leadership in the private and public sector with an opportunity to begin to grapple with the broader questions of life, death, and the human condition. Struggling with these concepts will only reinforce Franklin's recognition of his own fallibility and the need in our Republic to depend upon our "collective wisdom" in monitoring abuse of power and finding political compromise.

The movement in higher education to develop "track systems" toward a more marketable applicant pool for immediate employment after graduation is understandable. Student indebtedness coupled with the ever constant fear of unemployment only serves to influence curricular choices in undergraduate education. One can only hope that an objective reexamination of existing vocationally oriented and "pre-professional" undergraduate programs will underscore the importance of critical thinking in their curricular requirements. Courses can be designed which reflect not only the essential substantive information necessary for a particular career or occupation and which also encourage the skill sets necessary for critical analysis. Opportunities for students to join in class discussions and thereby develop confidence in their extemporaneous oral communicative and critical thinking skills can easily be incorporated into existing or new course offerings regardless of discipline. And, with institutional encouragement, these programs can work with other academic disciplines in the creation of interdisciplinary course offerings which will provide their students with a wider exposure to faculty and the academic traditions that they represent. Similar to their colleagues in our colleges of education, faculty who reside in vocationally oriented or "pre-professional" programs must be prepared for the "push back" which too often is produced by professional accrediting organizations and university administrators who are responsible for the successful completion of "external review" of their programs. There is absolutely no reason that national or regional accreditation organizations should not value the importance of well-constructed interdisciplinary course offerings or the emphasis on critical analysis in program development. To accomplish this goal, the accreditation review processes may require a reprioritizing of the benchmarks used for measuring the strength or weaknesses of college and university programs. Professional or institutional recognition of the importance of critical analysis and its direct or indirect impact on students and their future participation as citizens, will have a positive and enduring effect in the process of developing an "enlightened citizenry." Professional education must also reassess its institutional commitment to citizenship education.

Even the most cursory review of the class requirements necessary to obtain a medical, dental, or even a law degree, will find a troubling absence of any commitment to a serious examination of the responsibilities associated with these professions in American governance. This is noted not to suggest that the educational models used in professional education seek to achieve reasonably different objectives than those in elementary, secondary, and higher education. There should be little debate that the obligations associated with the practice of medicine, law, and engineering, just to name a few professions, requires specialized training and targeted substantive course work. A physician without an understanding of the multitude of potential consequences that may occur with the use of certain drugs or an engineer unfamiliar with the basic scientific requirements necessary in the design of a nuclear power plant can have foreseeable devastating impacts. And, it is equally true that a lawyer without the rudimentary skills necessary to litigate in the defense of a client may seriously harm his or her client's economic interests or even personal liberty. The importance of demanding a rigorous curriculum loaded with the basic courses which will inform each student with the knowledge and skill to responsibly practice their chosen profession is without question. But it is equally important to recognize the special role that each practitioner has, not only to their clients or patients, but also to the broader community.

Lost in the necessary intense study and training in professional education is the need to constantly reinforce the privilege that licensure to practice provides. There may be no better time to remind students of the special status and responsibility they will have placed upon them than in a course with an instructor who has earned their respect because of his or her depth of substantive knowledge and commitment to their profession. Whether this nation's future professionals want the responsibilities which come with the rewards associated with their licensure to practice, they will have them. With all due respect to the many individuals within our national and state professional associations who have displayed a commitment to raise the importance of professional responsibility in the country and their community, much still needs to be done. The need for citizenship education has been recognized by the American Bar Association on numerous occasions in the relatively recent past. As was noted earlier in this Chapter, the ABA helped fund a survey of a wide array of citizens regarding their understanding of our governmental process including the functioning of our legal system. Their support for this and other future projects is commendable and necessary. Yet, similar studies of members of the Bar and students preparing for entry into legal practice inquiring into their level of knowledge of our Constitutional history and the functioning of American Government either have not been performed or are unavailable for review.

The importance of integrating the historical, philosophical and constitutional values of American governance in legal education would seem to be a given in the curricular requirements to obtain a law degree and secure admission to the Bar. One could not fault the casual observer of our advanced legal educational process to presume that those who are required to swear an oath to the Constitution and become "officers of the Court" would possess a sophisticated understanding and commitment to these values. This is particularly true when a significantly high proportion of our elected representatives are graduates of our nation's law schools. Yet, the requirements for admission to law school, the curricular requirements for graduation, admission to the Bar, and so-called "continuing legal education" offerings mandated for all Bar members continued licensure, reflect little to no relationship to each student's actual knowledge of the history and philosophical origins to which they swear an oath of fidelity. Our nation's lawyers hold a special status in the implementation of our rule of law and, by definition, are held to a higher standard of professional responsibility than citizens in other professions. It is only fitting then that we examine whether the intellectual traditions so important to the creation of the Republic are reinforced for purposes of admission, curricular development, and licensure.

The testing of qualifications for admission to law school differs significantly from the process for admission to other professional schools. Unlike medical or dental school which require a prerequisite knowledge of certain subject areas, applicants for law school have no such requirement. Students from any discipline or field of study can take the Law School Admission Test. While students interested in becoming physicians or dentists, for example, must possess a basic understanding of chemistry, physics, or biology, applicants for law school are tested for their skill at reading comprehension and so-called logical reasoning. All test takers must also provide law school admission officials with a "writing sample" which will not be counted toward their ultimate score on the examination. This intense approximately four-hour examination divided into five 35 minute multiple-choice sections and a 35-minute essay purportedly tests for "critical reading" skills and "analytical reasoning" which includes "conditional logic and logical deduction."[96] Not one section or question evaluates the law school aspirant's knowledge of the historical, philosophical, or structural origins of the political system to which they will be asked to swear an oath of enduring loyalty. Certainly one cannot diminish the importance that this examination places on the law school applicant's ability to demonstrate his or her capability to correctly answer around 100 multiple-choice questions under very intense time constrictions. And, if this process reflects what it purports, which is to demonstrate the test taker's "critical analysis" skills then one ingredient for advanced legal education has been measured. But the earlier observation made regarding the teaching of critical thinking without historical context is also relevant in this process. Indeed, it is intellectually dishonest to suggest that one's score on a four-hour examination which is completely devoid of measuring even the most basic substantive understanding of our governmental process, should be used as a major factor in admission to law school. But in fact the LSAT score is the most important variable for admission.

Depending upon the law school, the weight placed on the LSAT score often ranges from 60% to 70%—sometimes even higher—of the total "index" score necessary for admission. And, while the promotional materials marketed by our nation's law schools also note the importance of undergraduate grades and experiential activities, and sometimes faculty recommendations, these considerations pale in significance with the LSAT examination score. Why then do the institutions to which Americans entrust the training of many of our nation's leaders require so little evaluation of the substantive knowledge of their incoming students and rely upon an evaluative process so fraught with generalizability regarding the student's eventual success in law school and the practice of law? Maybe the commentary of one of this country's most popular "self-study" manuals sums up this process best with this observation to law school applicants:

> The schools all have access to your complete undergraduate transcript, your academic and professional recommendations, and your essays. They could also ask for some of your undergraduate papers if they wanted to. However, all this reading would take too much time and cost admissions offices too much money—hence, they've got a neat little shortcut in the form of the LSAT. When they combine this with your undergraduate GPA, they generate your index, a number that allows them to quickly sort your application into one of a few preliminary piles to make the process of evaluating the increasing number of applications more efficient.[97]

In short, it is cheaper and easier to use a score received on the LSAT as the most important factor in admission than to actually examine the substantive knowledge, character and overall intellectual record of each applicant. Regardless of whether the LSAT actually measures one's critical thinking ability as it applies to the study and practice of law, and there is good reason to believe that it does not, the real problem is not the test itself but the weight that our nation's law schools place on the examination for admission. No amount of academic hyperbole regarding the alleged intellectual excellence of an incoming class of students can be justified based upon their combined score on the LSAT exam. But year after year this marketing scheme is trotted out by each law school across the country in an effort to demonstrate that it deserves its continuing status as an "elite" institution or that it is quickly emerging as a law school which should be "ranked" higher by *US News and World Report*. While this process of reaching for the "gold star" associated with receiving this magazine's recognition is understandable in a consumer-driven society, much more should be demanded of both our professional associations and of our law schools regarding their continued acceptance and use of a process for admission which fails to measure or even require a modicum of knowledge of our governmental process.

Some will argue that the more equalitarian method of allowing students from a multiplicity of academic backgrounds coupled with an evaluative process which is more "objective" than one based on an applicant's undergraduate transcript and recommendations, will produce entering classes in legal education which reflect the many demographic sectors of American life and will reduce the inherent subjectivity associated with evaluating academic performance from differing undergraduate curriculums. There is merit in these observations. The study and practice of law should not be the domain of a select few of preset undergraduate majors. Our society is thankfully a diverse and dynamic collective of citizens representing every imaginable combination of backgrounds and interests. Those who are privileged to practice the law should also reflect the diversity of the country. It is also accurate to suggest that the difficulty of attempting to compare the academic performance of applicants based upon transcripts from widely diverse academic programs and institutions would be fraught with the potential for subjectivity.

But once again we are confronted with false choices. Similar to those who would argue for the superiority of teaching method over content in our schools of education, those who argue for the present process of law school admission miss the point. It is not either/or, it is both. That is, that we can require and test for a basic understanding of the origins and functioning of our governmental process and at the same time maintain a standardized evaluation of applicants. One potential alternative to the present system for evaluation would be to restructure the LSAT examination to include a section or sections which would require a fundamental understanding of our Constitutional system. Placing a co-equal weight of importance on these sections with the other sections of the examination in the calculation of the overall score of the applicant on the LSAT would begin to establish a balance between the so-called aptitude and substantive knowledge of the test taker. This relatively modest addition to the structure of the Law School Admission Test coupled with a modification of the weight placed upon the examination by the nation's law schools would begin to raise the importance of citizenship education in the minds of students from across the academic disciplines in undergraduate education.

Of course, this suggestion is but one of many reasonable modifications which could be made in law school admission processes if there is a collective will for change. Leadership from the American Bar Association, the American Association of Law Schools, and the myriad of other legal professional associations across the country will be essential in this effort. The first step in the process requires acknowledgment of the "elephant in the room"—that the present curricular requirements in legal education, the requirements for Bar membership and continued licensure are also in need of modification if the profession's commitment to citizenship education is to be taken seriously. Defenders of the status quo will argue that the present course requirements established, mandated and monitored by the AALS and other accrediting organizations are more than adequate academic mechanisms to remedy any lack of exposure of entering students to the structure and intellectual origins of our governmental process. They will point to a required first-year class in constitutional law and a course which considers issues of professional responsibility, usually taken in a student's third year of law school, as obvious examples of advanced legal education's commitment to an understanding of these values. If these classes are coupled with other courses such as Contracts, Property, or Criminal Law, it will be suggested that first-year law students will directly or indirectly gain exposure to the general principles which underscore our system of rules. Such an argument is defensible, depending upon the quality of instruction, the course content, and the commitment of each institution to integrate the jurisprudential principles which underscore the evolution of each of these areas of our common law traditions. But very little data is available to suggest that these required classes which total to approximately fifteen credit hours in a degree program requiring at least eighty-two credit hours adequately supports such an optimistic claim. There are a few reasons for skepticism. One in particular seems to overwhelm the rest—the Bar examination.

After four years of undergraduate education and three years of law school individuals who seek licensure to practice law must sit for, usually a two-day, bar examination. Each state and the District of Columbia require any person asking for admission to practice in their jurisdiction to satisfactorily answer questions concerning that State's laws and procedures as well as questions formulated by the National Conference of Bar Examiners. Each state places a different weight of importance for bar passage on the various portions of the two-day examination. All fifty states require applicants to take the "Multistate

Bar Exam" typically administered the first day of testing. Similar to the LSAT examination used as the evaluative mechanism for admission to law school, the "Multistate" requires the test-taker to provide the "best answer" to 200 multiple choice questions 190 of which are graded. The subject areas tested typically are classes which the applicants studied in the first of the three years of law school—Constitutional Law (31 questions), Contracts (33 questions), Criminal Law and Procedure (31 questions), Real Property (31 questions), Evidence (31 questions), and Torts (33 questions).[98]

This technique for measuring an applicant's knowledge of any of the aforementioned areas is open to debate. But once again, similar to the rationale used in the defense of the LSAT examination, the purpose of this required multistate exam as stated by the National Conference of Bar Examiners "is to assess the extent to which an examinee can apply fundamental legal principles and legal reasoning to analyze given fact patterns."[99] It would appear then that the need for measuring an "examinee's" knowledge of our governmental process and its origins in any depth is unnecessary. Or, that somehow the asking of thirty-one multiple choice questions requiring the test-taker to circle the "best answer" from among four superficial choices is a defensible method of evaluation. Suffice it to say, that another American Bar Association study inquiring into the level of understanding which applicant's to law school and prospective members of the Bar possess regarding the first principles of our governmental process would either support the continuance of the present system of evaluation or underscore the need for new approaches. Time will tell whether the leadership role that by definition comes with the privilege to practice law and faithfully represent the Founders vision of government will be reflected in our legal educational process and demanded by members of the Bar.

As has been noted, the first step in moving toward Jefferson's understanding of an "enlightened citizenry" which would prevent "the perversion of power into tyranny" is to "illuminate...the minds of the people at large...with those facts which history exhibits...from other ages and countries." He and the Founders were convinced that self-government would not be possible unless "...the citizens are educated sufficiently to enable them to exercise oversight." This requirement of republican government coupled with a confidence in and reliance upon what Franklin described as "joint wisdom," along with the structural separation of powers in a national government, would assist in the necessary monitoring of tyranny produced by concentrated power.

Citizen participation in government then was not some abstract concept to be inserted into a grade school textbook, relegated to the dustbin of irrelevancy by contemporary instructors of government more interested in quantitative research and publication of public opinion surveys, or trotted out once a year for a presentation at League of Women Voter meetings by local politicians. Instead it was and once again must become, an essential tool for requiring a national discussion regarding our Constitutional first principles, the role of each citizen in maintaining our shared values, and entering into a long overdue collective dialogue concerning the requirement of political compromise in the functioning of government. Demand for this reinvigoration of citizenship is essential if the present sense of alienation from government, observed in every sector of American life, is to be confronted and overcome.

Central in this effort is the need for access to objective fact finding and presentation by both our "elected" and the mass communication industry. Some of our political elite may be so intoxicated by the trappings of status which come with their successes at the polls or are so wedded to the "factions" who funded their victories that they are unwilling to initially respond to a call for unfiltered delivery of facts relevant for public policy decision-making. Other political representatives may believe that their constituents are simply incapable of understanding the complexities of the public policies issues and that they are better served by some patriarchal- or matriarchal-like decision-making offered in their constituents "best interests." Those in the boardrooms of the mass-media conglomerates which shape the content and delivery of information regarding the functioning of our government may also be emboldened by the protective walls of their corporate status and initially be unresponsive to calls for the need for the separation of entertainment and objective fact finding in their "news" programming.

There are checks against these types of hubris. Madison was once again eloquent and unwavering regarding the consequence for any of our "elected" who failed to demonstrate a "faithful discharge of their trust" to their constituents. He observed that they would "descend to the level from which they were raised." The power of our vote is absolute. As to those in our mass media conglomerates who continue to control more and more of the public's sources of information both in the print and broadcast media, rejection of requests for more acquisitions through mergers by the FCC and review of the Telecommunication Act of 1996 will send a not so subtle signal that monopolies are an anathema to the preservation of a "free marketplace of ideas."

These checks on our political and corporate power structures coupled with a resurrection of the importance of critical thinking in our educational institutions will begin to move our political elite into a much needed discussion regarding the so-called "gridlock" in legislative decision-making. In the next chapter, we will identify some of the underlying reasons for this phenomenon in American politics and examine the meaning of compromise in the context of our "least imperfect" governmental process.

6 In Search of Political Compromise in an Environment of Gridlock: A Return to the Founding First Principles

THE CONSTITUTION OF THE UNITED STATES of America is the by-product of compromise. From its inception its philosophical and structural first principles have required, by definition, a process of vigorous debate in search for "joint wisdom" in governmental decision-making on behalf of the American people. The Founders understood that this process of searching for political compromise would be fraught with rancor, sometimes lead by individuals or "factions" who represent absolutist positions on every subject of governance and American life. But Hamilton, Madison, Franklin, Jefferson and eventually the American people were not deterred from their quest to design a governmental process which would accommodate the diversity of opinions and needs of the country. They believed that the objectives established in the Preamble of the Constitution could be achieved and maintained by controlling "factions" through the legislative process, separating power throughout the national government, and relying on the people to monitor the abuse that can occur with the concentration of power in governmental institutions. This belief in the necessity of political compromise for self-governance was not the by-product of some utopian vision regarding the nature of man. Instead it sprung from their recognition of the fallibility of men. Perfection in governance was no more likely than perfection in the actions of mankind. Ours was to be the "least imperfect" form of government committed to the maximization of liberty within the protection of the public welfare. Political compromise was not desired, it was demanded if the experiment in self-government was to survive.

We will discuss some of the reasons for the seemingly intractable gridlock in the Congress of the United States in a moment. But first a closer examination of the meaning of the concept of "compromise" as reflected in the Founders words and actions is in order. James Madison in *Federalist* no. 62, confronting what appeared to be irreconcilable differences regarding the methods for representation in the proposed Constitution, defended the need for compromise with a bi-cameral legislative assembly. He wrote:

> The advice of prudence must be to embrace the lesser of evil and, instead of indulging a fruitless anticipation of the possible mischiefs which may ensue, to contemplate rather the advantageous consequences which may qualify the sacrifice.[100]

Whether the issue was finding a solution to disagreement over repayment or assumption of state debt by the federal government, the location of the Nation's Capital, or the inclusion of the three/fifths rule regarding the calculation of slaves for representation purposes, highly contentious disagreements were resolved by "embrac(ing) the lesser of evil...." It should be noted that the compromises which were agreed upon regarding these and other contentious issues involved finding common ground not only with those who continued to challenge the existence of the new experiment in government but also amongst the Founders themselves. The strongest proponents of the Constitution, Madison, Jefferson, Hamilton, Franklin, and Washington brought different experiences, personalities, and recommendations in search for resolution of the Nation's problems. They did not always agree. Indeed, their disagreements could have ultimately destroyed that which they fought so hard to create. But one overarching consideration ultimately bound them together—the survival of the Republic and the first principles reflected in the letter and spirit of the Constitution.[101]

The meaning of "political compromise" was not simply taking the diametrically opposed recommendations of special interest groups and then "splitting the baby" as too often is suggested by some of our contemporary political elite. Instead "political compromise" in the context of our constitutional democracy requires a balancing of co-equal aspirational objectives. This can be achieved only by a recognition that no one first principle can function without support for the others. To find political accommodation amongst these values does not mean that any one first principal has been sacrificed. Indeed, it may be that part of our contemporary problem is that "political compromise" has been presented as a capitulation of one first principle or another. Rather than viewing the balancing of our constitutional first principles as a necessary process in an effort to maintain the support of what Madison described as the "constitutional majority," our national dialogue has been hijacked by ideological absolutists. One does not need to abandon the importance of maximizing individual liberty by recognizing the fundamental importance of protection of the public welfare. It is also important to remember that the philosophical origins which helped provide the impetus for the American Revolution while committed to liberty also recognized that it must be achieved without producing "harm" to another or the collective society.

Whether the issue is federal funding of victims of natural disasters, the need for monitoring the sale and purchase of weapons in the country, immigration reform, or an objective review of our tax code and our social safety net programs, finding "political compromise" will require a commitment to the balancing process of constitutional first principles. It will require a transparent discussion, on a case-by-case basis, led by those among our political elite who are willing to accept the responsibility of leadership. A "faithful discharge" of their trust to the American people will require them to explain the merit of Emerson's observation regarding the need to reject "a foolish consistency" and allegiance to inflexible political positions. The presentation of objective information, distilled of ideological absolutism, shaped within the context of our constitutional first principles, would begin to rescue the country from the never ending ranting from those described by Hamilton as "… the snares of the ambitious, the avaricious, the desperate, by the artifices of men, who possess (our) confidence more than they deserve it…" The present gridlock in the halls of Congress will be significantly reduced when our "elected" are willing to accept what Madison and his colleagues came to understand—that the survival of the Republic depends upon a delicate balancing of sometimes competing co-equal aspirational goals. Recognition of this constitutional "given" is an obligation of leadership not a capitulation of principles.

A first step in the process of finding resolution to the aforementioned public policy issues is the need to strip away the noise produced by one-dimensional special interests clamoring for one absolutist position or another. Political compromise or accommodation can be achieved through three fundamental elements—(1) the creation of an environment of mutuality of personal respect, (2) recognition of the constitutional legitimacy of the competing interests involved, and (3) a commitment to stand together in defense of the "political compromise" crafted as representatives not just of a region, or political district, but of the country. There is no pretense that such a process is easily accomplished. With the scare tactics of fear discussed in the last chapter, the gerrymandering of political districts by state legislative assemblies, and the constant distortion of our Constitution's first principles by politicians more interested in maintaining their current status than finding solutions to the Nation's problems, the task of breaking the gridlock will require a selfless leadership rarely observed over the last six years. A "faithful discharge" of the trust placed within the hands of our political elite requires a devotion to the Constitution and sometimes the courage to educate their constituents of the unfiltered facts associated with the resolution of public policy questions and defend their willingness to find political accommodation. How would this process of political compromise and engendering support from constituents work? Presuming that there is recognition from our "elected" that the status quo of gridlock is unacceptable, which remains an open question, an analysis of the current debate surrounding so-called "gun control" will illustrate how political leadership with respect to constitutional first principles can be demonstrated.

As mentioned above, the first step in finding political compromise is the requirement of establishing an environment of personal respect among those assigned the task of breaking the gridlock regarding legislation of gun violence in the country. One of the most important considerations in this process is to identify individuals for participation in the process who have displayed an ability to defend their legislative decision-making within the context of constitutional principles. That is, each participant must be willing to find compromise within the contours of the aspirational goals of the Constitution as articulated within the Preamble and the limits imposed by the relevant sections of the Bill of Rights. This process of finding accommodation between co-equally important constitutional objectives requires all parties to the negotiations, regardless of each participant's ideological preference toward the superiority of one principle over another, to acknowledge the legitimacy of others who may hold a different preference. Such an acknowledgment builds a mutuality of respect and an environment of good faith essential for public policy resolution. It accentuates the overriding principles which bind us together as Americans. While the absolutists and the special interests will continue to claim the legitimacy of their positions, transparent and articulate constitutional rationales offered by those involved in the negotiations will demonstrate the dangers of one-dimensional responses and the need for balanced decision-making as demanded by our Constitution. The country is starving for objective thoughtful political leadership which requires "joint wisdom" and a commitment to principles which bind us together, not divide us.

The next step in achieving political compromise is to identify the competing constitutional principles at issue in the public policy debate. Crafting legislation regarding gun violence in America then provides both our political elite and the country with the opportunity to discuss the aspirational goals articulated in the Preamble of the Constitution and the rights and responsibilities associated with the application of our Bill of Rights. Therefore, a brief restatement of the language of both the Preamble and the sections of the Bill of Rights relevant to any discussion of the regulation of gun violence is essential.

The Preamble of the Constitution enumerated the aspirational objectives of our collective covenant. It reads as follows:

> We the People of the United States, in Order to form a more perfect Union, establish Justice, insure domestic Tranquility, provide for the common defence, promote the general Welfare, and secure the Blessings

of Liberty to ourselves and our Posterity, do ordain and establish this Constitution for the United States of America.

As was discussed in Chapter One, each provision reflected our collective commitment to forge a nation built upon these co-equal principles of governance. Each objective was inextricably wedded to the others. Any action or inaction of government which is defended by our "elected" based upon one principle then must account for its impact on the others. For example, governmental action which is intended to "insure domestic Tranquility" can be defended only if it is implemented with a fidelity to principles of "Justice," assist in the securing of our personal liberty and "promote" the "general Welfare" of the American people. While each legislative decision then, depending upon the public policy issues involved, may of necessity require more emphasis upon one overriding first principle than another, proponents of the legislation must still account for its impact on the other principles.

Requiring our political elite to provide constitutional rationales for their action or inaction then begins to refocus public policy debates such as the regulation of gun violence. A brief pontification by any member of the Senate or House of Representatives superficially citing one provision of the Bill of Rights will not suffice as a constitutional justification for legislative action or inaction. Indeed, part of our current dilemma in regard to Congressional gridlock generally and the achievement of standards for gun safety specifically, has originated from the intentional distortion of, or maybe even more damming, the ignorance by our political elite of the very foundational principles involved in governance.

Rarely are the overriding principles of the Preamble ever cited in regard to any public policy issue let alone gun safety. But no such reticence is involved with citing the Bill of Rights. Almost on a daily basis both cable television and the "main stream" broadcast media fill two-minute time slots with politicians or "political contributors" who defend their willingness or unwillingness to find compromise regarding "gun control" legislation based upon a quick recitation of the Second Amendment of the Bill of Rights without the slightest recognition of the delicate balancing required for its application. But the Founding mandate which requires recognition of the need for the balancing of co-equal first principles reflected in the Constitution's Preamble is essential also with the application of any provision of the Bill of Rights. The regulation of gun violence is not exempt from this constitutional requirement. That is, that the Second Amendment enumerated in the Bill of Rights takes on meaning only within the context of the overriding co-equal first principles of the Preamble and the other co-equal enumerations with the Bill of Rights. The so-called "right to bear arms" is no more absolute than is the absolute "right to freedom of speech" or "freedom of the press." Indeed, over the last 222 years, the Supreme Court of the United States has, on a case-by-case basis, interpreted the parameters of each Amendment.

For example, the Court has held that the First Amendment prohibition against the restriction of freedom of speech was not intended to include categories of speech such as "subversive speech"[102] or "fighting words."[103] Depending upon what the Court has described as the "time, place, and manner" of the speech, all forms of otherwise protected communication may be subject to constitutional restriction. Most Americans are familiar with the oft cited constitutional truism that one cannot yell "fire" in a crowded theatre. It has also been determined by the Court that there are occasions when even the press can be restricted from[104] or held liable for its publication of certain categories of information.[105] While the cases have been rare and cautiously adjudicated, the Supreme Court has held that the press may be restrained from publication in situations which involve movement of troops at time of war or in situations where "community life" may be protected from publications which incite acts of violence. So has been the case with the application of First Amendment protections against governmental regulation of the free exercise of religion. While the protection of religious freedom has been a constant in Supreme Court decision-making, even this liberty is not absolute. In the late nineteenth century, the Court upheld a federal law prohibiting polygamy as applied to a Mormon who argued his religious duty was to practice polygamy.[106] Later in the mid-twentieth century, the Court recognized the absolute right of "freedom to believe" yet the society's right to restrict the "freedom to act."[107] Of course, there are literally hundreds of Supreme Court decisions involving every prohibition within the Bill of Rights which involve balancing co-equal competing rights. Important for our analysis is that the Court has recognized, as do most Americans when provided with objective facts devoid of self-serving political rhetoric, that with rights come corresponding responsibilities of citizenship.

The Second Amendment reads as follows: "A well-regulated Militia, being necessary to the security of a free State, the right of the people to keep and bear Arms, shall not be infringed." As noted above, the meaning of the language of the Bill of Rights and the constitutionality of any governmental restrictions of the rights articulated within the document has been assigned by the American people to the Supreme Court of the United States. Legislative leaders selected to find "political compromise" regarding the regulation of gun violence, are obligated to understand and reflect in their decision-making the constitutional interpretation on the subject offered by the Court. Therefore, before we discuss the political implications associated with this specific public policy issue, a review of the Court's decision-making regarding the "right to bear arms" is essential.

The key case determining the meaning of the Second Amendment "right to bear arms" is District of Columbia v. Heller.[108] In this 2008 decision of the Supreme Court, the Justices grappled with the linguistic meaning of the words of the Amendment, the history in which the terms of the Amendment were shaped, and the contemporary ramifications of its protections. Regardless of one's agreement or disagreement with the Court's decision, absent new legislation regarding the subject, subsequent decisions which refine the Court's rationale, or a constitutional amendment, its findings in this case are the law of the land. In this landmark 5–4 decision the Court found that there was a fundamental constitutional right for individual citizens to possess firearms. More specifically, the Court held that a District of Columbia law which, among other prohibitions, banned handgun possession of an unlicensed firearm in the home, was an unconstitutional violation of a citizen's "right to bear arms" under the Second Amendment.

Writing for the majority of the Court, Justice Scalia cited provisions in State constitutions at the time of the drafting of the Second Amendment which he believed supported the "right to bear arms" in addition to what he described as the "interpretation by scholars, courts, and legislators immediately after ratification through the nineteenth century" which supported this conclusion. Contrary to the historical reading offered by four Justices in dissent, the majority of the Court held that the language in the Second Amendment referencing "A well-regulated Militia" was not intended by the Founders as a restriction upon individual citizens' right to possess firearms. Scalia posited that this phraseology must be understood within the context of the time in which it was written. Relying on what he believed was "Anti-Federalist" fear that the newly established Federal government could "disarm the people" or "disable a 'citizens militia' and enable a politicized standing army or a select militia to rule," Justice Scalia ultimately concluded that the Founders did not intend to restrict the Second Amendment language of the right to bear arms only to those citizens who were part of an organized militia. Instead he suggested that it was our historical fear of standing armies or politically controlled militias which compelled the insertion of this protection in the Second Amendment. For the majority of the Heller court then, governmental prohibition of firearms generally, and more specifically handguns, which are intended for a "lawful purpose" such as self-defense in a citizen's home, was a violation of the Founders understanding of the limitations of government. That being noted, the majority in Heller was unequivocal in its belief that the Second Amendment did not confer absolute rights, any more than did other prohibitions within the Bill of Rights. Justice Scalia wrote for the majority:

> There seems to us no doubt, on the basis of both text and history, that the Second Amendment conferred an individual right to keep and bear arms. Of course the right was not unlimited, just as the First Amendment's right of free speech was not... Thus, we do not read the Second Amendment to protect the right of citizens to carry arms for any sort of confrontation, just as we do not read the First Amendment to protect the right of citizens to speak for any purpose...[109]

Indeed, the Court reiterated what might be constitutionally legitimate governmental regulation of the Second Amendment. Constitutionally permissible restrictions on the possession of firearms by "felons" or the "mentally ill," or establishing "time, place, and manner" limitations on the possession of firearms in schools or government buildings, as well as "qualifications on commercial sale of arms" were noted as potentially legitimate regulations of the Second Amendment right to bear arms.[110] While four Justices disagreed with the majority that the District of Columbia law should be struck down, not surprisingly they concurred that the rights enumerated within the Second Amendment were not unlimited. And, they submitted that the District of Columbia law fell within the category of permissible governmental regulation.

Writing for the dissent Justice Stevens agreed with the majority that the Second Amendment was a response by the Framers to fears that the Constitution would empower the Congress "to disarm the State militias and create a national standing army" which would impose "an intolerable threat to the sovereignty of the several States." Yet, Justice Stevens argued, that:

> Neither the text of the Amendment nor the arguments advanced by its proponents evidenced the slightest interest in limiting any legislature's authority to regulate private civilian uses of firearms. Specifically, there is no indication that the Framers of the Amendment intended to enshrine the common law right of self-defense in the Constitution.[111]

He noted that if the Framers had intended to include such a right to "self-defense" in the Amendment they could have easily incorporated the language from existing laws in the States of Pennsylvania or Vermont, which specifically indicated the right to possess firearms for the purposes of hunting or self-defense. Citing a series of past precedents regarding the constitutionality of Congressional legislation which had placed restrictions on the possession of certain types of firearms for civilian use, the dissent cautioned that the majority interpretation of the Second Amendment violated basic jurisprudential principles of reliance upon and commitment to stare decisis.[112] That is, without more historical evidence to defend their opinion, the majority was potentially endangering the Court's time-tested reliance on past decisions to provide the consistency and predictability necessary for judicial decision-making. Putting aside the obvious lack of unanimity amongst the Justices on where the constitutional limitations on governmental regulation of civilian possession of firearms should be drawn, both the majority opinion and the dissent unequivocally support the proposition that governmental regulation of firearms can be constitutionally designed.

The political elite which have been assigned the task of shaping Congressional legislation regarding gun safety must then incorporate the findings of the Heller Court and its determination that the Second Amendment protects a citizen's right to possess an unregistered handgun for "lawful purposes" such as "self-defense" in one's home. They should also note that this right has its origin in the experiences of colonial Americans and their memories of monarchial attempts in England to outlaw possession of firearms in an effort to consolidate power and destroy the evolving movement for a new vision of the relationship of government and individual citizens. This eighteenth century fear of standing armies, controlled by concentrated monarchial power, was not and is not an irrational fear as it might appear to some unwilling to find political compromise on a subject as controversial as gun safety. Indeed, contemporary examples abound of dictatorial regimes that use their "standing army" to control the aspirations of millions seeking to be free from tyranny. Whether one accepts the majority interpretation in the Heller case as a historically correct analysis of the Framer's intent when crafting the language of the Second Amendment or not, our twenty-first century legislators attempting to develop an environment of mutual respect in an effort to balance the co-equal principles of maximizing liberty and the protection of the public welfare are obligated to demonstrate respect for this fear of concentrated power and its historical impact on liberty. This being said, due deference to those who believe that liberty is best protected by the possession of firearms does not require an abdication of reasonable regulation of weapons in contemporary American life.

It will be remembered that the Preamble of the Constitution placed the protection of the public welfare in a co-equal status with the other over-arching first principles including the protection of liberty. As was noted in Chapter One, the Founder's philosophical understanding of liberty was tethered to what was described as the "harm qualifier." Both Locke and the English libertarians recognized that the individual's right to liberty must be tempered by the harm or injury that one's action or inaction has upon another or upon the community. Their insights regarding the limits of liberty have direct relevancy to any "political compromise" regarding gun violence. John Locke understood that with liberty comes responsibility. He wrote that while each individual possesses the inherent right to "preserve himself" he also has a corresponding responsibility to "preserve the rest of mankind…" It will be remembered that the English libertarian writings of John Trenchard and Thomas Gordon, in *Cato's Letters*, while providing powerful polemical arguments for individual liberty, also recognized the legitimate role of government. They argued that government should not "meddle with the private Thoughts and Actions of Men, while they injure neither the Society, nor any of its Members." It is then the task of our political elite selected to shape gun safety legislation to reflect these visions of liberty and to defend whatever limitations it mandates on liberty upon a demonstration of "harm" for the protection of the public welfare. If this responsibility is coupled with the Supreme Court's analysis of the Second Amendment in the Heller decision and recognition of the relevant co-equal first principles enumerated in the Preamble, then absolutists arguments presented by self-serving political elites soliciting support from one special interest or another can be identified as such by the American people.

As suggested above, another essential ingredient for breaking gridlock in our legislative process generally, and finding "political compromise" on legislation regarding gun safety specifically, is political courage. That is, enough of our "elected" must be willing to stand together, regardless of political party and individual ideological preferences to support reasonable regulation of firearms on behalf of the country not only their politically gerrymandered districts. This will require some significant self-reflection on the part of those we have chosen to "faithfully discharge" the responsibility of balancing the first principles reflected in the Preamble and the Bill of Rights. Summoning the fortitude to challenge the forces of factions often supported by individual and corporate interests hidden behind corporate and so-called non-for-profit organizations which provide campaign funding has been "a bridge too far" for most of our "elected" over the last five years. But the issue of gun safety may provide an opportunity for the beginning of political accommodation and compromise.

Ironically gun safety regulation, which appears superficially to be a very divisive public policy question, may actually have the potential for significant support from the American people including constituents who are often portrayed as unyielding opponents of firearm regulation. Public opinion polling on the subject has indicated support for a variety of potential legislative proposals which include but are not limited to the regulation of "straw purchases" of firearms which typically occur at gun shows between so-called "private" sellers of weapons to unregistered purchasers, a requirement of background checks on purchasers of firearms in an effort to restrict the sale of weapons to "felons" and individuals who have been adjudicated mentally unstable, and on the sale of firearms via the internet.[113] Some legislation to ban the sale of "military-style" weapons which may allow for the continuous firing of large ammunition clips has been also proposed. Predictably, support for one or some combination of these proposed legislative efforts to confront gun violence in the country has been mixed in the Senate of the United States. In fact, efforts to find "political compromise" on the subject through a proposed Bill offered by Senator Manchin of West Virginia and Senator Toomey of Pennsylvania failed to receive the necessary votes for approval.[114] No similar effort reached the floor of the House of Representatives for a vote on the subject.

Yet, it would appear that the tragic shooting of school children and their teachers in Newtown, Connecticut and the bombing of Americans attending the Boston Marathon has focused the American public on the subject like no time in our recent history. Putting aside the methodological limitations of some public opinion polling, it would appear that large swaths of Americans, including gun owners, are supportive of reasonable requirements for limiting gun trafficking, background checks coupled with criminal punishment for any individual or individuals who maintain(s) a national registry of gun owners, and online sales of weapons. The so-called "political cover" necessary for our "elected" in the Congress of the United States to support legislation which could address some of the issues associated with the death of approximately thirty thousand citizens each year related to gun violence is real, not imagined. Recent polling in States and political districts which have historically supported the importance of gun ownership has indicated overwhelming support for reasonable federal regulation of firearms.[115]

Why then are efforts to achieve "political compromise" on this subject mired in gridlock? It may be that it is too soon in the process to provide a definitive answer. But one important element for reaching accommodation on this public policy question seems to be absent—the courage on the part of enough of our "elected" to reflect upon their obligation to represent the American people and the Constitution. It has been suggested that finding "political compromise" requires our "elected" to occasionally lead and educate their constituents on public policy questions which can be distorted by self-interested factions on the so-called political right or left. To do so the "elected" must answer the fundamental question of what constitutes a "faithful discharge" of my responsibilities. To whom did I swear an oath? What principles must be reflected in my legislative decision-making? There can be little doubt that Madison would have acknowledged a representative's responsibility to his or her direct constituents.

He would also note the all too human tendency for political self-survival. But no serious observer of the Founders efforts in debating and ultimately ratifying the Constitution could conclude that they believed that the ultimate responsibility of our political elite was their re-election.

Even if one accepts the argument that political survival is the driving force behind the decision-making of our "elected," the broad-based support from the American public for reasonable regulation of firearms should enhance not impede legislative efforts for "political compromise." But no such compromise has been achieved. It then would appear that even if "political cover" is available for our "elected" from constituents in their political districts and in the nation as a whole, that there is another obstacle in finding accommodation on this public policy question and maybe others—the never-ending chase for political campaign contributions, money. Wholly separate from the argument often presented by some politicians that they are simply reflecting the desires of their constituents in rejecting some proposal for "political compromise" on gun safety regulation is their reliance upon one special interest faction or another for financial support in the next campaign cycle. The dilemma for those in the political elite who subscribe to the credo of re-election above leadership is the need to choose between what appears to be an increasing surge of Americans from across the political spectrum who support reasonable firearm safety regulation and well-financed factions which may not wield the power in the next election cycle that their K-Street lobbyists suggest. Stated in a slightly different way, do the political "survivalists" place their faith in the accuracy of the constituent opinion polling on this or any other public policy question or do they secret themselves within the tried and true marketing schemes of their special interest benefactors?

Of course, the first efforts by those in the Congress of the United States who are unwilling to search for compromise on the subject of reasonable firearm regulation is to use procedural tactics within their legislative body to avoid having to make such a choice. When in doubt use whatever parliamentary rule available to prevent having to register a vote on the subject. If that strategy fails, suggest "poison pill" amendments to proposed legislation which will destroy any good faith effort to find ground for accommodation. Placing blame on the other legislative body for non-action and projected gridlock or castigating the Executive Branch for a lack of leadership have been also excellent insulators from the "electors." If none of these methods of avoiding leadership succeed, even the "survivalists," those who value re-election over all other legislative responsibilities, must confront Madison's insight regarding the efficacy of political compromise. It will be remembered that urged his colleagues to:

embrace the lesser of evil and, instead of indulging a fruitless anticipation of the possible mischiefs which may ensue, to contemplate rather the advantageous consequences which may qualify the sacrifice.[116]

Accepting Madison's advice may be more shear pragmatism than political courage on the part of the "survivalists" in the process of finding "political compromise" and breaking the gridlock surrounding gun safety regulation and other public policy issues. Whether these political representatives will be rewarded for their acquiescence in the process of compromise or punished for their timidity will be ultimately left to their constituents. One can surmise, however, that the public's desire for political accommodation is so overwhelming that their support for those who demonstrate leadership in their efforts to find compromise will also be extended to those who follow rather than lead.

While recent Senate proposed gun safety laws failed to receive the necessary votes for passage, some rarely observed signs of "political compromise" were exhibited and may signal a thawing of the gridlock surrounding this and other public policy issues. Indeed, lessons for future legislative proposals on the subject of gun safety as well as immigration reform, a review of our tax code, and a myriad of other public policy issues can be learned from the recent failure of the so-called Toomey–Manchin bill. Therefore, following James Madison's observation that legislators are obliged "…to contemplate…the advantageous consequences…" which may justify compromise rather than "…a fruitless anticipation of the possible mischiefs which may ensue…," a review of the process which led to the formulation of the proposed legislation and its outcome is in order. Central to our review of this process will be whether these three elements necessary for reaching "political compromise" were present in the negotiations, drafting and presentation of the proposed bill: the creation of an environment of mutuality of respect among the leaders proposing the legislation; recognition of the constitutional legitimacy of the competing co-equal first principles involved; and, a commitment to stand together in support of the compromise on behalf of the American people.

The Public Safety and Second Amendment Rights Protection Act was created through negotiations between Senator Charles Schumer of New York, Senator Patrick Toomey of Pennsylvania, and Senator Joe Manchin of West Virginia. Each Senator brought different constituencies and different political ideologies to the subject of firearm regulation. While Senators Schumer and Manchin are both Democrats, their personal, political, and regional backgrounds are markedly different. Senator Schumer's political career has evolved from a Congressman representing districts which encompassed much of the metropolitan New York City area to becoming the third-ranking Senator in the Democratic Party.

While hailing from urban political districts and a "blue" state, that is a state which consistently elects predominately democratic candidates at the national level, he has developed a reputation as an excellent negotiator who seeks positions of compromise. As a state senator, secretary of state, and governor of West Virginia, Senator Manchin brings a significantly different constituency to the process of finding compromise regarding gun safety. Unlike Schumer whose voting record is often labeled "progressive," Manchin's history as governor and his voting record during his relatively brief time in the Senate, has vacillated between "conservative" to "independent." His "conservative" credentials were reflected in his role as governor when the state sued the federal Environmental Protection Agency over their rulemaking under the Clean Water Act which mandated the coal industry to conform with proposed requirements relating to water usage in mining. His vote against Don't Ask Don't Tell also reinforced his reputation as a so-called right of center Democrat. More recently, his refusal to endorse either Barack Obama or Mitt Romney for President, has demonstrated his willingness to stray from obligation of party loyalty to so-called independent positions. Senator Toomey's political resume is also interesting.

Labeled as a conservative republican, Senator Toomey's constituency in the state of Pennsylvania may be less predictable than either Senator Schumer's or Manchin's. Pennsylvania has generally fallen into the broad political category of a "blue" state electing so-called "moderate" Democrats to national office. Even one of the longest serving Republicans from Pennsylvania, Harlan Spector, was amendable to legislative proposals which attracted support from both political parties. On the contrary, Senator Toomey's conservative credentials are impeccable. During his relatively short term in the Senate he has been most often an outspoken proponent of so-called fiscal responsible legislation. He came to office with a career as a Wall Street investment banker and as an owner and operator of a chain of restaurants. He also served as President of Club for Growth, a powerful special interest group which lobbied for numerous legislative proposals to lower tax rates and reduce government spending. More specifically, Toomey has trumpeted positions which may render him vulnerable in his bid for reelection, particularly among suburban Philadelphia voters. As President of Club for Growth he often could be heard registering his disdain for "big government" and calling for "limited government." That he would become a party in the movement to negotiate a "political compromise" on the drafting of federal regulations regarding gun safety has been surprising to some who have supported the call for "limited government."

One would have to be naïve to suggest that some element of political survival has not played differing degrees of importance in the cooperation of these three

Senators and the other members of the Senate who supported the proposed legislation. As Madison noted there are "advantageous consequences" for finding "political compromise." Both before the submission of the proposed bill and after its defeat, public opinion polling reflected significant support from large segments of the American public and in the political districts which have re-elected Senator Schumer, and voted for both Senator Manchin and Toomey in their relatively recent election to the Senate. Senator Toomey may be the most vulnerable of the three. He will stand for re-election and may face the full force of campaign opposition from so-called "gun rights" factions. But his willingness to participate in seeking "political compromise" may engender support from suburban "swing" voters anxious to see gun safety regulations instituted.

Of course, even with the use of the most sophisticated polling techniques available, attempting to quantify the degree to which political self-survival plays a part in finding "political compromise" is difficult at best. What may be more important is that each of these Senators displayed a willingness to sacrifice some level of their "political capital" in seeking compromise. Schumer was willing to take an uncharacteristic less visible role as public advocate for the legislation—even to the extent of not appearing with Manchin and Toomey when the bill was publicly presented. Manchin, often seen as a stronger supporter of the "right to bear arms," challenged the "gun rights" lobby by suggesting that the proposed legislation would preserve the right of responsible firearm ownership and strengthen American's Second Amendment rights. Toomey, while challenged by some that the proposed legislation was "gun control" under another name, responded that "I don't consider criminal background checks gun control."

Even the most cynical political observer must concede that these Senators exhibited leadership in beginning to establish an environment for compromise and the mutuality of respect necessary to break the gridlock which has paralyzed our legislative process. While the bill failed by a 54–46 vote, these Senators demonstrated a commitment to stand together as representatives of the American people, not just their political districts. But lessons may be learned from this failed attempt at finding "political compromise" on gun safety which can be used in subsequent legislative efforts on this important public policy issue as well as others. One may be that the relatively short time frame which was involved in the "negotiating" process between Schumer, Manchin, and Toomey, prevented an objective and comprehensive public discussion regarding the constitutional legitimacy of the competing first principles involved in the proposed "compromise." If proposals for regulation of gun safety in the country are to continue to receive the support from the

American people, those who reside in our urban centers and in rural areas of the country, an honest and balanced presentation of the "right to bear arms" must be grounded on a constitutionally directed discussion of the rights and responsibilities associated with the Second Amendment of our Bill of Rights. That the American public is willing to accept reasonable regulation of firearms seems, at the moment, to be a given. However, without a continuing discussion in our representative bodies, from respected legislators similar to Schumer, Manchin, and Toomey, who are capable of explaining how proposed legislation is reflective of our competing co-equal constitutional first principles, not an abandonment of any one objective but rather a necessary balancing, then the process of finding compromise will be hijacked by one special interest faction or another. Indeed, the commentary by those who refused to support The Public Safety and Second Amendment Rights Protection Act reflected a serious disconnect between the actual provisions of the proposed legislation and their alleged constitutional concerns. A much more extended explanation by the bill's co-sponsors of its constitutional legitimacy would have exposed the misrepresentations of some who opposed the bill. Such a discussion would have provided the much needed transparency necessary for an objective examination of the bill and established a precedent for future public policy debates such as immigration reform or tax code reform. And, equally important, such a process of discussion would have stripped away the constitutional distortions offered by some legislators to deflect criticism of their opposition to any regulation of firearms.

For example, an often repeated defense in opposition to the bill was that it violated the Second Amendment rights of "law abiding" citizens. Alleging that any requirement of providing background checks on potential firearm purchasers in an attempt to determine whether they had a criminal background or were adjudicated mentally ill, as the bill proposed, were presented by opponents as a direct challenge to the Second Amendment. Instead of actually providing historical or Supreme Court opinions which could support such a claim, they instead offered the tried and true "slippery slope" defense for their constitutionally indefensible opposition. Senator Grassley of Iowa opined that the proposed legislation which required background checks would ultimately "snowball" into federal gun registration. Arguing that the bill's proposal to require background checks of unlicensed dealers at gun shows and for online sales was an example of federal government "overreach" in response to the shootings in Newtown, he said "Expanded background checks would not have prevented Newtown… Criminals do not submit to background checks now, they will not submit to expanded background checks."[117] Other opponents to the bill justified their "no" vote on similar "slippery slope" arguments claiming that the legislation would violate "the right to keep and bear arms."

The junior Senator from Texas, Ted Cruz, a Tea Party supporter and self-pro-claimed protector of the Constitution, offered the following commentary. Arguing that the proposed bill would lead to the "creation of a national database of gun owners" he said "In my opinion, adopting mandatory federal government background checks for purely private transactions between law abiding citizens, puts us inexorably on the path for a federal registry." When pressed by Senator Schumer regarding this point reminding Senator Cruz that the proposed bill "explicitly barred a federal registry" and would impose a harsh penalty on any official who tried to create one, Cruz replied:

> It is not currently proposed, but if the bill that is being considered would be adopted, it would put us on that path. And I think that path would be profoundly unwise and inconsistent with the Second Amendment right to keep and bear arms.[118]

It should be noted that at no time during the relatively brief "debate" regarding the proposed legislation did Senators Grassley or Cruz provide any substantive constitutional discussion regarding the Supreme Court's rationale in the Heller decision regarding the limits of the Second Amendment or any of the Court's observations of what might be "reasonable" governmental regulation of firearms. It should also be pointed out that very little was provided to the American public by the bill's proponents that the proposed legislation was well within the Second Amendment parameters established in Heller regarding limiting legal access to firearms to "felons" and legally "adjudicated mentally ill" individuals. Instead of having a transparent discussion of the elements of Senator Cruz's "misunderstanding" of the rights and responsibilities associated with the application of the words within the Second Amendment of the Bill of Rights, the proponents of the bill failed to engage his conclusions with any serious rebuttal other than to respond that the bill prohibited the establishment of a national registry and that for the last seventeen years there had been no effort by the Federal government to establish such a registry.

A very important teaching moment for Americans was lost. Instead of discussing the objections of Senator Grassley and Senator Cruz regarding their "slippery slope" arguments, their specific concern regarding the bill's impact on "law abiding" citizens and the meaning of their usage of the term "private transactions," it appeared as if Senators Schumer, Manchin, and Toomey believed such an effort was futile in their attempt to persuade their colleagues. It may have been that they counted the votes and knew that the proposed legislation was not going to obtain the necessary approval to then be submitted to the House of Representatives. Whatever the reason, the failure to confront the specific "constitutional" objections offered by the opponents to the bill, left a lingering legitimacy to their concerns that could have easily been rebutted. Such a discussion would have created a rarely observed opportunity to evaluate public policy discussions beyond political spin and transform it into the most powerful example of citizenship education.

To sustain support from the American people on this issue, as well as the other public policy issues mired in political gridlock in the House of Representatives and the Senate, demonstrations of continued efforts to create "political compromise" must build on the failed attempt to pass The Public Safety and Second Amendment Rights Protection Act. Senators Schumer, Manchin, and Toomey should be credited with beginning what may be a long process of negotiation regarding gun safety regulation. Their efforts reflected two of the three necessary elements for achieving "political compromise"—that is, establishing an environment of mutuality of respect among those in the political elite willing to work for accommodation of differing political interests; and encouraging others from the "elected" who are willing to define the "faithful discharge" of their responsibilities to include the entirety of the nation, not just their political electoral district. But the one missing component of their attempt at breaking the gridlock on this public policy issue was their failure to demand an extended, transparent discussion of the need to balance the competing co-equal constitutional first principles reflected in both the Preamble and the Bill of Rights.

Such a public discussion by Senators Schumer, Manchin and Toomey could have reflected the historical concern of the Founders which shaped the language of the Second Amendment. That is, they could have recognized the Founders' fear of concentrated power and its potential for totalitarian government. Instead of remaining to a large degree in the background of the "marketing" of the proposed legislation, Senator Schumer, the most "progressive" of the three, could have taken the lead on this concern of the Founders. In so doing, he would have reinforced his respect for those Americans who possess a healthy irreverence of so-called government "overreach" by sometimes supporting an absolutist position on the "right to bear arms." What such a discussion would have produced is a recognition which has been reflected in recent polling data—that background checks of sellers and purchasers of firearms, public and private alike, coupled with severe criminal penalties for any individual or individuals who attempt to create a registry of gun ownership, are overwhelmingly supported by the American people. Additionally, by having Senator Schumer present the findings of the Heller decision which underscored the historical legitimacy of the

Second Amendment "right to bear arms" in the context of their fear of tyranny from dictatorial actions of government, he would be demonstrating his respect for good faith citizens who are too often placed in one-dimensional "boxes" as ideological extremists preparing for the inevitable next revolution by those on the political "left." Additionally, by acknowledging this historical concern he would begin to expose the distortion of special interest factions which profit from the marketing of "right-wing" conspiracy theories claiming governmental control of every aspect of American life.

The next part of the discussion, led by both Senator Manchin and Toomey, could have been a point-by-point discussion of the proposed bill's provisions which reflected the Heller decision's recognition that the Second Amendment, similar to all the Amendments within the Bill of Rights, is not absolute and that certain regulations similar to the ones proposed were well within the protections of the Second Amendment and even presented by the Court as examples of po-tential constitutional regulations. With a more extended defense of the proposed legislation by a "progressive" recognizing the Founding fear of the potential for tyranny derived from governmental overreach, and an open discussion and de-fense by two members of the Senate with strong "conservative" credentials re-garding the bill's provisions which mirrored the Heller decision, would have pro-vided the opportunity to illustrate how the Constitution's mandate for balancing liberty within the context of the public welfare was reflected in their proposed legislation. Opponents of the bill would then have been obligated to respond with more historically and constitutionally grounded objections than to simply cite the Second Amendment language without Supreme Court interpretation and then run to the loudest media political spin doctor to demagogue the issue.

It will be remembered that the Founders constructed the bi-cameral repre-sentative process understanding that the role of the Senate of the United States was to be a deliberative body with members whose term of office would allow for debate and reflection of public policy issues facing the nation. While the process of negotiating in an effort to find "political compromise" requires varying levels of public transparency, once "a coalition of the willing" is constructed, a full blown debate of the constitutional legitimacy of the positions used to support or oppose proposed legislation is absolutely essential if Jefferson's requirement of an "enlightened citizenry" is to be achieved. But any effort to engender the support of the American people on the issue of gun safety or any of the other public pol-icy issues mired in the existing gridlock of our legislative process will require an extended participation of our print and broadcast media. After The Public Safety and Second Amendment Rights Protection Act failed to receive the necessary votes for passage in the Senate, the attention of the "press" quickly turned to other "breaking news." Even during the "debate" regarding the proposed Man-chin–Toomey bill, the main stream broadcast media provided only superficial coverage, and along with their cable channel compatriots, provided the public with two-minute sound bites or "analysis" using what we have earlier described as the "false equivalency" technique through the commentary of political spin doctors disguised as "political contributors."

That these practices do not fulfill the essential role of the "free press" in our democracy should be obvious. If the gridlock in the Congress of the United States is to be resolved and "political compromise" is to be found there must be a sustained effort by our broadcast media to fulfill what Alexis de Tocqueville in 1832 observed was the important role of the press in our democracy:

> ...It causes political life to circulate through all parts of that vast terri-tory. Its eye is constantly open to detect the secret springs of political de-signs, and to summon the leaders of all parties in turn to the bar of public opinion...[119]

Without this commitment to educate, not only to entertain the American public, any efforts to reinvigorate citizenship education and to confront the alienation of the country with its institutions of government will fail. Breaking the gridlock in Congress then will entail, at the minimum, a reexamination by enough of our political elite of what constitutes a "faithful discharge" of their duties to their country, an undaunted commitment by our print and broad-cast "free press" to demand transparency from our political representatives re-garding the facts which support their proposed public policy positions through sustained objective journalism on the subjects, and an engaged public open to balanced solutions from those who defend their positions on constitutional first principles. To believe that these elements for "political compromise" are achiev-able one only has to point to the process instituted during the gun safety nego-tiations. While the initial efforts to find accommodation were unsuccessful, the time still remains ripe for compromise—that is, if the press returns it attention to the issue once again. Time will tell.

7 "That The Public Good is Disregarded in the Conflicts of Rival Parties"

AMERICA IS AT A CROSSROAD. WE are at a time in our history when the diverse nature of our society can either propel us into positive collective actions to secure liberty and promote the public welfare or divide us into the abyss of class, regional, racial, or religious tribalism. There are many factors which have contributed to this state of affairs. While no one event can be identified as the sole reason for our seeming frustration with government and the actions of some in our private sector, in this chapter we will identify a few of the most troubling reasons for what appears to be our inability to reject the politics of "divide and conquer" and find strength in our collective capacity to shape a positive future for our children. As has been noted throughout our investigation many of our contemporary problems can be resolved through an understanding of and commitment to the visions of the Founders enshrined in the Constitution. Both the letter and spirit of the document can provide us with guidance as we confront the seeming intractable problems associated with our experiment in governance. An understanding of their recognition of the need for an "enlightened citizenry," dependence upon our "joint wisdom" and their confidence in the balancing process of "first principles" to resolve our differences is essential if we are to overcome the constant attempts at shredding the body politic for personal gain. In this chapter then we will begin the process of "piercing the veil" of those who knowingly or unintentionally misrepresent the Founding vision to the American people. In so doing, we will offer an alternative path for future public policy decision-making which is a more accurate reflection of the Founder's fears and aspirations.

Confronting "the Snares of the Ambitious"

The near collapse of our financial system in 2007/2008 and its impact on millions of citizens remains a slow healing wound to the American economy and psyche. And while the gaming industry euphemistically described as "Wall Street" currently has achieved "investment gains" secured by billions of dollars printed by the American people through the auspices of the Federal Reserve, the select "too big to fail" so-called "banks" continue to participate in domestic and global proprietary trading with little or weak governmental regulation. The influence of money emanating from the American oligarchy under the guise of corporate "job creators" and with the assistance of K-Street lobbyists often staffed by the "revolving door" of politicians turned influence peddlers, threatens the Founders reliance on the system's ability to control the "Mischiefs of Factions."

With the assistance of "institutes" and "foundations" funded by the same corporate and individual benefactors that support the K-Street lobbyists, those who have profited the most since the near collapse of our financial system are provided with "academic" and "intellectual" justifications for their wealth creation and power. Another bi-product of the "great recession" has seen the further erosion of trust in our governmental institutions nurtured by the constant ranting of media demagogues and politicians eager to decry the actions of government intrusion into the lives of Americans. Even with the recent Presidential campaign and the reelection of Barack Obama and his call for immigration reform, tax reform, gun safety regulation, and a modest national jobs bill, Congressional action has been tepid at best. The once healthy irreverence of our "elected" noted by the Founders seems to have evolved into a growing national malaise with government fed by those who profit from gridlock legitimized as "limited government." Some of the actions of a few government officials have only served to fuel the ever-present conspiracy theorists and politicians eager to score points with some of their most vocal constituents.

For example, the activity of some Internal Revenue Service employees tasked with the responsibility to identify illegal tax avoidance through the use of certain not-for-profit categories in our tax code, produced Congressional investigations seeking to determine whether the IRS was in fact targeting only so-called "conservative" contributors in the recent campaign and thereby creating a "chilling effect" on political speech. Continuing "investigations" into the tragic killing of State Department employees and our ambassador to Libya have identified serious issues of security at our foreign embassies in countries rife with civil unrest and violence. Additionally, a third inquiry regarding Department of Justice wiretapping of AP journalists and a Fox news reporter's phone conversations in an investigation of alleged "leaking" of national security information regarding North Korea, has raised questions about the government targeting the press. While these Congressional subcommittee hearings have elements of important issues associated with government "overreach" or "incompetence," very little factual information which would support a "big brother" White House conspiracy to target political opponents or "cover up" incompetent decision-making by a potential future presidential candidate has been produced.

Sadly, what at least on the surface, appear to be legitimate concerns about the functioning of some of our bureaucratic institutions, has the distinct flavor of but another political show trial by those eager to score points with their political base still reeling from their defeat in the presidential election of 2012. These so-called "scandals" continue to be presented by the marketers of "fear," "distrust," and "big brother conspiracy" as justifications for a myriad of public policy positions which would restrict the role of the federal government in regulating the activities of the "private sector." With terms such as "limited government" or "big government" used as the reason for the need for privatization of traditionally public service entities or the abolition of federal governmental agencies such as the Department of Education and the Environmental Protection Agency, these self-anointed "free market" devotees tout the benefits which governmental non-regulation can produce. The entrepreneurial spirit of the American people can only be unleashed if "big government" is reduced to "…the size where we can drown it in the bathtub," as Grover Norquist, the voice of so-called responsible tax reform in America, so confidently suggested.

At a time when the "gains" produced by Wall Street have been acquired by a disturbingly small percentage of the American public and the household wealth of the great majority of Americans has stagnated, seen only slight gains over the last thirty years or even fallen further into poverty, legislative efforts to enter into an objective examination of our tax code have been met with sophisticated opposition marketing campaigns by Norquist and his benefactors. Any increase in taxes, even to those who have achieved close to two hundred percent increase in wealth creation over the last thirty years and who have been the beneficiaries of numerous provisions of the tax code which limit their tax responsibilities are presented by the oligarchical front organizations as assaults on the American "free enterprise" system and as precursors of "big government" socialism.

As was discovered in Chapter Two, many of the known benefactors of "not-for-profit" political advocacy groups such as Freedom Works and the Tea Party Patriots are the same supporters of earlier special interest groups such as the American Petroleum Institute, Citizens For A Sound Economy, and Empower America. Under the public leadership of Dick Armey, a retired Congressman from Texas who along with others in Congress during the 1990's successfully "deregulated" the banking and telecommunication industries, Freedom Works along with Americans for Tax Reform have marketed what they have described

as "Key Issues" in their assault on "big government." With the necessary funding coming from members of the American oligarchy, such as the Koch brothers
and Steve Forbes, every conceivable "hot button" public policy term has been
trotted out by Freedom Works under the guise of fundamental "conservative"
principles in an effort to "limit" the role of the federal government in almost
every sector of American life. They have been assisted in this effort through the
machinations of so-called Tea Party Republicans in the Congress of the United
States and with the continual marketing of the "Key Issues" without serious
analysis by political ideologues disguised as broadcast journalists.

With the assistance of who we have described in our investigation as the
modern day snake oil salesmen—political marketers—these contentious issues
are presented to the American people through the same tried and true methodologies used in consumer product advertising. That is, with creatively produced
commercial images often accompanied with unsubstantiated claims of product
effectiveness. As most citizens have come to understand in our commercialized
market economy, much can be learned regarding the quality of any product or
the rights and responsibilities of any contractual agreement, by reviewing the
"fine print"—or the disclaimers regarding the product's proven effectiveness.
While consumer safety regulations mandate that some "notice" be provided
to the public in the marketing of some products, little is required regarding
the source or the accuracy of the claims made in the marketing of political
opinion sold as fact to the American public yearning for a "miracle cure" to
the problems of a diverse society. Wrapped in the cloak of our Constitution's
commitment to freedom of political speech and necessarily cautious to restrict
the communication of political opinion, it is presumed that the veracity of the
claims will be tested in "a free marketplace of ideas." It would seem only reasonable then that we explore some of the "Key Issues" presented by Freedom
Works and molded into "model bills" by the American Legislative Exchange
Council—a consortium of corporate special interest groups—in an effort to determine whether the solutions offered regarding these public policy questions
are factual presentations grounded in what are claimed to be the visions of the
Founders or are as Hamilton forewarned derived from "…the artifices of men
who possess (our) confidence more than they deserve it."

The "Key Issues" include: Budget/Spending, Tax Reform, Workplace Freedom,
HealthCare Reform, Energy and the Environment, School Choice, Red Tape,
Hidden Taxes, Regulations and Entitlement Reform, Medicare and Social
Security.[120] Each of these subjects of American life and government possess
the social and political "red meat" used by political marketers to create images
of intrusive Orwellian government actions. This brilliantly constructed list of

divisive public policy issues provides the perfect cover for sloganeering and the politics of "divide and conquer." Any one of these so-called "Key Issues" generates initial emotional responses from Americans regardless of their political preferences. One line sound bites can be produced on each topic which can be used to market simple solutions to a public who as Hamilton observed "...commonly intend the public good" and yet should be constantly vigilant of "...the arts of men who flatter their prejudices to betray their interests." While any of these subjects can be used to reinforce Hamilton's concerns and deserves a separate critical analysis, each "Key Issue" possesses a common theme which was expressed in the 2012 presidential campaign by Mitt Romney's belief that we have become a country almost divided equally between those who he described as "takers" and those who bear the responsibility of paying for the "takers" "entitlements."[121] At the core of both Romney's commentary and those who have so masterfully identified the subjects which produce the most divisive reaction in contemporary America, is the unresolved question of government's role in the regulation of, as James Madison described "...Those who hold and those who are without property..." There should be little question that, at the core of the contemporary gridlock in the Congress of the United States, is the body's inability to withstand the influence of literally billions of dollars of lobbying on behalf of those "who hold property." That being noted, it is important to indicate that those "who are without property" also have advocates who constantly seek an audience with our political elite in an effort to counter the influence of the American oligarchy. But after five and now almost six years of Congressional inaction on actual "job creation," reformation of our tax code, establishing real protection for the American people from "too big to fail" so-called banking institutions, and their failure to confront the Nation's long-term debt with balanced proposals, it would seem Madison's vision of competing factions forced into compromise has momentarily failed.

Part of the reason for the success by those who have marketed "government" as the problem not the solution, as Ronald Reagan once opined, is their ability to "reshape" Reagan's actual decision-making from this now much cited campaign sloganeering. President Reagan understood the very nature of negotiation and the requirement of compromise. Indeed, from the inception of our collective covenant and its implementation over more than two hundred years, our political elite—federalists/antifederalists, republicans/democrats—have ultimately recognized the difference between political rhetoric and governing. While one can generate short-term support for one public policy or another through the use of political rhetoric, to maintain the confidence of a majority of the American people actual statesmanship is required. That too few of our political elite are willing to or capable of challenging the self-interested lobbying/marketing of the K street front men/women continues to embolden those who anonymously fund their efforts. And as important as the influence peddlers are to the decision-making of our "elected," even more powerful is the ability of marketers of the so-called "key issues" to wrap their product under the guise of a political philosophy to the American people.

Instead of being exposed as the windfall financial beneficiaries of a well-developed "model bill"—that is, a proposed piece of legislation allegedly confronting one or more of the "key issues" facing the Nation—the anonymous profiteers can call upon otherwise traditional "conservative," or now popular, alleged "libertarian" principles, to legitimize their scheme(s) to "shrink government down to the size where (it) can be drained in the bathtub." Reminiscent of the tobacco industry's marketing campaigns of the 1950's and 1960's which touted the individualistic nature of the Marlboro Man riding a horse on an open plain with one hand on the reins and one defiantly holding a cigarette, each "model bill" allegedly addressing one of the "key issues" offered by Freedom Works or the other front organizations call upon the similar uniquely American values of rugged individualism and freedom. Having captured the hearts, if not the minds, of some citizens it is not so much of a "reach" to portray the recommended legislation as a protection from the ever present governmental bureaucracy always ready to destroy the aspirations of individual citizens in their "pursuit of happiness." Once the political marketers have now received the attention of their targeted "consumer"—selling their particular vision of "entitlement," "workplace freedom," etc., etc., becomes remarkably straight forward. Those who yearn for "liberty" and "freedom" to build a better future for themselves and their families are being strangled by those "others" who demand government "handouts" as a form of ransom from "real" Americans. Therefore, "Red Tape" signifies tyrannical government intrusion, "Workplace Freedom" becomes the eradication of unions and collective bargaining, "Tax Reform" presented in the context of "flat tax simplification" will be "fairer" to hard-working Americans, and most importantly, "Entitlement Reform" will send a message to all the "takers" that no longer will the largesse of the American people be available as an endless money pit for their sloth and non-productivity.

Only those who market one of the most addictive drugs known to man and have been able to continue the drug's legal status in this country and around the planet, could devise such a scheme. With unemployment still at unacceptable levels in the general population and even more elevated in other portions of our citizenry, the re-election of the country's first African-American President, and a continuing anemic economy placing more and more demands on the middle class, the last thing the country needs is further profiteering from the oligarchy under the guise of protectors of American "free enterprise" and "limited government." The presentation of these important subjects of contemporary America in the "them and us" methodology, only serves to drive the forces of tribalism into more reactionary responses and reduces the potential for an objective discussion of the role of government as the necessary mechanism to balance the overriding first principles of the Constitution. But this tactic does divert attention from those who profit from the politics of division. The strategy is brilliant. Always keep the enemy on the defensive. Identify the "weakness" of your opponent's position in stark "black and white" terminology allowing for no discussion of the "gray." Couch each "model bill" or recommendation with the glow of American entrepreneurialism and self-reliance. And most importantly, constantly reinforce the destructive impact of the "federal government" on individual liberty. An examination of how Freedom Works defines and markets the terms "regulation" and "entitlement" will illustrate the point.

"Regulations and Entitlement Reform"
Entering the World of Alice in Wonderland

Similar to Alice's extraordinary experience of falling down the "Rabbit-hole" and being confronted with a tempting offer to consume a bottle with a "beautifully printed" label, Americans are being asked to swallow an unknown concoction—but let Alice (Lewis Carroll) described her dilemma:

> "It was all very well to say "Drink me." But the wise little Alice was not going to do that in a hurry. "No, I'll look first," she said, "and see whether it's marked 'poison' or not"; for she had read several nice little stories about children who had got burnt, and eaten up by wild beasts, and other unpleasant things, all because they would not remember the simple rules their friends had taught them; such as, that a red-hot poker will burn you if you hold it too long; and that, if you cut your finger very deeply with a knife, it usually bleeds; and she had never forgotten that, if you drink much from a bottle marked 'poison,' it is almost certain to disagree with you, sooner or later."[122]

With no marking on the bottle that indicated that it was 'poison,' it will be remembered that Alice drank the mixture. Her response after drinking the bottle was, "What a curious feeling!"

Such is the experience that one has when confronted with the concoction blended by Freedom Works and their compatriots in Congress and the mass media regarding "Regulations and Entitlement Reform." Using the terms "red tape" and "hidden taxes" Freedom Works markets to the American "everyman (women)," the self-serving potion of their benefactors, that government oversight stifles "liberty" and surreptitiously steals the "fruits of one's labor." Predictably, distortion and fear also assist in selling their pitch of an impending fiscal Armageddon to the American public. In starkly vivid images the "front men (women)" of Freedom Works, the American Legislative Exchange Council, and so-called "libertarian" think tanks, sometimes cloaked within the prestigious walls of academic institutions, decry "unnecessary governmental regulation" and the stifling impact of "federal government" taxation for the benefit of the "takers" on hard-working Americans struggling to keep their financial heads above water. It is, indeed, a potentially poisonous mixture of "them and us isms" blended with half-truths and served with an always present aura of constitutional legitimacy through the use of terms such as "enumerated powers" and "limited government." What is so potentially poisonous to the American body politic is the creation of both a societal and political environment which is so strident that an objective examination of the country's challenges is rendered impossible. Similar to Alice's experience of innocently consuming the content of a "beautifully labeled" bottle, acceptance of the presumptions and conclusions regarding "entitlement" and "regulations" presented by Freedom Works creates an equally "curious" wonderland.[123]

For example, by identifying only the Nation's social safety net programs such as Medicare and Social Security as targets of "entitlement reform" Freedom Works and its marketers inexplicably exempt the myriad of other forms of "government" largesse which could also be described as forms of "entitlement" and could also be reviewed for modification or abolition. In fact, when one places a "cost benefit"—not to mention a social welfare impact—on other sectors of American commerce and life which are the beneficiaries of government support, a completely different image of the "takers" begins to emerge. One needs to search no further than our tax codes, both on the federal and state levels, to provide literally hundreds of examples of government sponsored exemptions from taxation or significantly reduced levels of tax rates for selected individuals or corporations.

In addition to Americans who fall below the poverty level and are exempt from federal taxation, retirees on Social Security and who may receive Medicare benefits, or millions of children living in poverty who receive "entitlements," farmers, hedge fund managers and investors, and corporations and businesses both large and small are also provided with tax exemptions or significantly lower taxation rates than the majority of American middle class taxpayers. Absent from any discussion by Freedom Works and their K-Street compatriots who attack the dispensing of such government largesse through Social Security and Medicare are equally scathing assaults on the constant tax windfalls provided to their corporate and individual benefactors. One such example is the continuing special tax breaks provided for the oil and gas industry. Apparently, Freedom Works and their supporters' silence regarding the billions of dollars which the industry will have accumulated via reduced tax rates over the next decade is to be exempted from any critical analysis or that it should be included in the category of "entitlement." Any serious examination of how the country is to pay down its indebtedness and secure opportunities for our children requires, at the minimum, an objective analysis of the sources of revenue available to the American people and a transparent accounting. While facts may not matter in the "wonderland" of Freedom Works and their benefactors, they are fundamental to any public policy debate on where the line(s) should be drawn between incentivized wealth creation and retention and unconscionable corporate or individual greed.

The Congressional Joint Committee on Taxation reported that the five largest oil companies receive a $2.4 billion per year tax exemption. Additionally, they calculated that because of the existing tax rates and exemptions the industry over the next ten years will have accumulated over $40 billion. In 2011, a year before the presidential election, the tax rate of the three largest oil companies were, Exxon Mobil –13%; Chevron –19%; Conoco Philips –18%. It should be noted that the industry spent $70 million in campaign contributions in 2012. The five largest oil companies spent $50 million lobbying Congress in 2012 which totaled to one-third of the industry's expenditures. The special tax status that the industry receives remains in effect in 2013. In fact, the profitability of the oil and gas industry continues to call into question its need for government "incentives" provided through our tax code.[124]

Of course, arguments abound regarding the efficacy of the industry's special need for lower rates and exemptions. The most often presented rationale is that they are necessary to encourage exploration and development of new resources. Yet, while the initial rates and exemptions were allegedly crafted at a time when dire predictions were presented regarding the Nation's dirth of new sources of oil and the need to become "energy independent" from "foreign oil," the United States is now quickly becoming one of the largest exporters of oil and gas in the world. Regardless of one's view concerning the need for the continuance of government support for this industry, at the minimum one would expect that those who are fearful of "big government" and outraged by the "coercive power of government" would include this form of corporate welfare as a subject for discussion concerning "reform." Indeed, this practice of providing numerous methods in our tax code by which corporations can reduce, or in some cases, eliminate any tax obligation to the American people can certainly be described as but another form of "entitlement" for select individuals—after all "corporations are people too."

It would seem then that in the "wonderland" of Freedom Works and other so-called Tea Party organizations such as the Tea Party Patriots, their outrage regarding government wealth redistribution which benefit some sectors of the population and are presented as unconscionable government taking of property, does not apply to government sponsored tax exemptions provided for select corporations and individuals. It continues to get "curiouser and curiouser," to coin a phrase, as Alice falls further down the rabbit-hole when the contemporary devotees of selective government largesse remain silent on the benefits provided to some of their most enthusiastic supporters from the American oligarchy. For example, the tax "write off" or exemption provided in differing forms through our federal and state tax codes to "farmers." A snapshot of one state property tax, presumably enacted to incentivize the survival of an important business sector of our country, will illustrate the point.

The state of New Jersey, similar to many states, imposes a property tax on its citizens' ownership of land. Depending upon the size of each parcel of land owned by any individual there is a corresponding level of taxation. However, not unlike other states, New Jersey provides various forms of "tax relief" to land owners. The state's public policy of encouraging and protecting "farming" has produced a "curious" by-product—what has been coined as "faux farmers."[125] That is, individuals who owned large—defined by state tax code—tracts of land which are exempted from significant property tax obligations because the land holding is used for agricultural or farming purposes. Numerous wealthy citizens—millionaires and billionaires—in New Jersey have received significant tax exemptions or tax reductions by returning "back to the land" from their "day jobs" as captains of industry, musical performers, media moguls, or outspoken critics for a "fairer tax code." Indeed, the confusion that Alice experienced as she was introduced by the white rabbit to a world filled with inexplicable events, again begins to emerge when advocates for sweeping reforms of the social safety net programs fail to murmur even the slightest outrage at the application of laws similar to New Jersey's to the benefit of the American oligarchy.

The property tax levied by New Jersey pursuant to its public policy to encourage "farming" as it applied to a consistent supporter of Freedom Works is an excellent example. Multi-millionaire, Malcolm Steve Forbes, an outspoken critic of the federal tax code, owns 450 acres of land in New Jersey. It has been reported that his tax obligation on his property was $2,005. He received this extraordinarily modest tax responsibility because he raises "show cows" on the property and therefore is qualified to receive a significant reduction in what would otherwise be a more substantial property tax. It should be noted that he also receives reduced tax obligations pursuant to the federal taxation process. But he was not alone in being rewarded under the New Jersey property tax process of incentivizing "farming" in the state. Other prominent citizens of the Garden State also have filed for reduced property tax relief because of their commitment to the importance of agriculture. "Woody" Johnson, heir to the Johnson and Johnson family fortune and owner of the New York Jets, along with billionaire print and broadcast media owner Donald Newhouse and musician Bon Jovi also are beneficiaries of the tax program.[126]

The point, of course, is not that any of these individuals who avail themselves of these types of incentives provided by our federal and state tax codes have violated the law. But rather that so little is said regarding these programs obvious largesse to a select few. It would appear that those who eagerly attack the so-called "entitlements" provided through the federal and state governments "discretionary budgets" for programs such as food stamps (SNAP), head start, and Medicare/Medicaid/Social Security, are unwilling to have an objective public debate regarding acceptable incentives for wealth creation and retention within the context of the competing constitutional obligations to the country. It may be that Freedom Works and its supporters simply believe that the possession and protection of "private property" is the sole purpose for our collective covenant. Such a discussion then is not required. Cite the Declaration of Independence, without any historical or philosophical context, interpret the Constitution as a one-dimensional agreement to protect individual liberty—meaning the absolute right to protect the fruits of one's labor regardless of "harm to another," and return the "governing" of the country to an Anti-Federalist vision of so-called state and local decision-making—a "beautifully labeled bottle," indeed.

But while our journey through the "wonderland" of Freedom Works and its marketers may not discover any correlation between the Founding visions reflected in the Constitution and the "concoction" being sold, one can appreciate Alice's confusion as she attended what Lewis Carroll described as "A Mad Tea Party" with the "Hatter." It will be remembered that after attempting to join in a rational discussion with the Hatter and the other attendees at the tea party in an attempt to understand the strange events she was experiencing after consuming the contents of the bottle, she found herself even more befuddled and angry. And while the constant rudeness of the Hatter's "answers" to her questions eventually compelled her to leave the tea party and conclude that she would "never go there again," she did decide to continue her exploration with the assistance of a "little golden key" and a nibble of the mushroom which had miraculous powers. As Carroll wrote "...she found herself at last in the beautiful garden, among the bright flower-beds and the cool fountains."[127] The American oligarchy's pitchmen (women) promise an equally "beautiful garden" for America if only the "red tape" and "regulations" of government were eliminated. Absent the mushroom, let us venture, just for a moment, into the world of "bright flower-beds and the cool fountains" presented by our modern day Tea Party advocates.

If Freedom Works and their benefactors are to be believed, the eradication of "regulation," particularly from the federal government, will release our free market economic system from the shackles of unnecessary bureaucratic intervention and produce a new spirit of innovation across the country. The underlying claims marketed are the following: 1) Politicians lack the necessary expertise to shape regulatory policy; 2) Politicians have abdicated their regulatory policy making responsibilities to unelected bureaucrats; 3) Unaccountable bureaucrats produce regulatory mandates which strangle the economy and stifle economic growth; 4) The federal government has used regulatory rulemaking as a method to "hide" spending programs by requiring business to bear the cost of the mandates; 5) Ultimately, American consumers pay the cost of the regulations by the increased cost of products. A quick sampling of three commentaries produced by Freedom Works will underscore these presumptions.[128]

One commentary was published on June 21, 2013, the next in April of 2013, and another was provided in June of 2011. While presented to their readership over a span of two years their message is consistent—deregulate, deregulate, deregulate. In 2011, in a commentary entitled "The Hidden Cost of Regulation," James Hammerton, suggested that the voluminous size of the Federal Register, the publication required by Congress to provide notice to the American people of proposed rulemaking by both Executive and Independent Administrative Agencies, was evidence that "the lost to business is staggering." He wrote:

> ...It is not just large corporations but the entire economy that ends up bearing the cost of regulation. Complying with regulations is not cheap. The cost of complying with federal regulations increases businesses' expenses by billions of dollars every year. Some of the compliance cost associated with federal regulation comes out of business profits, but much of the costs are passed down to consumers in the form of higher prices...Because regulations create artificial costs that must be paid by both producers and consumers, they cost the economy money and act as a drag on economic growth. (Citing the Competitive Enterprise Institute's analysis of the cost

of regulations, he continues)...Government regulations are also used by the government as a means to hide spending programs. Instead of creating expensive government initiated programs, the government can create new regulations requiring businesses to carry out and bear the cost of the same initiatives.[129]

In the same commentary Hammerton expands his general observations on the negative impact of regulations, into a more transparent political attack. He writes:

> ...And the Obama administration appears to be doubling down on regulations, with massive new regulations in the works at the Environmental Protection Agency, new health care regulations, and a host of yet to be written regulations covering financial services...Unfortunately Obama's bureaucrats continue to crank out new expensive regulations at an incredible rate. Continued overregulation will only drag the economy down. On the other hand, pursing a policy of deregulation would free up the economy to grow and prosper.[130]

After the re-election of Barack Obama, under the category of "Red Tape, Hidden Taxes, and Regulations" Freedom Works continues to predict the devastating impact of federal government rulemaking.

> ...the coming years will see a significant increase in regulations as the federal agencies write new regulations to implement Obama Care and the Dodd-Frank financial services reform legislation, as well as major environmental regulations being pushed by the EPA. Regulatory reform is essential to ensure these regulations do not impose costs that exceed their benefits. Cost benefit analysis, risk assessment, risk protection, and market-based incentives are fundamental components that should be included in any reform of the process. In a global market place, the United States cannot afford to hamper its economic system with excessive and unnecessary regulations.[131]

In April of 2013 Freedom Works published and yet another warning concerning the creation of "governmental regulations." After trashing politicians' lack of substantive expertise to solve public policy problems, Logan Albright turned his wrath on the ever available whipping boy (girl) of "conservatives" and so-called "libertarians"—bureaucrats. He wrote:

> ...However, perhaps a bigger problem than the politicians themselves, are the unelected bureaucrats who end up designing the bulk of regulatory policy. Whereas politicians can be removed from office by popular vote,

bureaucrats are, for all intents and purposes, accountable to no one. Organizations such as the Transportation Security Administration or the Environmental Protection Agency have been given a free reign to regulate as they see fit, with no observable consequences for their failures. If we are to be free from the grip of endless, pointless, economically unproductive regulations, we must find a way to strip these agencies of their now nearly limitless authority and return the power to the people and their duly elected representatives.[132]

Similar to Alice's attempts at having a rational discussion with the Hatter at the "Mad Tea Party" one fears that any objective analysis of the claims and presumptions within the aforementioned commentaries will be only met with further attempts to market their product without any discernable disclaimer(s) to the American public. Indeed, without a requirement through "regulation" that their "concoction" may have deleterious consequences to the unsuspecting consumer of their presumptions, citizens are left with the age-old maxim of our common law—that is, *caveat emptor*—"buyer beware." But before Americans are left with the irrefutable power of determining which path they want their country to follow, at a minimum, the "facts" supporting public policy positions must be distilled from the debatable conclusions presented by those who seek our approval. The task of separating fact from fiction is always a difficult enterprise. But, one is again reminded of Senator Patrick Moynihan's remark that we are all entitled to our own set of opinions, not our own set of facts.

The commentary offered by Freedom Works is without question opinion marketed as fact. The masterful use of certain words or phrases reiterated throughout their publications then coupled with sweeping conclusions regarding government and recommended reform can create for the susceptible reader a method by which to enter a world filled with "bright flower beds and cool fountains." An examination of what are presented as "facts" and their techniques of persuasion should assist in determining whether their claims are worthy of our acceptance or mere illusions presented in the form of a political philosophy benefitting their benefactors. First let us examine the underlying claims or "facts" presented by Freedom Works and their supporters.

1) Politicians lack the necessary expertise to shape regulatory policy.
2) Politicians have abdicated their regulatory policy making responsibilities to unelected bureaucrats.
3) Unaccountable bureaucrats produce regulatory mandates which strangle the economy and stifle economic growth.
4) The federal government has used regulatory rulemaking as a

method to "hide" spending programs by requiring business to bear the cost of the mandates.

5) American consumers pay the cost of the regulations by the increased cost of products.

As with many of Freedom Works claims and presumptions there is an element of accuracy. But the first two claims are either woefully superficial descriptions of the powers of our political representatives or intentional misrepresentations offered to further the political agendas of Freedom Works and their benefactors. It is accurate to suggest that our "elected" do not possess the expertise to shape rules to objectively balance the specific requirements of commerce and its impact on the multiplicity of interests of the American people. But to suggest that they do not possess the constitutional power of oversight regarding the functioning of the so-called administrative state is simply untrue. It is also important to note that the evolution of our contemporary regulatory process is a by-product of the demands of citizens who have felt the too often deleterious impact of unmonitored commercial transaction.

The Founders accounted for what some predicted would be a future Congressional responsibility to create additional levels of expertise throughout the national government as the needs of the American People evolved. Article I, section 8. Clause 18 of the Constitution, authorizes the Congress to "... make all laws which shall be necessary and proper" to implement the enumerated responsibilities identified in Article I and any others which may be required to assist in the fulfillment of the Congress' law-making functions. With the evolution of the country in both land mass and population, a devastating Depression, and the trials and tribulations of surviving two world wars, the American people demanded and received political support for a federal government which would regularize government oversight of a rapidly expanding economy. Congress responded to the challenge by creating administrative agencies which would possess the expertise to assist Congress in implementing their law-making function under the Constitution. By 1946 the Congress, recognizing the need to establish a process which would create consistency in the functioning of its administrative agencies, enacted the Administrative Procedure Act.[133] Since the creation of the APA, federal administrative agencies located both in the legislative and Executive branches of our national government have systematized their quasi-legislative, quasi-executive and quasi-judicial decision-making.

The growth of the administrative state at the federal level is without question a by-product of the explosion of our population since its Founding, the seeming never-ending need for more specialized knowledge to meet the needs of the country, and the demands of citizens that our government encourage the growth of our private sector within the context of the public good. But while the People's representatives have acknowledged that they may not possess the necessary expertise to investigate, propose, and potentially institute administrative rules in an attempt to balance the needs of all sectors of American life, they have not abdicated their ultimate authority to "unaccountable bureaucrats" as Freedom Works contends. It is true that Congress has sub-delegated a portion of its lawmaking function to civil servants who have been insulated from political machination by a series of legislative enactments in an effort to separate political decision-making from the rulemaking and implementation of its administrative agencies. However, Congress still retains the power of oversight. It can restrain the functioning of any independent administrative agency by denying budgetary requests, monitoring the appointment process of each agency's leadership, or passing legislation which constrains the delegated powers assigned to a particular administrative agency. It is, therefore, absolutely true to suggest that our public servants in regulatory agencies are "unelected," it is quite another thing to conclude that they are "unaccountable."

There is no question that public administrators at the federal and sometimes at the state level have been legislatively insulated from the influence of the political process. The passage of the Pendleton Act[134] and the subsequent enactment of the Civil Service Reform Act of 1978[135] were legislative responses to numerous events in our history which produced governmental corruption through political cronyism fed by the influence of money and the need to provide more accountability within the system. While it may not serve the purposes of those who market the political dogma of so-called "limited government" in an effort to deregulate selected sectors of our economy—from the writings of Freedom Works and its supporters it would appear those businesses are the oil and gas industry, the so-called "financial services" industry, and the health "insurance" industry—the need for regulatory oversight by politically insulated public servants still remains an important element in the process of striking a balance between protecting the public interest and encouraging competition in commercial enterprises.

Our reliance on public administrative agencies and their mandates to provide objective expert judgment regarding the need for regulation is an appropriate subject for debate. But that debate must be shaped by the unfiltered facts devoid of misrepresentations or distortions. It may be that the administrative state has grown too large to fulfill its original mission to the American People as Freedom Works and its benefactors conclude. But as we examine the regulatory agencies that they rail against and their claims of the devastating impact of regulations on the economy, one is once again thrust down the "rabbit hole" with Alice as we try to decipher the real from the imagined.

Peering Through the Looking Glass:
Searching For the "Facts"

At the core of Freedom Works attack on "big government" is the claim that regulations strangle the economy and stifle economic growth. To legitimize their conclusion they present "data" collected and presented by the Competitive Enterprise Institute, a "conservative" research organization funded by the Koch brothers and other so-called "free market" supporters. CEI's analysis of the cost of regulations concluded that the cost of regulations was higher than the corporate pre-tax profit and therefore a "tax" on business which compelled them to pass the cost of regulations on to consumers. Other "progressive" research organizations have described CEI's findings as "misleading." James Goodwin, a policy analyst with the Center for Progressive Reform has observed that the CEI's study of the cost of regulations fails to account for the "positive effects" that regulations have on the functioning of the markets. He wrote:

> As we all know, this money is promoting goals Congress intended: a cleaner environment, safer workplace, etc. Moreover, it ignores the indirect economic benefits of regulatory compliance spending, which spurs economic activity (something our economy by and large is lacking).[136]

One can hardly argue that if most Americans were polled regarding the importance of clean air and safer workplaces they would support regulatory requirements which protect both. But Mr. Goodwin's observation presumes that Americans are willing to pay for the "pass through" cost of the regulations routinely instituted by targeted businesses more interested in maintaining or increasing their profit margins then promoting the public good. At a time of economic distress for too many citizens, and for those who believe that "global warming" or protection of the "spotted owl" are by-products of some "liberal" conspiracy, it may be wishful thinking on his part to conclude that Americans understand or see the "indirect benefits" of regulatory rulemaking.

Freedom Works and their benefactors are betting that they do not. They understand that if they can market the underlying fear of a continuing "jobless recovery" and tie the weak economic growth to a scenario of job loss created by government bureaucrats then they will have more success on "shrinking government to the size where we can drown it in the bathtub"—and presumptively, leave the defining of the public good to the so-called "free market." A compelling strategy—mount a campaign against "unaccountable bureaucrats," present sweeping attacks on "government regulations" generally, defend their conclusions based on "research" supported by those in the industries which would profit the most from "deregulation" and market it as the reason for "job loss" to a country with an unemployment rate not seen in decades. But similar to Freedom Works claim that bureaucrats are unaccountable their claim that the reason for "job loss" and the continuing slow return to acceptable levels of employment within the country is due to "government regulations" is also highly questionable.[137]

It has been reported that based on the Bureau of Labor Statistics data government regulations were a minor reason for private sector layoffs. In the first quarter of 2013 only 0.5 percent (5) of the 914 reported layoffs were attributable to government regulations. What then has been the reason for "job loss" in the labor market over the last few years? The answer given by the Bureau of Labor Statistics is—"lack of demand." The number one reason for more than 39% of all layoffs reported in the first quarter of 2013 cited by respondents was not government regulations but rather "business demand." As early in the so-called "recession" as 2011 self-described "conservative" small business owners reported that "demand" was the single most important factor in their need to downsize their employees. The findings reported that only 13.9% believed that regulations were the reason for layoffs while 20.8% identified taxes as the reason, 29.6% responded that poor sales was the basis of their decision to "downsize."[138] Other studies which have focused on the "cost of regulations" versus their "benefits" also call into question the sweeping generalizations and conclusions of Freedom Works and their supporters.

The Office of Management and Budget 2011 Annual Report traced the growth of federal regulation from 2002 to 2011 and calculated what they described as the "Total Annual Benefits and Costs of Major Rules." Among numerous findings they concluded that in 2011 while the cost of regulation was $8 billion, the benefit was $62 billion. Without question this finding is important. The overall "cost" of the federal regulations identified for study fell well below the "benefits" attributed to federal administrative rulemaking. The OMB report was quick to acknowledge that its extensive study of the cost/benefits of regulations was a general finding of most regulatory rulemaking instituted at the federal level. Some independent administrative agencies' rules were not examined for cost/benefit impacts.[139]

For example, the General Accounting Office pursuant to its responsibility to provide oversight and assessment of federal administrative rulemaking found that numerous rules impacting the "financial services" industry did not access their cost/benefit impact. This has particular significance since the passage of the Dodd-Frank legislation in which Congress authorized the Security and Exchange Commission to shape rules providing increased oversight of the industry. It should be noted that the SEC and its commissioners have yet to agree to the implementation of numerous proposed rules regarding the functioning of our "banking" system and other areas of securities trading because some members of the commission argue that new rules will have a negative impact on the industry.

Despite the limitations that some will note are present in any study instituted by any unit of the Executive Branch of our government, particularly one year prior to a re-election campaign where issues of government "overreach" are sure to be at issue, very little serious criticism has been levied against the study. Indeed, the number of qualifiers attached to some of the report's findings, in addition to the macro-economic nature of the report, leave open for discussion its generalizability to industries which may have been "targeted" for more oversight through regulatory rulemaking. Freedom Works and its supporters have been quick to point to what they believe is the crippling "cost" of regulations on both the "financial services" industry and on the producers of coal, oil and gas. Not surprisingly, they and their industry-funded "institutes" and "foundations" insist on the need for more "study" on the impact of rulemaking on these industries. While social science investigations may provide even more objective "data" regarding the impact of "regulations," it may be too much to expect that any finding which supports regulatory oversight of these industries will not be met with further claims that the cost of governmental monitoring far outweighs the benefits of any "big brother" intervention into Freedom Works version of "free markets." But with the passage of health care and financial services legislation—Obama Care and Dodd-Frank—for the moment it appears that they have accepted the fact that some form of regulatory rulemaking will be instituted which will impact their most favored industries.

The tactic now is to continue to decry the "excessive" nature of the laws and under the guise of so-called "regulatory reform" demand the need for "cost benefit analysis, risk assessment, risk protection, and market-based incentives." But what is meant by "cost benefit analysis" to Freedom Works may mean something significantly different to those who support regulatory oversight. Similar to Alice's interaction with the Hatter at the "Tea party" we once again find ourselves struggling to see if we can establish some mutual understanding of our individual experiences. Presuming "good faith" on behalf of all participants at the party, it may be that we, like Alice, require a closer examination of the terms that are at the heart of our "misunderstanding."

For example, to come to any objective evaluation of the positive or negative impact of regulatory oversight of any private sector activity we need to define what is meant as a "benefit." Then we must delineate the "cost." Finally, we are obligated to determine whether the actions of government or of individuals (corporations) reflect the concerns of the Founders. Because Freedom Works and their supporters regularly castigate the rulemaking activities of the Environmental Protection Agency as major contributors to "overregulation" which "only drag the economy down," a closer examination of the EPA's ruling making is in order. Rules promulgated by both the EPA and the National Highway Transportation and Safety Administration in 2010 provide an excellent backdrop in our journey to determine whether a "beautifully labeled bottle" marketed as "deregulation" produces the promised "garden" filled with wonderful benefits to the American people as Freedom Works and its supporters contend.

These administrative agencies issued a "joint rulemaking" in November of 2010 to regulate pollution from large pickups and vans, vocational vehicles, combination tractors, and heavy duty engines. It was reported that these rules were estimated to cost $7.7 billion, but were projected to generate close to seven times as many benefits—$49 billion. Richard L. Revesz, Dean of New York University Law School, and Michael A. Livermore, Executive Director of the Policy and Integrity Project, wrote in the *Huffington Post* on February 23, 2011, the following analysis of the "benefits" of the proposed rules:

> The benefits of the heavy duty truck rule include reducing emissions by almost 250 million metric tons and saving over 500 million barrels of oil over the life of the vehicles sold between 2014–2018. The agencies report that an operator of a semi-truck, after paying for technology updates, could have a net savings of up to $74,000 over the life of the vehicle.[140]

The authors suggested also that when calculating the costs of pollution "…it is often the case that the price of regulations is far less than the social costs of unchecked emissions." They ultimately concluded that "…strong protections do cost businesses and taxpayers money, but when compared to the price of weak regulations, it turns out that they can be more than worthwhile."[141] Presuming that the findings regarding the impact of these proposed rules are accurate, the "benefits" produced regarding fuel emissions from the vehicles and engines described appear to be significant. It would also appear that over a period of four years the owner/operators of reconfigured vehicles will also "benefit" from the proposed rules. But while the authors spend very little time discussing the "cost" associated with the implementation of these rules, they do note that they do "cost businesses and taxpayers money."[142] This observation when coupled with their conclusion that the rules are "worthwhile" as compared to what they describe as the "price of weak regulations" highlights the crux of our dilemma—that much of any analysis of "cost/benefit" calculations often depend upon claims originating from dramatically different world views.

The use of the term "worthwhile" by Dean Revesz and Executive Director Livermore, when juxtaposed against Mr. Hammerton's conclusion in Freedom Works commentary that "…In a global market place, the United States cannot afford to hamper its economic system with excessive and unnecessary regulations," only reinforces the sense of our bewilderment similar to that felt by Alice as she attempted to discuss her predicament with the Hatter. As we know Alice left the party declaring that she would "never go there again."[143] Let us at least try to parse the real from the imagined. Or, stated in a different way, let us try to delve further into the presumption of "worthwhile" and the claim of "excessive and unnecessary" governmental regulation in the context of what we have found to be the sometimes competing "first principles" of our Constitution.

"Cost/benefit" calculations obviously have limitations. They are an essential first step in an objective analysis of public policy considerations. But, as evidenced by the on-going debate regarding the impact of environmental regulations, they may not account for the too often unverifiable "given(s)" undergirding the "study" or "report" presented to the American public as fact. Indeed, the use of "cost/benefit" analyses which do not place their "findings" within the balancing process demanded by the Constitution creates a fertile environment for the "box makers" who create uncompromising public policy positions. In a country that has such a diversity of life experiences originating from our educational, social, and political interactions, it behooves those who solicit the support of the American people to articulate why their position(s) reflect(s), in the case of environmental regulatory action, a promotion of the public welfare. It is not enough to presume that a consensus necessary to build political support for regulatory oversight of our environment can be created by citing empirical data noting perceived "benefits" without discussing the potential "costs." It is equally important to note that conclusions for the restrictions of environmental regulations cannot be taken seriously by the public without a clear articulation of how they "hamper" our private sector in competing in a world marketplace. More extended analyses by good-faith advocates for public policy environmental decision-making certainly must present their rationales by objectively exploring the ramifications of both the "cost" and the "benefit" of their positions.

For example, Dean Revesz and Mr. Livermore's analysis of the proposed EPA/ NHTSA rules would have been even more compelling if they had addressed the impact that the rules will have on small farmers and small businesses which depend on the vehicles effected. While the "costs" of the "technology updates" on the semi-trucks and other vehicles described in the proposed rules more than likely could be absorbed by large agribusinesses and private sector transportation companies, a potential unintended consequence of the rules may have been the "cost" to struggling small farmers and "independent" transportation businesses dependent upon farm equipment and big engine vehicles for their survival. And instead of presuming that citizens interested in this important public policy issue understand the significance of the "cost/benefit" data noting the reduction of 250 metric tons of vehicle emissions with the implementation of the proposed rules, more emphasis could have been placed on available data which demonstrates the health-related "benefits" associated with the proposed rules such as a reduction of childhood asthma as but one of many diseases caused by air pollution. In other words, discuss the connection between the "data," the proposed rules, and the promotion of the public welfare.

Why? Isn't the data self-evident? Isn't the reduction of fuel emissions obviously "worthwhile"? One could think that it is the case. But, too often our daily experiences shape completely different understandings of what is real and what is imagined. Americans living in congested and highly populated metropolitan centers may have a completely different response to the question than citizens residing in rural or low population density regions of the country. And, as was noted, the projected savings of $74,000 with the advent of new big engine technology may be a long term "benefit" for businesses capable of absorbing the initial cost of purchasing these semi-trucks and farm vehicles. But the short-term impact may have serious financial consequences to small farmers and small businesses. Recognition by supporters of "strong" environmental regulations regarding the need to provide a balanced presentation of the potentially unintended consequences of such rulemaking will only enhance a national dialogue of what constitutes the public good.

For those who would conclude that the country must accept as fact that environmental regulations will handicap American industries in competition with other global businesses which have weak or no environmental regulations impacting their functioning, much more data is needed to defend such claims than the hyperbole presented by Freedom Works and their supporters. Just as those who would promote "strong" environmental regulations are obligated to demonstrate how they will promote the public welfare and have a minimal impact on the country's economic sustainability, so too do those who suggest that such regulations will "hamper" our ability to compete in the "global economy."

Proponents of this argument must begin to answer the question of whether there are any limits to our participation in global capital markets too often driven by the acquisition of short-term profit captured by standards of production which would be unacceptable to most Americans. Are all bets off when "competing" in the world markets? Does unbridled capitalism trump our collective efforts over the last 222 years to aspire to achieve and maintain the "first principles" articulated in the Preamble of the Constitution? Defend how providing so-called "cheaper" consumer products produced by little children in the "sweat shops" of the developing world creates jobs for our citizens or reflects the values of justice or human aspiration that we project to the world. Present the facts to the American people. Be transparent. Submit the "cost/benefit" data and any other argument to the "joint wisdom" of the country. What value is the overall health of the country through the reduction of pollution as against the presumed higher cost of production associated with environmental regulation? Defend the position that "cost" associated with environment regulations which are allegedly "excessive" by implication is forcing American corporations to flee to low wage labor pools across the planet. Bring the discussion devoid of ideological harangue before the American people.

Where the balance should be struck between the importance of wealth creation through a vibrant economy and the preservation of a quality of life which promotes the public good is the responsibility of an "enlightened citizenry" under our constitutional process. Such decision-making cannot be left in the board rooms of the American oligarchy or with the sometimes experientially limited but well-meaning advocates for environmental regulation. The submission of "cost/benefit" analyses by all stakeholders to this discussion then must be placed within the context of our collective covenant which mandates a balancing of these co-equally important objectives. What is "excessive" and "unnecessary" regulation to Freedom Works and their supporters is "essential" and "worthwhile" to supporters of regulatory oversight regarding environmental policy and other subjects such as regulation of "too big to fail" so-called "banks." The separate realities continue. The Keystone pipeline will create jobs. "Fracking" will produce energy independence and create jobs. The pipeline will endanger the environment with the potential for oil spills and its production will contribute further to global warming. Shattering the shale layers of earth threatens the water supplies so essential for millions of Americans. "Beautiful gardens" will be produced for economically struggling communities. Americans must be ready for an environmental holocaust.

And we felt badly for Alice as she struggled to understand the observations of the Hatter? Nevertheless, with her head spinning from her interactions with the surreal characters attending the Tea Party and throughout her "adventures" down the rabbit hole, Alice ultimately awoke from her dream. While she experienced fear at some points throughout her journey it did not overwhelm her ability to remain focused on what was real and what was truly "curious." As the country slowly emerges from the impact of divide and conquer politics driven by the "snares of the ambitious" one can only hope that we too are focused on what is real and what is imagined.

As has been noted throughout our investigation, the Founders understood that too often the "public good is disregarded in the conflicts of rival parties." James Madison found this to be particularly true when our governmental process must regulate "those who hold and those who are without property." The "conflicts of rival parties" based on the acquisition and retention of wealth may always plague those who yearn for a country, if not a world, committed to economic equality. Others believe that government is the antithesis to liberty and a dark force against the human spirit of individual accomplishment. Both world views are built upon images of "perfection" which were alien to the Framers of the Constitution.

The American experiment in governance was crafted by individuals who wished for the best in the interactions amongst citizens but planned for the worst. It is a system of governance which is grounded in the recognition of the essentiality of political compromise. It requires our "elected" to "faithfully discharge" their responsibilities to the American people, not just their direct constituents. It protects "freedom of the press" as a mechanism to inform the public and assist in the creation of an "enlightened citizenry" in the fundamentally important process of soliciting our "joint wisdom" as a society and exposing the "secret springs of political designs." This protection was not crafted to provide unregulated media monopolies with the power to transform these objectives into "entertainment" programming driven by profit not public interest.

Our investigation has called into question whether these and other important "first principles" have been overlooked, dismissed, or distorted in the Nation's public policy debates. For over the last six years the country has been mired in political gridlock which has failed to resolve some of the most important concerns of American life. In the next chapter we will return to the visions of the Founders in an effort to consolidate their "first principles" and to identify some of the most important contemporary issues facing the nation which must begin to be addressed within the context of these co-equal objectives.

8 Designing the "Least Imperfect" Government Eighteenth Century Insights for the Twenty-First Century

WITH THE ADVENT OF SOCIAL SCIENCE and the technological advances of the centuries after the design and ratification of the Constitution it is not unreasonable for many Americans to question whether their problems could possibly be resolved by venturing back to the insights of those who came before. And, certainly some critics will reject the legitimacy of the perspectives on human nature presented by the Founders as the by-product of white, male, property owners, and in some instances, owners of slaves. To do so would be a fundamental mistake.

It is accurate to suggest that social science has provided us with a plethora of findings regarding the interactions of citizens and the functioning of our institutions and in so doing have enabled us to understand better our current realities. The technological innovations of the late twentieth century also have begun to "flatten" the world we live in and have facilitated the communication process by which we interact—whether we have "advanced" as homo-sapiens with the advent of social science and technology is another question altogether. But the inherent injustices associated with accepted colonial values regarding slavery, the role of women in civil society, and the prerequisite of property ownership for political participation in twenty-first century America have been confronted and changed within our legal system. And, one does not have to be an apologist for the continuance of slavery initially legitimized by the Randolph Plan to recognize that without the "three-fifths" calculation for political representation that ratification of the Constitution would have failed. A republic was crafted and a "More Perfect Union" was designed. But tragically it took the deaths of hundreds of thousands of citizens and subsequent amendments to the collective agreement to begin to resolve its initial "deal made with the devil."

As American society has changed, so too has our collective covenant. With some important exceptions, we have found accommodation between strongly held divergent opinions by calling upon the processes implanted in the Constitution which produce modification within the rule of law. At the core of this process we call American government are certain presumptions about human nature and the interaction of individuals. As we move forward in the twenty-first century it behooves us to reflect on these "first principles." If they remain compelling we should use them as a guide in evaluating public policy suggestions from both our "elected" and from those who seek our support for change. If they are in need of revision to reflect the ever modulating contours of American life, then we should cautiously readjust the balance between competing values. In the following pages we will highlight the visions of the Founders which underpin their eventual agreement to form a "More Perfect Union" and offer some observations regarding future public policy decision-making.

A Primer for Maximizing Liberty and Promoting the Public Good

As we have discovered the Constitution of the United States is a reflection of both the fears and aspirations of the Founders. It was an agreement to maximize individual liberty and promote the public welfare within a scheme of government depended upon broadly articulated enumerated powers. It was a covenant which placed ultimate authority in the collective People but which delegated governing to the People's representatives. The document was and is a device by which to balance the sometimes competing interests of human aspiration within the confines of an ordered system of rules. The ratification of the Constitution was a commitment to redefine ourselves from citizens of individual states to become citizens of a new nation—America. Ultimately, the collective covenant was understood to be a process of governance dependent upon certain presumptions regarding the interactions of the individual with civil society. Many of our contemporary problems can be traced to either our failure to remember or a distortion of the core presumptions which helped shape the design and ratification of the Constitution.

Some of the overarching principles and presumptions held by the Founders and reflected in the Constitution include the following:

- The maximization of personal liberty limited only by the demonstration of harm to another or the community

- The promotion of the general welfare of the American people

- A commitment to limited government through the division of power in the departments of government

- A vigilance of concentrated power created and supported by minority "factions" or by actions of the majority not in conformance with the rights of the minority protected by the Bill of Rights

- A commitment to "control" factions through political compromise

- A dependence on the "joint wisdom" of the American people by nurturing an "enlightened citizenry"

- A rejection of titles of nobility

These objectives originated from the Founders' reflections on the struggles of humankind to form civil societies across the millennia. They were well aware of the dangers of concentrated power in all of its forms. Whether it was wealth creation to the diminishment of the community, political institutions controlled through the use of military force, or the establishment of unchecked ruling political elites, they believed that individual liberty within the context of the public good could only be achieved if our institutions of government reflected these concerns in their design and implementation. But with all the delegated division of powers and the checks upon the potential of tyrannical governmental decision-making, the Founders were convinced that if the republic could be kept, as Franklin worried, it was the American people who must constantly be vigilant of the "ambition and avarice of a ruling class."[144] And Hamilton forewarned of the "snares of the ambitious," from those in government or from those who attempt to manipulate the governmental process for their own self-interest. Their "realities" were formed with this fundamental presumption about humankind—we are fallible. Consequently, so too are the institutions we design. But they were equally confident that individual liberty and the promotion of the public good were not mutually exclusive aspirations. As Madison noted when discussing the need for a blended representation model in our legislative process "the advice of prudence must be to embrace the lesser of evil…" as we demand that our representatives find common ground by which to move the country away from the precipice of racial, religious, and regional tribalism.

The so-called "great recession" has exposed the always smoldering underbelly of our society. That is, the constant struggle between those who Madison described as "with or without property." In fact, after almost thirty years of corporations fleeing to low wage "developing economies" and the subsequent loss of millions of jobs and its corresponding impact on the American middle class, we may need to rephrase Madison's observation to "those with, slowly eroding, or without property." It has been reported that four out of five Americans at some time in their lives will require some form of public support. Presently, 46 million citizens live in poverty—approximately 15 percent of the country. Calculating for inflation the salaries of working class Americans in 2013 is less than the average salary earned in 1964. Study after study over the last few years have indicated that the significant gains made since the beginning of the "great recession" have gone to the top 1% of Americans. The disparity of salaries between workers and corporate "leaders" has ballooned beyond belief. Unemployment remains at or hovering near 7%–8%. If the numbers of citizens who have simply given up searching for employment, and therefore are not calculated in the aforementioned statistic, are coupled with the number of underemployed workers the percentage of Americans caught in the economic aftermath of the collapse of our financial institutions is much higher.[145]

The fragility of our social fabric should be obvious to any citizen brave enough to confront our current economic situation. It may be that for the first time in our Nation's history that Americans cannot be confident that their children will be "better off" than they are. There are a multitude of reasons for our current economic dilemma ranging from under regulated domestic and international "financial" markets, weak political leadership, and the constant marketing by the self-interested oligarchy through "divide and conquer" strategies of one-dimensional solutions resulting in more and more concentrated economic power to a select few. One does not need to subscribe to some apocalyptic futuristic scenario to foresee a country of "have and have-nots" with a dramatically reduced middle class becoming the America of the twenty-first century if the disparities in wealth creation are not addressed. A first step in this process of reexamination is to understand and then apply the overriding principles and presumptions of the Founders to the public policy recommendations of some of our "political elite" and their benefactors.

The first principle of maximizing individual liberty regulated by the "harm" qualifier is reflected in one form or another in all the other Founding presumptions noted above. The aspiration of providing a civil society which encourages individual accomplishment includes, but is not limited to wealth creation, was at the core of Locke's treatises and the colonial pamphlets written by John Trenchard and Thomas Gordon.[146] Their insights regarding the limits of liberty were contingent upon a demonstration that the actions of the individual did not "injure" another or the community. As was noted in Chapter One, Locke observed that while every individual needed to "preserve" himself he was obligated "as much as he can, to preserve the rest of mankind, and may not... take away, or impair the life, or what tends to the presentation of the life, the liberty, health, limb, or goods of another." He went on to note when discussing the importance of each individual possessing the right to enjoy the "fruits of his labour" that it was "useless, as well as dishonest, to carve himself too much, or take more than he needed."[147] The revolutionary tracts on liberty written by Trenchard and Gordon under the title of *Cato's Letters* also mirrored Locke's understanding of the legitimate limits of the actions of the individual. While lauding the importance of liberty and questioning the role of government interceding into the sanctity of personal decision-making, they wrote "And it is foolish to say, that Government is concerned to meddle with the private Thoughts and Actions of Men, while they injure neither the Society, nor any of it members..."[148] If some of Locke's language sounds vaguely familiar to Americans they would be correct. Jefferson borrowed without citation some of the language from his Virginian colleague George Mason who drafted the state constitution and borrowed the language from Locke. As can be seen, some of Locke's language found its way into the Declaration of Independence.[149]

Over the last six years Americans have been asked by some within our "political elite" and their political marketers funded by the American oligarchy, to support their "answers" to public policy questions regarding taxation, regulations, and entitlements based upon their commitment to a questionable interpretation of the language in the Declaration of Independence and without any discussion of the Founders aspirations as articulated in the Preamble of the Constitution. Absent any recognition of Locke's, the English Libertarians', and subsequently, the Founders' understanding of liberty, the electorate is asked to accept an almost absolutist version of liberty which celebrates the so-called "makers" and denigrates the "takers" in a winner takes all world of "free enterprise" and unregulated "entrepreneurialism." That this conception of liberty serves to legitimize the policy objectives of those who promote it is without question. That it is an accurate understanding of the objectives enshrined within the Constitution is historically unsupportable. In fact, it contradicts each of the other overarching principles noted above and demonstrates the continuing importance of evaluating contemporary legislative proposals with the Founders' fears and observations in mind. Another important concern of the Founders as noted above was the fear of the impact of a ruling class created by the granting of Titles of Nobility.

It may seem for many Americans that any discussion of the Founders' rejection of titles of nobility is ludicrous. It is a subject which has long since been addressed. No citizen is tapped for knighthood; we have rejected any tinge of primogeniture in our inheritance laws; our educational system provides for equal access to all children through public education; and, the "best and brightest" rise in a system of meritocracy across our economic system regardless of social class. While these observations as to our collective aspirations are generally accurate, closer examination calls into question our success as a country in actually achieving these goals.

The Founders disdain for titles of nobility did not originate from their desire to establish some equalitarian state whereby each citizen would be restricted to equal divisions of property. It will be remembered that Madison described such a scheme as "improper or wicked."[150] But they did understand the destructive impact that a concentration of wealth in a select few would have on the promotion of the public good. If each citizen was to have the opportunity to break free from the caste society of the English aristocracy, they knew that limits needed to be established which would reduce the potential of a new form of noblesse oblige. Rejection of the granting of titles of nobility was then more than a symbolic act of rejection of the English monarchial system, it was a commitment that the aspirations of Americans would not be held hostage by, as Franklin feared, the "avarice of a ruling class." Rejection of titles of nobility by the Founders was a reflection of their belief that concentrated wealth creates concentrated power which in turn creates social castes making economic mobility difficult if not impossible. Their understanding of the "pursuit of happiness" did not guarantee economic equality amongst citizens. But it did signal a revolutionary aspiration of establishing a process which would maximize economic opportunity for all citizens by limiting the political power of concentrated wealth through the "control" of their "factions" by requiring political compromise in lawmaking and through an electoral process which was open to all of the citizenry regardless of social class or economic status. One of the most important questions which must be resolved through the processes of our governmental system then remains the same as that which confronted the Founders: How do we "control" the influence of a ruling class, reduce income inequality by encouraging a vibrant middle class, and yet encourage wealth creation as one of many rewards which can be gleaned from maximizing liberty?

An important requirement in addressing these questions is to acknowledge our current realities. While we have rejected the granting of titles of nobility, we have our own version of an aristocracy—absent knighthood. After the "great recession," the cloak which shielded the lives and times of our nobility from the view of the vast majority of citizens has now been lifted. Old wealth has now been joined by an "in your face" corporate "bonus" salary system which continues to enrich the short term decision-making of corporate officers and has left American workers with few, if any, salary increases.[151] The wealth creation of a relatively small number of our corporate "leaders," along with hedge fund and private equity managers, has created a contemporary band of oligarchical elites who have now joined the beneficiaries of inherited old wealth in establishing an American version of the once popular public television program "Upstairs and Downstairs."

Another important consideration as we struggle to determine how best to address the potential deleterious impact of concentrated wealth in the context of our commitment to balance individual liberty with the promotion of the public good is the fact that income inequality in America is directly tied to inheritance. It has been suggested that up to eighty percent of household wealth originates from inheritance.[152] As the vast majority of the economic gains since the "great recession" continue to be achieved by only an extraordinarily small percentage of Americans it is then not unreasonable to predict that the wealth creation for our citizens will reflect an ever expanding unequal distribution. Therefore, while our inheritance laws have rejected the monarchial system of primogeniture, the method of controlling concentrated wealth by requiring the transference of land to the oldest male survivor of the aristocracy and thereby solidifying concentrated political power to a select few families, the retention of sometimes enormous concentrations of wealth in America still remains in a relatively small proportion of our citizenry passed through via inheritance. It would appear then that the vast majority of Americans who are not fortunate enough to be the beneficiaries of the estates of the 1%–0.5%, will have estates which were produced through some other wealth creation process totaling up to 20% of their household wealth added to whatever inheritance they have been afforded by their parents. Stated in another way, most Americans can expect that their accumulation of wealth compared with the beneficiaries of the American aristocracy through inheritance will be dramatically smaller regardless of life choices and career successes. With what appears to be a growing income inequality gap between those at the top of those with the most household wealth and the vast majority of citizens the myth of an American meritocracy—the engine that drives the American Dream—has now been called into question.

In fact, recent studies of social mobility across the planet have challenged our often touted superior status as compared with other countries. Whether the methodologies associated with these studies can be questioned as potentially distorting their findings by comparing relatively homogeneous populations with more open and diverse societies or not, they do call into question the generations' old mantra of American Exceptionalism based on our so-called meritocracy. While this myth is perpetuated throughout many of our social institutions, it is most often spun in our educational system.

Our collective commitment to establish universal public education for all children was hailed as an essential "equalizer" in leveling the social economic playing field. It was to be the instrument which would reward personal accomplishment based on merit and provide economic and ultimately social mobility. The "best and brightest" would evolve from this merit-based educational process, regardless of racial, religious, or social class. Equal educational opportunity would then provide our children a path to achieve the American Dream. While there was no pretense that all who entered the process would achieve at the same levels, it was presumed that economic security for a vast number of Americans would be created through entry into the middle class. Just as sobering as the fact that inheritance more than any other variable creates income inequality, so too is the realization that our well-intended efforts through universal education is struggling to provide equal educational opportunity for our children. Recognition that our educational system is not a meritocracy is the first step in addressing the multitude of issues facing pre-school, elementary, secondary, and higher education.

The constant perpetuation of the idea that our "best and brightest" are to be produced from the ranks of graduates of exclusive preschools who are then placed in "college preparatory" public or private secondary schools, and finally receive "acceptance" letters from the nation's so-called "elite" colleges or universities continues to reinforce the mythology of a meritocracy. Without diminishing the sacrifice of the families and students who are the winners in this race for the brass ring, the results of this educational marathon were for the most part predetermined. Study after study has provided overwhelming data which has found the continuing correlation between social economic status and educational achievement or "success" on college entrance examinations.[153] It is truly remarkable that in a society where personal accomplishment through self-sacrifice and hard work are so valued that the term "best and brightest" is not only dispensed upon those students who have had the financial support to propel them through their educational journeys which may include the subjectively ranked "elite" institutions of higher learning but is not also applied to the multitude of other students who overcame the lack of financial support and have graduated from excellent colleges or universities which are not on some highly subjective ranking system created to sell more magazines. The game continues to an even more dangerous level for our democracy when the myth is perpetuated further by the political elite, regardless of political party, who recommend appointees to powerful positions in our government allegedly based upon the nominee's "best and brightest" credentials originating from only a few "elite" institutions. It is true that political party affiliation, race, gender, professional associations and numerous other characteristics may influence this process. But the inescapable fact that only a select few institutions of higher learning seem to be identified as producing the best fit for appointment to some of the most influential positions in American government is another example of the impact of the myth of meritocracy. A snapshot of relatively recent appointments to the Supreme Court of the United States will illustrate the point.

The legal educational background of the current members of the Supreme Court is as follows: John Roberts, Harvard; Antonin Scalia, Yale; Anthony Kennedy, Harvard; Clarence Thomas, Yale; Ruth Bader Ginsburg, Columbia/

Harvard; Stephen Breyer, Harvard; Samuel Alito, Yale; Sonia Sotomayor, Yale; Elena Kagan, Harvard. While a more extensive recording of relatively recent past members of the Court will produce a slight variation on the theme with the University of Chicago and Stanford joining the illustrious pantheon of mostly Ivy League law schools, the selection process for the highest court in the land has harvested the "best and brightest" from only a very limited number of our country's law schools. The personal and professional backgrounds of our Justices are certainly to be admired. But it is truly puzzling that so few of the literally thousands of graduates from the hundreds of law schools across the nation have been worthy of selection to the most important judicial body in the country.

Of course, the same point can be made when describing the educational backgrounds of the last four Presidents of the United States—Bush, Yale; Clinton, Yale; Bush, Yale; Obama, Harvard. If the reality of our appointment process is coupled with the nominees offered by our political parties and the eventual victors in the last seven presidential elections, not to mention the socio-economic backgrounds of our "elected" in the Congress of the United States, it would appear that the path(s) to public service at its most important levels of decision-making is dangerously becoming a club for a select few. As was noted in Chapter Three, the potential impact of this process is the creation of a political class which, even with the most honorable intentions, may reflect a world view which is extraordinarily different than that of the vast majority of citizens. Even with all the posturing of our "elected" who purport to understand the needs of the American people, as they so fondly love to submit when on camera, millions of citizens are unemployed or underemployed, the income inequality gap continues to widen for most citizens, and the potential for more manipulation of our so-called financial industry without strong and coordinated regulation insulating the country from another "recession" becomes a real possibility.

Apparently the 113th Congress' answer to these and other public policy issues facing the country was to—take a five-week recess! For some of our "elected" the immediacy of the issues facing the nation are not compelling. Indeed, their interpretation of the Founders' vision of "limited government" means no government. And for many other members of Congress the immediate issues having a potential negative impact on their lives were resolved. For example, exemptions for the airline industry were created to avoid the inconveniences to their travel plans produced by the across the board cuts of federal funding of essential airline employees and the exemption of some of the requirements of the new health care legislation on their staffs found "bi-partisan" support in a relatively short period of time. And, after all, the stock market is continuing to remain strong, housing prices—a key indicator of household wealth for many Americans—in select markets are allegedly rising. In the world of so-called meritocracy all is well. Additionally, for those who have reaped the rewards of being born into the correct gene pool, managed to translate their undergraduate degrees from an "elite" institution into a six-figure or higher job on Wall Street, or have been the beneficiaries of having equity in a house in a market which has been stable or seen only slight decreases in home value over the last five years, the American Dream is alive. For the elderly who must make a monthly decision to cut their prescription pills in half or not be able to pay the heat bill, for the children who comprise a large and often forgotten segment of the "takers" in the debate over so-called "entitlements," preschool opportunities and school lunch programs are slashed in ideological budget battles, and the working poor and shrinking "middle class" wait while members of the Congressional club muse about the importance of raising the minimum wage in an effort to establish a "working wage." For these citizens the American Dream has become a nightmare.

Recognition of the realities associated with the present status of the American Dream, while reinforcing many of the Founders' fears, also can serve as a "wake up call" for all our citizenry regardless of political party affiliation and social class. It can be a catalyst for an honest examination of the public policy issues facing the nation and a long overdue national discussion regarding the ultimate objectives of our constitutional democracy. Noting the dramatic gaps regarding income inequality and its potential to shred the social fabric of the country is not a call for an abandonment of "free enterprise" or an attack on individual liberty. It is, however, an important indicator that readjustments in public policy regarding taxation and regulation, in addition to other issues, need to be debated in the public forum with an ever-present eye toward the "snares of the ambitious." Such a national discussion, however, will require a balanced analysis of the co-equal aspirations noted by the Founders, devoid of the current self-interested political demagoguery disguised as constitutional mandates. Our collective amnesia regarding the importance of both liberty and preservation of the public good has been fostered by those who have hijacked the Constitution and the visions of the Founders. Indeed, examples of the distortions of their overarching principles and presumptions crafted into the Constitution and the Bill of Rights and noted above can be found on an almost daily basis in our local, regional, and national print and broadcast media. In the final chapter we will examine their claims and "solutions."

9 Marketing a Twenty-First Century Anti-Federalist Vision for America
An Examination of the Claims and Solutions

As was discussed in Chapter Four, the seemingly mindless submission by publishers and network programmers of syndicated columnists or "political contributors" opinions regarding the directives of the Constitution or the Founders Visions which shaped its design and ratification, without any substantiation of their conclusion(s) based on the document and its philosophical or historical origins, has created an aura of legitimacy which may serve the political agenda of the columnist/contributor/politician or publisher but too often goes unchallenged. The result of this practice has produced an environment whereby political ideology is marketed and defended by highly questionable interpretations of the Constitution and the Founding vision. To the millions of Americans who for a multitude of reasons are unfamiliar with the origins and evolution of our collective covenant and are only casual consumers of the daily round of public policy debates circling their everyday lives, it becomes extremely difficult to identify the political agendas hidden within the aura of constitutional interpretation presented by syndicated columnists, paid political commentators or some of our political elite. This practice of challenging the actions of political opponents by couching arguments with language selectively plucked from one section of the Constitution in an effort to provide cover for one political opinion or another without rebuttal can produce an undeserved legitimacy of both the interpretation and its application to whatever public policy issue the columnist or "political contributor" finds most disdainful.

This technique of selectively citing constitutional language to legitimize claims of "unconstitutional" acts by the Executive Branch or "unelected" government bureaucrats have originated, for the most part, from whom the political marketers would describe as the "conservative" or "right-wing" in American politics. Depending upon the targeted market, syndicated columnists, talk show hosts, or politicians have also sold their "constitutional" interpretations as "libertarians." Few, if any, "liberals/progressives" from the so-called political "left" have offered any sustained rebuttal to these claims of "unconstitutional" governmental usurpation of the Founding vision. In fact, it would appear that the Constitution and the Founders vision, has become the exclusive domain of those fortunate enough to be invited as speakers at "foundations" and "institutes" sponsored by our American oligarchy. With images of the American flag, the words of the Declaration of Independence and the Constitution as a backdrop behind the podium of the speaker, the message is always the same— our Constitution has been violated and our liberties are at risk from those who have usurped power through the federal government. Almost always the pitch being promoted is devoid of any recognition of any other values reflected in the Constitution than the "institutes" or "foundations" absolutist view of "liberty." In an attempt to direct our analysis away from responding to the politically motivated rhetoric used to glean the support of a political party "base," we will return to the observations of the Founders regarding the necessity of "controlling" factions and identify both the legitimate and illegitimate claims being marketed as constitutional imperatives to the American people.

It will be remembered that James Madison cautioned that the American people need to always be vigilant of abuse of power from whatever source— minority factions or majoritarian legislative bodies. Clarion calls regarding abuse of power from either the political "right" or political "left," or any other source, must always be taken seriously if our constitutional system is to survive. Therefore, the contemporary claims of unconstitutional decision-making by so-called "conservative" or "libertarian" columnists or politicians should not be dismissed in their totality as ploys to delegitimize their opponents. In fact, they should be credited with bringing the discussion of what constitutes constitutional governmental action within the purview of public discourse. As we have discovered from our analyses of the initial concerns of the Tea Party, the Occupy Wall Street protests, and some of the broad concerns marketed by Freedom Works and their supporters, there are important public policy questions which must be addressed through our governmental process and an informed debate regarding our collective commitment to find compromise between the co-equal aspirations of maximizing individual liberty within the context of promotion of the public good. That discussion presupposes that there exists an understanding and agreement that these Founding values are not mutually exclusive. And, that support for one does not portend the eventual destruction of the other. Instead mutual agreement that both aspirational objectives are of co-equal importance allows Americans to have an honest discussion about how to balance the maximization of individual liberty through a system of rules which also is committed to the promotion of the public good. Of course, recognition of the co-equal importance of these Founding values may not serve well those who reject Locke's "harm qualifier" and the Founders' admonition to seek political compromise. As was noted in Chapter Five, one-dimensional black and white absolutist concepts are much easier to market than those which require critical thinking and the rejection of false choices. An examination of some of the claims of "unconstitutional" actions of the federal government will illustrate the consequence of raising important questions regarding the need for governmental oversight and then providing highly questionable rationales to support their recommended "solutions."

Revising the Founding Visions—Fact or Fiction?

A syndicated radio talk show host has introduced a book into the contemporary "analyses" of so-called unconstitutional federal government actions which encapsulates most of the arguments found scattered across the airwaves or in our print media.[154] Another syndicated columnist, in a recent column entitled "A Constitutional Cure for What Ails Us," described the book as a "serious work that can serve as an action plan" for controlling the federal government's "lust for power."[155] The book's author addresses what he believes to be breaches of the Framer's intent regarding the limits of the federal government and offers what he describes as "liberty amendments" to the Constitution. While a point-by-point examination of each claim made by the author is beyond the scope of this investigation and should be the subject of a separate analysis, a description of his general claims and the alleged intentions of the Founders which he believes supports his conclusions is essential. Such a general overview is required not only because it will provide a consolidation of the claims asserted by other self-described "constitutionalist" but also because it will begin to demonstrate the strengths and weakness of the assertions and remedies offered.

In an attempt to lower the rhetoric and increase the potential objective review of the provocative claims most often submitted by our contemporary critics of federal government decision-making, the following analysis shall intentionally reject the temptation to respond to the divisive commentary so often in their critiques. That being said, the history of humankind is filled with examples of ideological true believers who promoted change by demeaning both the intentions and actions with whom they disagreed. In so doing, what might be legitimate claims of governmental or institutional dysfunction are dismissed as the ranting of political ideologues. At a time in our history when the country is vulnerable to any suggestions presented to resolve the gridlock in Congress and which is susceptible to "solutions" which purport to be grounded in the visions of the Founders, failure to address these claims would be irresponsible.

In a book entitled, *The Liberty Amendments: Restoring the American Republic*,[156] Mark L. Levin has proposed the adoption of a series of amendments to the Constitution. His vision of a conspiratorial federal government involved in "sinister" acts of abuse of power designed to "disfigure and mangle the constitutional order and undo the social compact" with the assistance of "philosophers, experts, and academics" and a "delusional governing elite" sets the stage for his alleged historical/constitutional defense of the proposed amendments. He unabashedly believes that the institution of his "liberty amendments" is a matter of "necessity and urgency" for the restoration of what he describes as the preservation of "civil society from the growing authoritarianism of a federal Leviathan."[157] He is convinced that a cabal of the aforementioned conspirators has established "a centralized and consolidated government with a ubiquitous network of laws and rules actively suppressing individual initiative, self-interest, and success in the name of the greater good and on behalf of the larger community."[158] He notes that the successful enactment of his proposed amendments will be politically difficult because of "powerful and strident" "governing masterminds" who will seek the assistance of "a corroboratory media to vanquish such a movement and subdue the public."[159] But regardless, he believes that there are "untold numbers of citizens who comprehend the perilousness of the times and circumstances" and that "a restoration of constitutional republicanism" is imperative.[160] Mr. Levin writes that:

> The Framers anticipated this day might arrive, for they knew that republics deteriorate at first from within. They provided a lawful and civil way to repair what has transpired. We, the people, through our state legislatures—and the state legislatures, acting collectively-have enormous power to constrain the federal government, reestablish self-government, and secure individual sovereignty.[161]

The general claims and subsequent recommended "liberty amendments" are as follows:

Claims:

- Individual liberty and the protection of private property have been suppressed by a "centralized" government.

- The electoral process for Congress has produced a political class which is nonresponsive to the People and operates without their knowledge or consent.

- The Congress has unconstitutionally delegated its law-making function to an unelected administrative bureaucracy which creates draconian rules.

- The Supreme Court is just another political institution staffed by individuals who act only on their political loyalties.

- The regulation of "commerce" within each State by the federal government, legitimized by Supreme Court decision-making, has unconstitutionally restricted "free enterprise."

- The solution to the Leviathan of the federal government is to follow the alleged "original" mandate of the Tenth Amendment to return ultimate power to State government.

Amendments

- Term Limits for Members of Congress

- Repeal the Seventeenth Amendment—all Senators shall be chosen by their state legislature

- Term Limits for Supreme Court Justices

- Create a 3/5ths Congressional Override of a majority opinion of the Supreme Court

- Promote Free Enterprise by restricting Congressional power to regulate only commerce between the states and thereby grant to the States the power to regulate all commerce within the state regardless of whether it affects interstate commerce

- Protect Private Property by requiring that governmental Eminent Domain proceedings which are instituted through seizure or through regulation compensate fully the property owner if the taking results in a market value reduction of the property, interferes with the use of the property, or results in a financial loss to the property owner exceeding $10,000

- Establish Specific Budgetary Restrictions on Federal Spending by requiring "caps" tied to the GNP of the last fiscal year

- Limiting Congressional taxing to no more than 15 percent of a "person's" income—"Person" shall include natural and legal persons

- Congress shall not collect tax on a decedent's estate

- Grant the States Authority to Directly Amend the Constitution

- Grant the States Authority to Check Congress—Upon three-fifths of the state legislatures, the States may override a federal statute

- Enact an Amendment to Protect the Vote—Mandate state legislative "citizen-designated photographic identification" funded by the state.[162]

Many of his claims have been echoed in the publications of Freedom Works, Americans for Tax Reform, the American Legislative Council's and its auxiliary group's "model bills," or the numerous "reports" produced through "institutes" and "foundations." But unlike many of these groups, his justifications for each claim and subsequent "solutions/amendments" are produced allegedly by a return to the guidance of the Framers. As was noted above, a point by point examination of each of his "solutions" is beyond the scope of our investigation. What are directly relevant to our investigation are the historical, philosophical, and constitutional sources that he uses to defend his mandate to "restore" the republic.

As we examine his sources it is important that we place into context his alleged Founding visions with the overriding first principles which this investigation has identified originating from the writings of Madison, Jefferson, Hamilton, and Franklin during the ratification process. Additionally, we are obligated to stay focused on both the specific language of the Constitution, the political compromise which produced the language and the overarching fears and aspirations which compelled the ratification of the agreement with the People. As we do so it should be remembered, as was noted in Chapter One, that the Constitution provides for amendment and allows for revision of the document and was intended to be the ultimate check on abuse of power originating from the actions or inactions of any department of our governmental system. It also should be noted that the constitutional amendment process was designed to be rigorous, to reflect the will of the American people and ultimately to be the failsafe against abuse of power. On that point, Mr. Levin and his cohorts and this investigation concur. Whether or not the institution of this process is required based upon his "analysis" of the functioning of the federal government is quite another matter as are his recommendations.

Thankfully, he has been clear as to his opinion regarding both the evolution and the present status of our "least imperfect" governmental process and has provided us with "solutions" which reflect his preference for an America dramatically different than that which was proposed by the Founders. He has every right to present his claims to the American people. If, on close examination and public debate, a majority of Americans agree that his recommendations should be instituted, then the design of a new experiment in government should be established. But to be clear, Mr. Levin is not calling for a restoration of the American republic as he would have us believe. Indeed, his so-called "liberty amendments" signal an outright rejection of some of the most important Founding values discussed throughout our investigation and noted in the last chapter. A consolidation of his claims and subsequent recommendations for change through the constitutional amendment process produces one overriding mandate—establish state legislative assemblies as the ultimate source of governmental power in American life.

As noted in Chapter Two, this call for a return to state legislative power has been marketed by others who yearn for an America without taxes, reflective of their regional or cultural values, and controlled by a more homogeneous citizenry capable of monitoring their political representatives and as a result limiting the impact of those citizens not within the sovereignty of their state or in a political majority. The so-called "liberty amendments" mirror this vision. A "return" to the "American Republic" *à la* Mr. Levin and his supporters would prohibit taxation of any individual's estate, create a "flat tax" under the guise of a 15% income tax on individuals and corporations, and empower the states to "directly amend the Constitution" and override a federal statute. The implications of these and his other "amendments" which would place term limits on members of Congress and the Supreme Court, would certainly serve select "factions" well. The so-called "liberty amendments" do provide the American oligarchy with a guarantee of concentrated economic power enabling even more ready access to more easily control state legislative political processes. Income inequality will become even more pronounced in American life. And, with the institution of term limits for the federal courts, it allows for an increase in political partisanship in the functioning of the judiciary. But before one accepts these "amendments" as remedies to the functioning of our governmental processes based upon an alleged "restoration" of the Founding principles a series of questions must be asked and answered.

Did he overlook Locke and the English Libertarians acknowledgment of the limits of liberty? Has he accurately described Madison's concern regarding the necessity of protecting the public good? Or, did he forget to mention Madison's commitment to "controlling" factions through political compromise in a national government? Why did Madison believe that a national government would best protect against powerful factions that controlled state legislative assemblies? Who does Mr. Levin believe are the Framers? Do the arguments and observations of the Anti-Federalists and strident opponents to the Constitution serve as the authors of the founding visions?

The short answer to all of the questions is that he both failed to acknowledge Madison's and the other Framer's concerns on how best to control "factions" and protect the "public good," conveniently avoided Locke's condition regarding the limits of reaping the "fruits of owns labor" by evaluating whether the acquisition of such harmed any other individual or the society as a whole, and cited opponents to the Constitution to defend his movement to "restore" the republic. Instead Mr. Levin and his supporters herald Madison's oft-quoted observation concerning the role of government in the protection of property without placing his commentary within the context of his other arguments for a national government whose fundamental responsibility would be the "regulation" of "those who hold and those who are without property." Apparently he believes that the Founder's concern about the manipulative impact of "factions" within state legislatures was unfounded or that the present composition of state legislatures which appear to represent his and his supporters' world view would be more likely to protect the interests of the majority of the American people. Once again he has a right to make that argument—but it certainly was not James Madison's and those that ratified the Constitution.

It will be remembered that one of Madison's overarching concerns was "to break and control the violence of faction." In the *Federalists Papers* no. 10 he wrote that if liberty for each citizen was to be protected and preserved then the "conflicts of rival parties" which threatened the "public good" must be addressed in a new centralized national government. "A well-constructed Union" would require these groups to bring their interests into a national forum where they must compete for power with others from across the country. Such a scheme would result in public policy making which would find compromise "according to the rules of justice and the rights of the minor party" and would minimize the impact of a "superior force of an interested and overbearing majority." He was convinced that such a process would act as a mechanism to protect liberty and the public good from factions created by a either a "majority or a minority of the whole, who are united and actuated by some common impulse of passion, or of interest, adverse to the rights of other citizens or to the permanent and aggregate interests of the community." His position on this subject and the absolute necessity of shifting law-making authority to a national assembly which would reduce the power of "local prejudices and schemes of injustice" bears repeating before one accepts Mr. Levin's "liberty amendments." As we noted in Chapter One, Madison argued in *The Federalist Paper* no. 10:

> ...The influence of factious leaders may kindle a flame within their particular States, but will be unable to spread a general conflagration through the other States. A religious sect may degenerate into a political faction in a part of the Confederacy, but the variety of sects dispersed over the entire face of it must secure the national councils against any danger from that source. A rage for paper money, for an abolition of debts, for an equal division of property, or for any other improper or wicked project will be less apt to pervade the whole body of the Union than a particular member of it, in the same proportion as such a malady is more likely to taint a particular county or district than an entire State.[163]

Apparently those similar to Mr. Levin believe that Madison and his colleagues had it wrong. The country and its citizen's liberties would be best protected by state legislative assemblies. Returning the selection of Senators to the wisdom of state politicians and their campaign funding sources would protect American's economic and personal liberties from the "sinister" actions of "unelected" bureaucrats and a "nonresponsive" political class in the Congress of the United States. For some reason Madison's insight on the essentiality of creating a "blended" representation process which would stagger election cycles and length of terms of office between the House of Representatives and the Senate was ill-conceived. Madison's rationale of providing the American people with a political process which would require co-operation between two legislative bodies now would be better protected by empowering state politicians to select members of the Senate. If such a scheme, as proposed in the so-called "liberty amendments" is essential to control a political class which is "nonresponsive to the People," then why did Madison and those who ratified the Constitution believe that those who would serve then in a second branch of the national legislative assembly, with longer terms and different individual qualifications for office than their counterparts in the House would be less likely to, as Madison wrote in *Federalists* no. 62, "…yield to the impulse of sudden and violent passions and to be seduced by factious leaders into intemperate and pernicious resolutions?" Of course, the answer is that, the fear of the Founders, based upon their experience with the functioning of the Articles of Confederation, was that the power of a few factions increased significantly as the governing of the American People was concentrated in state legislative assemblies. Indeed, at the core of Mr. Levin's proposed amendments to the Constitution is his highly questionable reading of both the language of the document and its proposed objectives. This is particularly evident when he argues that the "Framers rightly insisted on preserving the prominent governing role of the state legislatures as a crucial mechanism to containing the power of the proposed new federal government."[164]

Mr. Levin is correct to suggest that Madison and the Federalists recognized the fundamental importance of the role which state governments would play in the functioning of the proposed Constitution. It is also true to submit that one of Madison's major objectives was to confront the numerous attacks against the ratification of the Constitution by the Anti-Federalists, similar to George Mason who Mr. Levin seems to confidently rely on to justify his positions on numerous points to "restore" his version of the "American Republic." But to suggest, as he does, that the Framers intended to provide the states with "plenary governing authority" as opposed to what he describes as only "limited, specified powers" in the federal government,[165] is both a misuse of the term "plenary" and once again fails to place into context Madison's other observations regarding the subject in the very sections of the *Federalist* which Mr. Levin cites to support his conclusions.

For example, in *Federalist* no. 14, Madison did note, as Mr. Levin suggests, that the "general government is not to be charged with the whole power of making and administering the laws…" and that the jurisdiction of the proposed federal government would be "limited to certain enumerated objects, which concern all the members of the republic…"[166] And it is also correct to indicate that he recognized that other issues would by necessity be addressed presumably by state and local governments. But by this did Madison mean that state legislative assemblies would "(retain) for themselves plenary governing authority" as Levin suggests? Nowhere in *Federalist* no. 14, 45, or 46—the sources that Mr. Levin cites—does Madison infer that the proposed Constitution would place "plenary" (absolute) governing power in state legislative assemblies.

If one reads Madison's entire response to the Anti-Federalists who challenged the proposed Constitution, in *Federalist* no. 14, a significantly different conclusion than Mr. Levin's is reached. Madison wrote:

> …In the first place it is to be remembered that the general government is not to be charged with the whole power of making and administering laws; its jurisdiction is limited to certain enumerated objects, which concern all the members of the republic, but which are not to be attained by the separate provisions of any. The subordinate governments, which can extend their care to all those other subjects which can be separately provided for, will retain their due authority and activity. Were it proposed by the plan of the convention to abolish the governments of the particular States, its adversaries would have some ground for their objection; though it would not be difficult to show that if they were abolished the general government would be compelled, by the principle of self-preservation, to reinstate them in their proper jurisdiction.[167]

Madison's observation then is neither an abdication of "plenary" (absolute) governing authority to state legislative assemblies nor an argument for dissolving state lawmaking authority. Instead he believed that the state legislatures would fill a "subordinate" and yet necessary function in their "proper jurisdiction." The Federalists recognized the important role that state governments must play in securing the particular needs of its citizens. As noted by Madison, no attempt was being instituted to abolish the lawmaking authority of the states. To do so would be the height of folly. But to suggest as does Mr. Levin that "The debates during the Constitutional Convention and the state ratification conventions are 'unequivocal' that the Framers 'insisted' that the 'states retained for themselves plenary governing authority'" is an inaccurate reading of Madison and the Framers proposal. Certainly the Federalists understood the practical necessity of continuing the lawmaking functions of state legislatures for the well-being of their respective citizens. And the experiences of the Founders reflected the need for a multiplicity of laws and administrative processes which would be necessary at the state and local governmental level. But there was no doubt in the minds of the Framers that such lawmaking authority would be "subordinate" to the lawmaking functioning of the proposed national government. State sovereignty would, by definition, be "subordinate" to that of the nation. While Mr. Levin did not note Madison observations regarding this subject in his writings in *Federalist* no. 44, they are too important to the subject to overlook. Madison responded to Anti-Federalist critics of proposed language in Article VI, clause (2) of the Constitution which unqualifiedly addressed the lawmaking authority between the national and state governments. As was discussed in Chapter One of our investigation this section of the Constitution states:

> This Constitution and the laws of the United States which shall be made in pursuance thereof, and all treaties made, or which shall be made, under the authority of the United States, shall be the supreme law of the land, and the judges in every State shall be bound thereby, any thing in the constitution or laws of any State to the contrary notwithstanding.

Madison noted in no. 44 that without a commitment to this overriding mandate the Constitution would be "...evidently and radically defective." He then went on to observe that "...we need only suppose for a moment that the supremacy of the State constitutions had been left complete by a saving clause in their favor." The result of such would render "all the authorities in the proposed Constitution, so far as they exceed those enumerated in the Confederation... annulled and the new Congress would have been reduced to the same impotent condition with their predecessors."[168] He concluded that:

> In fine, the world would have seen, for the first time, a system of government founded on an inversion of the fundamental principles of all government; it would have seen the authority of the whole society everywhere subordinate to the authority of the parts; it would have seen a monster in which the head was under the direction of the members.[169]

It is one thing to suggest that the Founders recognized the essentiality of state lawmaking authority in the functioning of the proposed Constitution but it is quite another to conclude as does Mr. Levin that the "...Framers rightly insisted on preserving the prominent role of the state legislatures..."

Describing Madison's observations in *Federalist* no. 14, 45, and 46 as evidence of the Founders belief that the liberties of the American people would best be protected by providing state legislative assemblies with "plenary" (absolute) power simply does not reflect either the language of the Constitution or James Madison's observations noted above. Nevertheless, Mr. Levin is convinced that:

> ...without these assurances (presumably that the Founders granted absolute power to state legislatures)—and the additional pledge that the First Congress would offer amendments to the Constitution further ensuring that individual and state sovereignty would be safeguarded against the new federal government (what became the Bill of Rights, including the Ninth and Tenth Amendments)—the Constitution would not have been ratified.[170]

Therefore, without any discussion of the importance of finding political compromise through the "three-fifths" plan or the shaping of a blended representation process, he presents a revisionist or contemporary Anti-Federalist "interpretation" of Madison's observations, and confidently concludes with the often heard mantra that the "states established the American Republic, and through the Constitution, retained for themselves significant authority to ensure the republic's durability."[171] Whether "significant authority" and "plenary governing authority" are intended to be interpreted as to possess the same meaning we will leave for another analysis. But his commentary noted above does require a response.

Once again, Mr. Levin's reliance on the one-line sound bite that "the states established the American Republic," while an excellent marketing slogan for his version of our constitutional history, it is only partially accurate. It is absolutely true that the state representative bodies already in existence at the time of the Constitutional Convention and functioning under sometimes very disparate state constitutions during the Articles of Confederation period were the mechanisms by which the desires of the American people were determined regarding the adoption of the Constitution and the Bill of Rights. But to conclude as do our twenty-first century Anti-Federalists that the Founders believed that the proposed national government was the creature of state legislatures is historical revisionism at its best. As was noted in Chapter One, the argument to reject the proposed Constitution on the grounds that it was not an agreement between the states and instead was constructed upon the premise of "We the People" failed to receive support even in a state which provided for enumerated "rights" within their state constitution. It will be remembered that Patrick Henry, a Virginian and outspoken Anti-Federalist opponent to the proposed Constitution, railed against the plan for numerous reasons but two in particular were the

center of his arguments to reject the proposed Constitution at the Virginia Ratifying Convention in 1788. He argued that:

> The fate of... America may depend on this: Have they said, we the States?
> Have they made a proposal of a compact between the States? If they had,
> this would be a confederation: it is otherwise most clearly a consolidated
> government. The question turns, Sir, on that poor little thing—the expres-
> sion, We, the people, instead of the States of America. I need not take much
> pains to show, that the principles of this system, are extremely pernicious,
> impolitic, and dangerous...[172]

Henry lost the argument. Instead another Virginian, James Madison, and his
vision of the future of the country was supported by the citizens of Virginia's
representatives at the convention. He and his fellow Federalists ratified a new
experiment in government which rejected the supremacy of state legislative
power and instead found the locus of all legitimate governmental power to be
found in the citizens of the Union. Under the Constitution no longer would the
interests of Virginians or New Yorkers be placed over the interests of the nation.
But Henry's other argument that the proposed Constitution should be rejected
because it failed to enumerate fundamental protections of individual liberty
did receive eventual support. Madison drafted amendments to the document
becoming what we know today as the Bill of Rights.

To be clear, the Constitution did not render the state governments impotent. As we indicated above, Madison and his supporters fully understood the
important "subordinate" role that state governments would play in the newly
established federal system. Mr. Levin is correct to point out that one of the re-
sidual powers left with the state legislative assemblies was their responsibility
to select members of the newly proposed Senate. But once again in an effort to
justify his "solution" of returning selection of Senators to state legislative assemblies and thereby abolishing the Seventeenth Amendment of the Constitution
which mandates direct state elections of Senators via popular vote of the citizens of each state, he selectively quotes Madison's discussion in *Federalist* no. 39
regarding the "Nature and Powers of the New Government."

"Restoring" or Reinventing the American Republic
A Historical Slight of Hand

Because the Framers' understanding of the proposed federal system is
often at the core of contemporary debates regarding the role of the national
and state governments, it is important that we examine both Madison's
observations regarding the subject and the actual constitutional language

ratified by the American people through their state legislative assemblies. None of the foregoing analysis, of course, precludes Mr. Levin or his supporters in continuing their efforts to persuade the American public of "the malignancy of the Progressive mind-set and its destructive impact on the way we practice self-government..."[173] The question for our investigation instead is whether the changes which are being offered originate from the draftsmen of the Constitution. The amendment process is open to all who can carry the support of the American people. Whether the selective quoting of Madison coupled with a generous sampling of the observations of those who opposed the Constitution blended into a revisionist marketing model of the "American Republic" will be successful remains to be seen. The question before us is not whether the Seventeenth Amendment to the Constitution should be abolished, but rather whether our contemporary critics of a "sinister" federal government can legitimately claim that its creation was a rejection of the Founding principles.

As he does with so much of his "analysis" of the Founding visions, Mr. Levin's disdain for any and all things "progressive" and for what he believes are conspiratorial motivations by the "Statists" in conjunction with the "governing masterminds" to "attack relentlessly the individual's independence and free will" results in a highly one-dimensional understanding of Madison's rationales for his "blended" proposal of representation and republican government.[174] His commentary regarding the creation and ultimate passage of the Seventeenth Amendment is a case in point. What is so troubling with his "analysis" is not whether the change for direct election of Senators by popular vote should be challenged and once again amended, but rather his facile defense for such a change, based upon a misconstruction of Madison's arguments for his electoral proposal specifically and his understanding of republican government generally. He observes correctly that the Framers, including Madison, were concerned with creating two legislative bodies which would be selected through a similar electoral model—that is, direct representation through popular vote. But, without discussing Madison's vision of the entire Constitutional proposal, Levin seizes upon the electoral selection process which would provide the states with the authority to select Senators and fails to discuss the ultimate compromise— the Three/Fifths Plan of Randolph—which brought the smaller populated states into the representation process.

Whether acceptance of the selection process for senators through the mechanism of state legislative bodies underscores Madison's belief that such a process would be, as Mr. Levin suggests "balanced with dispassionate, considered judgment through a stable and diffused governing construct"[175] or was a necessary compromise, in addition to the Randolph Plan, to solidify support for ratification, is certainly open for discussion. What is not unclear is that Madison offered a "blended" model of representation and argued throughout the ratification process that the proposed Constitution was neither a national governmental model nor a federal model—he believed that it possessed elements of both. And while Levin notes Madison's reiteration of his proposed "blended" model of representation in his comments before the Virginia Ratifying Convention where he explains that it is an attempt to "exclude the evils of absolute consolidation (of the national government), as well as of a mere Confederacy" and that the "powers of the federal government are enumerated…," Levin never returns to *Federalist* no. 39 to place Madison's comments in context with his previously more developed rationale for the different modes of selection of representatives and senators in the proposed national Congress.

Madison's explanation of the characteristics of the proposed Constitution and its integration of both "national" and "federal" powers in *Federalist* no. 39 reflects his commitment to provide two different modes by which the desires of the people could be ascertained and implemented and yet protect against tyranny from whatever source. His commentary in no. 39 is a direct response to those, similar to Henry and his Anti-Federalist colleagues, that the proposal was rooted in principles of republicanism reflecting the essentiality of self-government and receiving its powers "…directly or indirectly from the great body of the people…" He described the general criteria understood to reflect republican self-government with the following observation:

> If we resort for a criterion to the different principles on which different forms of government are established, we may define a republic to be, or at least may bestow that name on, a government which derives all its powers directly or indirectly from the great body of the people and is administered by persons holding their offices during pleasure, for a limited period, or during good behavior. It is essential to such a government that it be derived from the great body of the society, not from an inconsiderable proportion or a favored class of it; otherwise a handful of tyrannical nobles, exercising their oppressions by a delegation of their powers, might aspire to the rank of republicans and claim for their government the honorable title of republic…[176]

After describing the methods by which such a republican government could be instituted, Madison then reminded the critics of the proposed plan that many of the techniques being presented were found in numerous existing state constitutions. Whether it was the appointment or electoral process, he argued that the proposed Constitution mirrored principles of republicanism reflected in similar processes in state governance. In fact, he noted that their proposal offered additional checks against abuse of power. For example, the proposed Constitution would provide for impeachment of both judicial appointees and the President of the United States and prohibited titles of nobility from being granted by either the federal or state governments. What was essential in the functioning of republican government for Madison was that "the great body of the people," either, directly or indirectly, selected and controlled those who administered their government.

It was Madison's task to persuade the Anti-Federalist critics that the proposed process for ratification was both a reflection of republican principles and yet provided each state with the independent sovereignty to solicit its citizens' desires regarding the construction of a new government. The proposed ratification process did not require a national referendum from the majority of the people of the Union or even agreement from a majority of the states, but rather Madison stressed the "federal" nature of the process. He explained that "It is to be the assent and ratification of the several States derived from the supreme authority in each State—the authority of the people themselves." He argued that "The act, therefore, establishing the Constitution will not be a national but a federal act." Responding to his opponents attempt to define the overall proposal as a dangerous consolidation of power to the rights and liberties of the people, Madison argued that the desires of the "great body of the people" would be determined through the existing mechanisms provided by each state government not "…from the decisions of a majority of the people of the Union nor from that of a majority of the States."[177] Madison and the Framers were committed to continue and protect the sovereignty of each state for the purpose of the ratification process. They were cognizant of the fact that without this understanding, while the desires of a majority of citizens in the country might support the proposed Constitution, citizens who resided in states which were smaller in population may be persuaded to reject the proposal because their interests might be disregarded. Therefore, Madison was particularly sensitive to the process by which the will of the people would be determined regarding ratification. A balance needed to be struck between the desires of the "great body of the people"—the essence of republican government—and the protection of the interests of citizens who might not form a majority in a "consolidated" government. His solution was to argue that the desires of the people regarding ratification could best be determined by soliciting their support through "the distinct and independent States to which they respectively belong." In so doing, each State's ratification would originate from "the authority of the people themselves."[178] Such a process, he argued was federal in nature and would result in a determination regarding the proposed Constitution which is "…neither from the decisions of a majority of the people of the Union nor from that of a majority of States."[179] Therefore, Madison skirted the allegations that he was proposing a national government which was constructed solely on the desires of a majority of citizens from the most populated States by recognizing that an "indirect" method by which to discern the desires of citizens could be determined through the mechanism of State legislative assemblies. But this recognition of State sovereignty as an indicator of the people's desires for ratification of the Constitution, while federal in nature, did not satisfy his opponents. He then turned to the hybrid nature of the proposed representation model.

As we discussed in Chapter Three, Madison's rationales for a bi-cameral legislative process were numerous. He presented his arguments not only in *Federalist* no. 39, but also in no. 52, no. 53, no. 57 and in no. 62. After citing some of Madison's arguments in no. 39, Mr. Levin would have us believe that Madison's ultimate objective of providing a selection process for Senators which relied upon State legislative assemblies was based upon his commitment to preserving the "plenary" authority of state legislatures as co-equal governmental units with the proposed national government. Once again placed within the context of his other arguments throughout the *Federalist Papers*, such a reading of Madison's defense of the "blended" nature of the proposed Constitution in no. 39 is at best a limited interpretation of his commentary.

Madison's commentary in no. 39 should be read as a vigorous rebuttal of his Anti-Federalist opponents by illustrating the "federal" nature of the electoral selection process for members of the proposed Senate. It is absolutely correct to suggest that one of his overall concerns was to construct and defend a governmental process that would provide checks against abuse of power from whatever source. The selection of Senators through the processes established by the people through their respective state legislative assemblies was an additional mechanism in that effort, along with the other requirements for electoral office at the national level. But Madison's recognition of the role which the States would play in this selection process should be understood as but one of many methods by which to balance the inherent competing interests of a republican government dependent upon majority rule with the Founders' commitment to protect the interests of those not in the political majority. Unlike the House of Representatives which derived its power directly from the "great body of the People," another check would be established by delegating authority to State legislatures to solicit the desires of its citizens regarding their representation in the Senate.

While the powers which were to be utilized to determine the wishes of individual citizens were derived through "direct" or "indirect" electoral processes each Congressmen or Senator would be ultimately answerable to the

People. It will be remembered that Madison's perspective on the ultimate check on abuse of power originating from those who were ultimately selected to hold positions of public trust was to always be "...compelled to anticipate the moment when they must descend to the level from which they were raised—there forever to remain unless a faithful discharge of their trust shall have established their title to a renewal of it."[180] While his observations were noted in his commentary in *Federalist* no. 57 when he was discussing the "direct" representation process for members of the proposed House of Representatives, he most certainly did not abandon his commitment to this principle when the "indirect" method of the selection of members of the Senate was proposed. Indeed, when placing Madison's fundamental concern regarding the potential deleterious impact that "factions" play on all levels of the legislative process but most particularly on the state level, it strains credulity to suggest that the ultimate reason for Madison's recommendation for a different selection process for the proposed Senate was based fundamentally on his trust in the legislative authority of state governments.

The challenge for Mr. Levin and his contemporary Anti-Federalist supporters who would repeal the Seventeenth Amendment is to persuade Americans that a vote by majority of state representatives in their respective state legislatures is the best method by which to reflect their interests as American citizens. After a bloody Civil War, the institution of the Thirteenth, Fourteenth, Fifteenth, and Nineteenth Amendments, the population growth of the country and the impact of *laisse faire* economic theory on late nineteenth century, early twentieth century Americans, one wonders whether Madison would be persuaded by Mr. Levin's call for an abolition of the Seventeenth Amendment. Or, whether James Madison might remind those concerned with "unelected bureaucrats" or "non-responsive" members of the political elite that the most powerful method by which to protect against tyranny is to search for its source and control it through the power of each citizen's vote. Time will tell whether the argument of contemporary Anti-Federalist who would return the selection of Senators to intermediaries of the People—state politicians—will be persuasive, or whether twenty-first century Americans, regardless of their place of residence, will be reminded of the varied history of state legislative assemblies in the preservation and protection of their most fundamental rights.

Mr. Levin's claim that the Framers intended, through the insertion of the Ninth and Tenth Amendments within the Bill of Rights, to place "...structural limits on federal governmental action and respect for individual sovereignty and local community interests..." should also be closely examined. He asserts that their intentions were "altered fundamentally" through the actions of

Progressives who pursued "...utopian objectives of economic, social, and cultural egalitarianism and reformation... and this distortion of these amendments ... reveals itself in relentless social engineering and lifestyle calibrations."[181]

Surprisingly, he is unclear as to what particular actions, with the exception of the standard objections regarding the institution of the federal income tax by the enactment of the Sixteenth Amendment, are examples of "social engineering" or "lifestyle calibrations" and therefore are "distortions" of the Ninth and Tenth Amendments. What we do know is that he arrives at his conclusions without any discussion or analysis of the meaning of We the People and the entire Preamble of the Constitution; the impact of the Three-Fifths Plan on securing a compromise for ratification of the Constitution; an entire period of American history torn apart by a Civil War and the subsequent enactment of the Thirteenth, Fourteenth, and Fifteenth Amendments; the dramatic population growth of the country since the ratification of the Constitution; or, the impact of monopolies on our free market system. Instead, he focuses on what he describes as the "original meaning" of the Ninth, and by implication, the Tenth Amendments to the Constitution to demonstrate how a "top-down centralized government" has usurped "individual sovereignty and local community interests."[182] It might be helpful if the language drafted, debated, revised and defended by James Madison is examined in an effort to determine the legitimacy of our contemporary Anti-Federalists claims.

Repackaging the Bill of Rights for Contemporary Consumption

The Ninth Amendment reads as follows:

> The enumeration in the Constitution, of certain rights, shall not be construed to deny or disparage others retained by the people.

The Tenth Amendment states:

> The powers not delegated to the United States by the Constitution, nor prohibited by it to the States, are reserved to the States respectively, or to the people.

It should be remembered that Madison's task was not only to draft this "least imperfect" contract with the people, but also to seek ratification of the agreement. As noted when we discussed the bi-cameral electoral process above, compromises needed to be struck with political coalitions both within the Federalist camp and the Anti-Federalist opposition. And, he needed to be cognizant of internal disagreements within each group. Madison's political skill to find support for the Constitution can be best understood, as was noted in Chapter One, from his observation regarding his blended representation model discussed above. In his effort to solicit support for his proposal he wrote:

> The advice of prudence must be to embrace the lesser of evil and, instead of indulging a fruitless anticipation of the possible mischiefs which may ensue, to contemplate rather the advantageous consequences which may qualify the sacrifice.[183]

His understanding of the importance of developing a consensus for ratification through political compromise is also reflected in his ultimate willingness to draft both the Ninth and Tenth Amendments. Initially, many Federalists, and even some Anti-Federalists were unconvinced of the necessity or the legitimacy of such proclamations for very different reasons. But with a continuing effort by Anti-Federalists, particularly in Virginia, to oppose ratification of the Constitution on numerous grounds including the absence of an enumeration of rights in the proposed document, Madison agreed to draft a series of amendments. But he did have reservations. Madison explained his reasoning on the matter to Thomas Jefferson in a letter, he wrote:

> My opinion has always been in favor of a Bill of Rights; provided it be so framed as not to imply powers not meant to be included in the enumeration…I have not viewed it in an important light—1. because I conceive that in a certain degree…the rights in question are reserved by the manner in which federal powers are granted—2. Because there is great reason to fear that a positive declaration of some of the most essential rights could not be obtained in the requisite latitude. I am sure that the rights of conscience in particular, if submitted to public definition would be narrowed much more than they are likely ever to be by an assumed power.[184]

Always concerned with establishing the correct balance between republican government grounded in principles of majority rule, and the necessity of protecting individual liberty, Madison's observation to Jefferson reflects his worry. He understood that without an articulation of the fundamental rights of Americans which no government could infringe, the proposed Constitution would be open to attack by its opponents as evidence of a dangerous conspiracy to deny individual liberty. But he also recognized that once specific enumerations of fundamental rights were inserted into the document, failure to articulate with unqualified language the limit of governmental restrictions on each citizen's liberty could potentially legitimize unintended governmental restrictions from political majorities or powerful minority factions. The importance of protecting the right to freedom of conscience, a right specifically protected by the

Virginia Constitution unlike some other state constitutions during the Articles of Confederation, was particularly important to Jefferson. So while Madison may have believed that no honest reading of the proposed plan could have concluded that it—even absent an enumeration of certain rights—would legitimize any governmental (state or national) usurpation of each citizen's fundamental right, the political necessity of carefully drafting such enumerations needed to be instituted. But first he needed to reassure his Federalists colleagues like Alexander Hamilton that he respected their concerns regarding creating such enumerations. Then he must draft language which would reflect the good-faith objections on both sides of the debate regarding a Bill of Rights generally, and the specific concerns regarding the fundamental rights of each citizen—the source of all legitimate governmental action.

The House of Representatives established a Select Committee to draft proposed language for the institution of a Bill of Rights. Madison, as a member of the committee, presented drafts of proposed language regarding the Ninth and Tenth amendments which were then offered to his colleagues and then to state ratifying conventions. While there is disagreement within the legal community regarding the intended historical meaning of the Ninth and Tenth Amendments[185] there is no question that the initial draft proposal language of these two amendments presented to the Virginia ratifying convention by Madison was modified in the final draft. The original drafts of the Ninth and Tenth Amendments presented to the convention read as follows:

The Ninth Amendment

The exceptions here or elsewhere in the Constitution, made in favor of particular rights shall not be so construed as to diminish the just importance of other rights retained by the people, or as to enlarge the powers delegated by the Constitution but either as actual limitations of such powers, or as inserted merely for greater caution.

The Tenth Amendment

The powers not delegated by this Constitution, nor prohibited by it to the States, are reserved to the States respectively.

A comparison of the eventual language which was ratified and the draft language cited above underscores Madison's and the supporters of the proposed Constitution commitment to recognize the source of all legitimate governmental power. Both the draft language of the Ninth Amendment presented to the Virginia Ratifying Convention and the final language offered for ratification reflect Madison's commitment to the preservation of individual liberty within the context of a uniquely American system of republican government. While certain rights could and should be enumerated, he understood that in so doing he needed to reiterate that the source of all rights are derived from the people delegated to government upon their consent. There should be little debate as to Madison's intention of providing notice through both of these amendments that the rights enumerated and others which each citizen retained would be protected from attempts to restrict them by the newly designed national government. That being noted it is also important to remember Madison's and the Framers' concern with the impact of factions on liberty at the state and local governmental level. The addition of the language "or to the People" in the final draft of the Tenth Amendment only reinforces their recognition that state sovereignty was not the only residuary of power within the proposed Constitution. Individual citizens of the states also were beneficiaries of the reserved powers. It shouldn't be surprising that those who opposed ratification on the grounds that it was not an agreement between the several states but instead between government and "We the People" would find the insertion of "or to the People" in the final draft of the Tenth Amendment to be justification for rejection of the amendment and the entire document.

Mr. Levin's conclusion that the meaning of these two amendments has been "altered fundamentally"[186] has received some support from those within and outside of the legal community who believe that the source of each citizen's immutable liberties was intended to be determined through the actions of local government. They contend that the Ninth Amendment language of "rights retained by the People" were exclusively found in the writings of the Anti-Federalists. One legal researcher has concluded that the Founders believed that rights were a "matter of local concern."[187] This same researcher contends "...the Ninth and Tenth Amendments declare that all non-delegated powers and rights are retained by the people who may delegate them to their respective state governments as they see fit." He then asserts that "...The Ninth Amendment prevents the nationalization of these powers and rights through expansive readings of the Constitution."[188]

While this analysis of our constitutional history and the "original meaning" of the Ninth and Tenth Amendments certainly conforms with the marketing strategies of "institutes" and "foundations" which decry the destruction of liberty by the actions of an out of control federal government, a few points need to be made.

It is absolutely correct to note the Founders' reliance upon immutable rights derived from principles of natural law. Any discussion then of their understanding of the phrase "rights retained by the people" requires an examination of the philosophical tradition from which the Founders legitimized both a revolution and the eventual creation of the Constitution. As we noted in Chapter One, John Locke's vision of these inalienable rights flowed not from government but attached to each individual as they entered civil society. Once an individual joins with others into a collective enterprise called government while not relinquishing the rights, they must of necessity delegate their protection and implementation to individuals accountable to the community. The English Libertarian's whose writings were so well received prior to and during the revolution also mirrored this understanding of the need for government. Both understandings of the relationship between the individual and civil society were constructed upon the premise that government—regardless of its configuration—must maximize the freedom of the individual within the context of an ordered society. The key principle upon which they relied to determine the legitimate limits of individual liberty was what we have described earlier in our investigation as the "harm qualifier." It would be government's responsibility to demonstrate how the actions of the individual were harmful to another or the community as a whole. Any discussion of what constituted the Founders' understanding of "natural rights" must account for this fundamental given.

The assertion that the meaning of the phrase "rights retained by the people" found in the Ninth Amendment can be best understood "in the writings of the Anti-Federalists" and are "matters of local concern" is troubling. First, the debates surrounding the ratification of the Constitution by both the Federalists and Anti-Federalists abound with arguments declaring how best to protect liberty. While the Anti-Federalist, Patrick Henry and George Mason defended their rejection of the proposed Constitution based on their fear that liberty would be usurped by a national government, Madison, Hamilton and their supporters argued that liberty was best protected from the actions of factions by balancing the demands of republican government through the process of political compromise in a union of all citizens. Another questionable conclusion regarding the "correct" interpretation of "rights retained by the People" is that these "natural rights" while being protected from usurpation by a national government, could be "delegated" to state governments "as they see fit."[189]

Stated within the context of contemporary Anti-Federalist commentary—the "original meaning" of the Ninth Amendment language only limits the federal government from defining the rights of citizenship retained by each American—state legislatures operating with the delegated powers provided to them by a majority of its citizens may determine the limits of liberty. This interpretation of the language while rejecting "…the nationalization of these powers and rights through expansive readings of the Constitution,"[190] submits that the Founders intended that the limits of liberty vested in state and local governments. This is an interesting analysis of Madison's and late nineteenth century Americans' understanding of liberty. Indeed, this interpretation is fundamentally at odds with concerns he expressed to Jefferson. It will be remembered that he worried that without the insertion of unqualified language regarding any enumeration of rights left to each citizen such proclamations may lead to unjust restrictions by the actions of a legislative majority. While he was addressing that potentiality in regard to the national government, are we to take seriously the assertion that he was unconcerned with the immutability of these rights and willing to leave their protection to state and local assemblies sometimes controlled by powerful minority factions?

The language of the Ninth Amendment, the subsequent incorporation of similar language in numerous state constitutions, and the insertion of the "or to the People," language in the final draft of the Tenth Amendment are compelling actions which would reject any such conclusion. The "rights retained by the people" were immutable. No government national, state, or local, would be permitted to restrict those rights enumerated within the first eight amendments of our Bill of Rights, or any others so determined through the delegated powers of government provided by the Constitution without a demonstration that those rights "harmed" another or the "community as a whole." That task it will be remembered was assigned to an independent judiciary whose only power was that of the "power of judgment."

Controlling the "co-conspirators": The Contemporary Anti-Federalist's Response to Supreme Court Decision Making

If you believe that "expansive readings" of the Constitution have been created by the Supreme Court which have rendered these amendments "mere truisms," it would be consistent to submit that state legislatures were better guardians of our liberties. Citing the Court's apparently legitimate interpretation during its early decision-making regarding "natural rights" cases and its "attendant rule of construction" throughout most of the nineteenth century which deferred to state lawmaking, it is entirely predictable that so-called "New Deal" judicial decision-making which reexamined the balance of state and federal lawmaking authority would be unacceptable to our contemporary Anti-Federalists. Indeed, at the core of Mr. Levin and his supporters push for term limits for Justices of the Supreme Court is their selective disdain of the Court's decision-making throughout our history. Apparently Supreme Court decisions throughout the nineteenth century which restricted federal power and by implication correctly deferred to the "original intention" of the Ninth and Tenth Amendments by using an "attendant rule of construction" are examples of legitimate constitutional decision-making. But decisions from the Court which supported the constitutionality of federal legislation enacted to remedy either the vestiges of state sponsored discrimination or the impact of a Depression are decisions which are egregious examples of judicial fiat.

It is one thing to argue as most "original intent" jurisprudents contend that only through adherence to a "strict construction" of past decisions can consistency and predictability be attained in the application of our system of rules. But it is quite another to imply that the Court does not also possess the responsibility to determine whether past precedent conforms with evolving social mores determined through the legislative process in the Congress of the United States. Where the balance should be struck is an important and interesting jurisprudential question for another investigation. Suffice it to say for our purposes that ultimately the legitimacy of Supreme Court decision-making is determined by the American people through their compliance. And, that compliance will be, for the most part, depended upon their respect for the objectivity of the decision-making of the Court.

Mr. Levin and his supporters have every right, maybe even an obligation, to rail against decisions which they believe are produced through a politically biased judicial process—as do all Americans who may disagree with a particular determination of the Court. But similar to many of his rationales for the establishment of his "liberty amendments," Mr. Levin's call for term limits for Supreme Court justices relies on the failed arguments of opponents to the proposed Constitution—not its proponents. His technique of correctly identifying, but out of context, selected language from one of the Framers and then sprinkling his "analysis" with the observations of Anti-Federalist vehemently opposed to ratification of the document in an effort to reinforce the historical legitimacy of his "solutions" to control what he believes to be the despotic decisions of the Court requires a response.

By interweaving the arguments presented by the Framers of the Constitution with those who vehemently opposed it, he presents an "analysis" of the Court which renders it as but another political branch of a federal government acting with "far-reaching and breathtaking rulings on the whole society, for which there is no effective recourse."[191] Of course, he fails to note all of the structural checks discussed in Chapter One of our investigation in regard to the Founder's creation of an independent judiciary. But nevertheless, seizing upon the "flesh and blood" characteristics of Supreme Court Justices and their "human imperfections and frailties,"[192] he identifies the Supreme Court cases of—Dred Scott v. Sandford,[193] Plessy v. Ferguson,[194] and Korematsu v. United States[195]—decided early in our history and which would find little support from contemporary

Americans—to legitimize his "solution"—term limits for Supreme Court Justices. In so doing, he failed to note later decisions of the Court which either reversed their previous eighteenth century decisions regarding the constitutionality of separate but equal, or their post-Korematsu decisions which narrowed the application of that case to exceptional circumstances such as times of war so determined by the actions of Congress.[196] That he noted these "notorious holdings" of the Supreme Court is indeed gratifying. Supreme Court legitimization of slavery prior to the Civil War or state sponsored racial segregation instituted more than three decades after the Civil War—not to mentioned the internment of thousands of Americans in camps based predominately on their national origin—are truly egregious examples of failures by the institution of the Court to provide the country with guidance with who we can be as a people not who we are in that particular moment of societal conflict.

What is curious, however, is that our modern day Anti-Federalists seem to want it both ways. That is, while they decry the lack of adherence to past precedent in decisions of the Court which in their minds abandoned the "original intention" of the Ninth and Tenth Amendments, they seem perfectly willing to attack the findings of the Court in the cases of Dred Scott v. Sandford and Plessy v. Ferguson which are compelling examples of the limitations of that methodology in judicial decision-making. Mr. Levin is consistent, however, on one area of Supreme Court decision-making which he believes needs to be controlled by the establishment of term limits—the regulation and taxation of American commerce.

While he and his cohorts in the variety of oligarchical supported "institutes" and "foundations" cite the Court's past decisions regarding "personal policy preferences relating to social, cultural, and religious issues..." as unacceptable examples of judicial fiat, the real target of their movement to control the Court via term limits is their interpretation of, Article I, Section 8., Clause 3, of the Constitution—the so-called "Commerce Clause."

Using the similar marketing strategy of Freedom Works and other front organizations of our American oligarchy, but under the guise of constitutional analysis, Mr. Levin cites what he believes are examples of a Court sanctioned out-of-control federal government. Noting federal regulation of everything from the Nation's debt and "pension guarantor" to "things in your bathroom, laundry room, and kitchen" and even "lunch menu(s)," he concludes and asks "...the question is not what the federal government regulates, but what it does not. And it makes you wonder—how can a people incapable of selecting their own light bulbs and toilets possess enough competence to vote for their own rulers and fill out complicated tax returns?"[197] Regulations—the bane of American life. Our individual and collective existence would be so much better if we transferred the protection and quality of the products we purchase to the wisdom of those in the corporate boardrooms of our captains of industry. "Beautiful gardens" would be once again observed through the efforts of unencumbered free enterprise.

How do we return to such a Utopian state? It would appear that one part of Mr. Levin's strategy along with his compatriots from the Tea Party, Americans for Tax Reform and the other oligarchical-funded organizations, is to "persuade" current and future members of the Court that the regulation of commerce—if it is to be done at all—should eventuate through the actions of state legislative assemblies. Return the protection of the American people and the food they consume, the medicine they require, the protection of their savings or retirement pensions, etc., to the wisdom of state and local politicians and the factions which fund them. No longer would the constitutional language within Article I section 8. Clause 3 which provides the Congress with the power to regulate "commerce … among the States…" be interpreted to include commerce generated within a state but which has a substantial impact on interstate commerce and the nation. While our contemporary Anti-Federalists are mostly silent on the impact of this "solution" to "restore the American Republic," a brief historical backdrop should be noted.

A reinterpretation of the interstate commerce clause *à la* Mr. Levin and his supporters would reject the Court's findings in two cases which upheld provisions of the Civil Rights Act of 1964. In Heart of Atlanta Motel, Inc. v. United States and Katzenbach v. McClung,[198] the Supreme Court held that the denial of motel accommodations and in-store service by these two private businesses based on race violated the interstate commerce clause. The Court, following the statutory language of the Civil Rights Act and the Congressional intention discerned through a search of congressional hearings on the act, determined that while each case presented differing elements of intrastate commerce the refusal to serve African-American travelers or consumers, had a substantial economic impact on interstate commerce and therefore fell within the purview of the Congress' power to regulate. In so finding, the Court rejected the arguments of the private business owners that their rights under the Fifth Amendment of the Bill of Rights were violated by the Civil Rights Act of 1964. Writing for a majority of the Court, Mr. Justice Clark concluded:

> Nor does the Act deprive appellant of liberty or property under the Fifth Amendment. The commerce power involved here by the Congress is a specific and plenary one authorized by the Constitution itself. The only questions are (1) whether Congress had a rational basis for finding that racial

discrimination by motels affected commerce, and (2) if it had such a basis, whether the means it selected to eliminate that evil are reasonable and appropriate. If they are, appellant has no "right" to select its guests as it sees fit, free from governmental regulation.[199]

While the Court could have grounded its decision upon Equal Protection violations by these private businesses, as some of the concurring Justices noted, the majority instead provided a rationale which it believed was constitutionally unassailable. That was, that Congress possessed the "plenary" (absolute) authority to regulate the free flow of commerce within the country. Commerce which was solely operative within the jurisdiction of each state would be within what Madison would have described as their "subordinate" regulatory purview. But commerce which originated within those jurisdictions which had a substantial impact on commercial activity "among the several states" must be monitored by the American people's representatives in the Congress of the United States. The impact of commercial enterprises, which refused accommodations or services to thousands of interstate travelers of a particular race, but were otherwise available to all other travelers, unquestionably impeded the free flow of interstate commerce, so the Court reasoned. While its finding reinforced the power of Congress to legislate against "moral wrongs," the majority of the Court found "overwhelming evidence of the disruptive effect that racial discrimination has had on commercial intercourse." The deleterious impact that this practice created on commerce alone justified Congressional prohibitions on businesses which provided "public accommodations" or services on the basis of race.[200]

The Supreme Court's determination in these cases and its application of the Commerce Clause in subsequent decisions was not created out of whole cloth as our contemporary Anti-Federalists would have us believe. That it was well within the "attendant rule of construction" of previous case law is without question. What these decisions do, however, is confront the always present issue of how constitutionally to balance the interests of the individual with that of the public welfare. What are the constitutional limits of personal liberty—including the use of "private" property—with the impact that such use has on "another or the society as a whole"? The issue then is not, as Mr. Levin would have us believe, whether the Court has followed past precedent. Instead it is whether the determinations of the Court conform to our contemporary Anti-Federalists' revisionist interpretation of the Founding visions.

For Mr. Levin and those who would place term limits on the justices of the Court, the Commerce Clause decisions are the foreseeable outcome of a branch of the federal government that early in American history created for itself an unintended power of judicial review and has eventuated in a Court that is but another political institution controlled by five individuals who "...pursue even newer and more novel paths around the Constitution..." We will briefly discuss a few of the decisions which he believes provide evidence of this claim in a moment. But these cases have not been decided based on the interstate commerce clause. However, he does identify the one decision which, calling upon the mandates of Article I, Section 8, Clause 3, directly confronts the question of the limits of the use of private property and its impact on "another or the society as a whole"—Wickard v. Filburn.[201] This case, which established the constitutional foundation upon which most contemporary Supreme Court decisions have been formulated regarding Congressional power to regulate commerce, is for Mr. Levin, a glaring example of a Court which "contort the facts and the law, as they must, to reach their desired result."[202] A brief review of the decision may be helpful in determining whether his evaluation is a constitutionally accurate description of the case.

The facts in Wickard v. Filburn are important. The case, decided in 1942 in the middle of a world war, with a country slowing mending from a deep economic depression and trying to determine how best to reinvigorate and stabilize the nation's markets, involved the imposition of a "marketing penalty" for an alleged violation of the Agricultural Adjustment Act of 1938. This act of Congress was but one of many pieces legislation instituted to repair numerous sectors of the national economy devastated by the Depression. This act placed limits on the amount of wheat which could be produced by farmers in an effort "to control the volume moving in interstate and foreign commerce in order to avoid surpluses and shortages and the consequent abnormally low or high wheat prices and obstructions to commerce." Mr. Filburn, an Ohio farmer, produced an amount of wheat crop in excess of the Act's per acre allotted amount. The amount of bushels of wheat he grew over the allotted amount set by Congress was small. He intended to sell a portion of the wheat produced, use some to feed his livestock and for home-consumed flour and seed. The act required whatever excess over the per acre quota "may neither be disposed of nor used except upon payment of the penalty or except it is stored...."[203] The Supreme Court upheld the "marketing penalty" assessed to Mr. Filburn and found the Agricultural Adjustment Act of 1938 to be constitutional pursuant to Article I, Section 8., Clause 3.

For our contemporary Anti-Federalists, this case is the quintessential example of the Leviathan federal government and its ever-ready servant, the Supreme Court, interceding into the sanctity of private property usage and self-sufficiency. After all, what is more ingrained in the American spirit than the values reflected in this case? A small farmer who plants enough wheat to make a little money on the open market, feed his farm animals and use the remainder of the wheat for home consumption—it is the very essence of the American experience since our founding. It is a powerful image and one that deserves recognition and support. Yet, as has been noted throughout our investigation, Mr. Filburn's actions cannot be constitutionally evaluated without examining the "harm" that the overproduction of wheat by others similarly situated would have on the market.

The Court provided an extended discussion regarding the "wheat industry" and the problems associated with the impact of "a large surplus in production" coupled with "an abnormally large supply of wheat and other grains" on the markets. It noted that those conditions "caused congestion in a number of markets; tied up railroad cars; and caused elevators in some instances to turn away grains, and railroads to institute embargoes to prevent further congestion." They went on to observe that in 1941 wheat producers who cooperated with the Act "received an average price on the farm of about $1.16 a bushel as compared with the world market price of 40 cents a bushel." Additionally, they found that on farm consumption of the crop was variable but was "in an amount greater than 20 per cent of average production...." They concluded then that "(The) effect of consumption of home-grown wheat on interstate commerce is due to the fact that it constitutes the most variable factor in the disappearance of the wheat crop."[204]

After identifying Congress' intention through the Agricultural Adjustment Act "...to increase the market price of wheat and to that end to limit the volume thereof that could affect the market," the Court reasoned that the variability and volume of home-consumed wheat by farmers across the nation would have "...a substantial influence on price and market conditions." They believed that it was altogether reasonable to conclude that this home-consumed wheat production "if induced by rising prices tends to flow into the market and check price increases." Another potential consequence of unregulated home wheat consumption the Court reasoned would be that if the production does not go into the market in the first scenario, and was used by the farmer for his own purposes then it would reduce the value of wheat already placed into the market by other producers. Justice Jackson, writing for the Court noted that "But if we assume that it is never marketed, it supplies a need of the man who grew it which would otherwise be reflected by purchases in the open market. Home-grown wheat in this sense competes with wheat in commerce."

Ultimately, the issue of the balance between individual self-sufficiency and the needs of the country at a time of significant financial uncertainty for farmers producing agricultural commodities such as wheat was addressed by the Court. They wrote,

...The effect of the statute before us is to restrict the amount which may be produced for market and the extent as well to which one may forestall resort to the market by producing to meet his own needs. That appellee's own contribution to the demand for wheat may be trivial by itself is not enough to remove him from the scope of federal regulation where, as here, his contribution, taken together with that of many others similarly situated, is far from trivial.[205]

Noting the past history of the wheat industry, the present uncertain condition of the price of wheat both in the domestic and foreign markets, the impact that unregulated production had on other sectors of commerce, and Congressional recognition of the importance of establishing a fair price for farmers who placed their wheat in commerce, the Court held that Mr. Filburn's actions coupled with others "similarly situated" would eventuate in reasonably foreseeable injury to the national markets.

One suspects that our contemporary Anti-Federalist will continue to cite the Wickard v. Filburn decision as an example of the Court's "defiance of the Constitution's structure and limits." But, did the Court really "contort the facts and the law" in this case? Did the Court's validation of an act of Congress demonstrate its agenda to "promote a trajectory of expanded federal power" or was the decision a reflection of their constitutional responsibility to determine whether the people's representatives could enact legislation which impacted the stability of an important sector of the nation's economy? Would the Founders who had felt the impact of disparate laws regarding commercial transaction throughout the Articles of Confederation period agree with Mr. Levin and his supporters that Mr. Filburn's private property usage was absolute and free from any regulation by other members of the community regardless of any demonstration of harm?

It is difficult to discern what is at the core of our contemporary Anti-Federalists' selective disdain of Supreme Court decision-making. In the case of the "New Deal" decisions is the reason because the Court "expanded" the power of the federal government by constitutionally validating the "plenary" power of the people's representatives to enact legislation in an attempt to stabilize sectors of the American economy during the great Depression? Or, is the problem with the Court's recognition that an individual's action, taken together with others who may act similarly, can be constitutionally balanced with the interests of others who may be harmed by such actions? Or, are they suggesting that such determinations are outside the constitutional jurisdiction of the Court to review?

One is left with the impression that unless and until the Supreme Court validates through its decision-making their revisionist interpretation of the

"American Republic" that they will continue to decry any decision which does not conform to their world view. Indeed, Mr. Levin is convinced that the Founders intention for the creation of an independent judiciary has been usurped by a "judicial oligarchy" whereby five justices of the Court can exercise "supreme power over the other federal branches and the states." His "solution"—reject Hamilton's and the Founders requirement of lifetime appointments; politicize decisions of the Court by providing the Congress with the power to overturn a decision of the Court; and, most importantly, return the interpretation of the Constitution to state legislative assemblies.[206] To understand more clearly why he believes term limits are essential to "control" the Court one only has to examine the decisions he cites as "politically determinative."

He identifies the decisions of Everson v. Board of Education,[207] Griswold v. Connecticut,[208] Plyler v. Doe,[209] Lawrence v. Texas[210] and National Federation of Independent Business v. Sebelius[211] as proof of his assertion that the Court has become a "judicial oligarchy." Taking a chapter from the marketing strategists who have identified what we described earlier in our investigation as the "red meat" issues of American life to rail against "big government," he has also identified decisions of the Court which he understands will continue to engender the wrath of some citizens. Without any analysis of the facts presented to the Court, the legal principles relevant in each decision, and the historical context in which the cases were determined, he parenthetically describes the result of these widely disparate and important Supreme Court decisions as examples of "defiance of the Constitution's structure and limits."[212]

These cases required the Court to address the balancing of First Amendment rights of Free Exercise of Religion with the prohibition of the Establishment of Religion (Everson v. Board of Education), to determine whether state laws which made it a crime to sell or purchase contraceptives violated a fundamental right "retained by the people" under the Ninth Amendment—the right to marital privacy (Griswold v. Connecticut), to decide whether the Equal Protection Clause in the Fourteenth Amendment was violated by the state of Texas which denied public education to the children of illegal aliens (Plyler v. Doe), to determine whether the state of Texas, which criminalized private, adult, consensual, sexual relations between members of the same sex was a violation of the right to privacy pursuant to the Ninth Amendment (Lawrence v. Texas), and to decide whether the Affordable Care Act of the Congress of the United States which established minimum standards of coverage for each insured to include such protections as no cap on health care coverage, no provisions which excluded pre-existing conditions, to provide coverage of the policy-holder's children up until the age of 26, and which placed a penalty on citizens who failed to purchase health insurance, was constitutionally permitted under provisions of Article I (National Federation of Independent Business v. Sebelius).

For our contemporary Anti-Federalists, these decisions, and others not mentioned by Mr. Levin which have limited state lawmaking authority and have upheld acts of the Congress of the United States, are vivid examples of "politically determinative decisions" in which the Court "contort the facts and the law...to reach their desired result." Apparently what they would have us believe is that the Supreme Court as a co-conspirator with the other two branches of the federal government in its thirst for power has defied the "Constitution's structure and limits" and has allegedly usurped the liberty of Americans which would be better protected by majorities in state legislative assemblies. What is so very interesting is that those who have marketed the importance of individual liberty would entrust the protection of this co-equal objective of our Constitutional system to state legislative bodies which—both historically and contemporaneously—have legitimized segregation, criminalized the sale and purchase of contraceptive devices, the consensual sexual acts of adults in their bedrooms, and have refused to establish minimum standards of coverage by "health insurance carriers" for millions of Americans who reside in their state.

The question(s) involved in these and a multitude of other contentious social, religious, and cultural issues have driven our political debates and eventually have found their way into legislative efforts both on the federal and state levels. Indeed, it is in those institutions of our governmental process where the interests of the individual and the collective were intended to be debated and find some level of resolution. But as we noted in Chapter One of our investigation, the Founders recognized the importance of creating a "final arbiter" of conflicts, absent a referendum of the people through the constitutional amendment process, which would be delegated the responsibility to review "all cases and controversies...arising under the Constitution."[213] While the individuals who were to be selected to fulfill this responsibility were vetted by and often were creatures of our political process, their independence from the legislative process and the Executive function was intended to insulated them from "political machinations" and thus secure the respect and compliance of the American people.

One suspects that Americans, regardless of political party affiliation, can point to a decision or decisions from the Supreme Court with which they have disagreed. Even Madison, once he accepted the responsibilities of the Executive branch, expressed frustration with the Court. And for those of us who possess more than a passing interest in the functioning and decision-making of the Court, departures from past decisions or public pronouncements from members of the Court signaling an entrenched political bias triggers both frustration and fear—frustration that if the rule modification is not articulately explained claims of arbitrary decision-making will most certainly be forthcoming; fear that continual public commentary by individual justices which signal their dissatisfaction with a particular decision or another will quickly lead the public to believe, sometimes correctly, that political ideology alone drives some members of the Court's decisions.

But one wonders what is at the core of our contemporary Anti-Federalists selective disdain of Supreme Court decision-making. Is it really the Court's blatant disregard for principles of republican government? Or, is it that Mr. Levin, et.al. have decided that the Founders once again got it wrong. That is, that an "independent judiciary" as they would define it, is one which is tethered to the political determinations of legislative bodies at the federal and state levels. Apparently, the "final arbiter" of the meaning of constitutional governance, absent the already prescribed amendment process created by the Founders, would not be left to "a mere five lawyers," but instead to our "elected" through a "supermajority vote."[214]

Regardless of Mr. Levin's efforts to persuade Americans that his proposal of term limits for Supreme Court Justices and the establishment of "legislative overrides" of select Supreme Court decisions will not eventuate in changing "the Court's core judicial functions or the independence of the Court as an institution,"[215] his scheme is a direct assault on the very principles espoused by Hamilton and the Founders. While his proposal does not directly impact the appointment process it most certainly inserts the political process into constitutional decision-making never intended by the Founders. One recommendation is a not-so-subtle threat to individual justices through the use of term limits and the other "solution" is a direct insertion of the political process in the role of the Court as the "final arbiter" of what constitutes the constitutional actions of government. It would appear that individual liberty will be better protected from the "overreach" of the federal government by legislative majorities. Why didn't Hamilton and Madison think of that? Abolish life terms for Supreme Court Justices—increase the cycles for political appointments to the Court; eliminate or significantly reduce the potential for providing finality to conflicting lower court decisions; and most importantly, segment any ultimate decision regarding the fundamental rights of all citizens regardless of state residency to the vote of legislative majorities.

Whether Mr. Levin and his contemporary Anti-Federalist cohorts' proposed "solutions" to the issues surrounding the seeming intractable paralysis of our political process will receive the support of the American people remains an open question. But what is apparent is that each of the "solutions" offered should be carefully examined to determine if they are grounded in the First Principles of the Founders vision of constitutional republican government. There is every reason to believe that they are anything but reflections of those who supported the Constitution and the establishment of the actual American Republic.

Conclusion

THE PERSPECTIVES ON HUMAN NATURE, ON government, and on the dangers of concentrated power provided by the Framers of the Constitution to contemporary Americans are important. Their insights can assist us as we evaluate public policy proposals offered by our "elected" and the "factions" which influence their decision-making. There is reason to believe, however, that a majority of citizens described to be "The New American Center,"[216] have serious doubt that the Constitution can assist us as we confront the issues of today. The last five if not six years of political gridlock in the country has only served to reinforce their frustration that our "least imperfect" process can be rebalanced on behalf of the majority of the citizenry instead of being driven by those unwilling to find compromise. Americans remain fearful of the future driven by the economic uncertainty surrounding their lives and that of the country. Those fears are not unfounded.

This investigation has been an effort to resurrect the Founding Visions, to provide the reader with the philosophical origins of our collective covenant and the Framers arguments for the establishment of a "More Perfect Union." Additionally, we have identified both the specific language of the Constitution and its mechanisms by which to protect individual liberty and secure the public welfare. Throughout the investigation numerous potential causes for the continuing gridlock have been noted and calling upon the insights of the Founders, some recommendations have been offered. In this final chapter of our journey through our constitutional history and its relevancy to contemporary public discourse, we will highlight some of the Framers' most important observations regarding their experiment in government. With these observations in mind, a list of public policy objectives will be offered for future analysis and debate. While an in-depth analysis of each subject is beyond the scope of this investigation, some issues which may be relevant in addressing the public policy objectives noted will be raised in an effort to facilitate a collective discussion of these and other related issues.

Messages from the Cavern Walls—The Founding Perspectives on Government and the Human Condition

In Chapter Eight, we identified the overarching first principles which form the basis of the Constitution and its aspirational objectives. While they originate from a world which at first glance appears to be dramatically different than that of America and the planet of the twenty-first century, the insights of Madison, Hamilton, Jefferson, and Franklin regarding the interaction of citizens remain relevant as we confront the underlying causes of gridlock in our political process. At the core of their vision of government was their belief that it must be a process—an enterprise between diverse individuals and groups which would reflect all the virtues and limitations found within the human condition. Therefore, they crafted a plan which they believed would maximize the aspirations of each citizen and yet protect against the abuse of power. While it was the "least imperfect" governmental system, they believed that its imperfections originated from as Madison observed "the nature of man." Their experiment in government then would depend upon a written contract which articulated divisions of powers, structural checks on the various departments of government, and a process by which to amend or abolish the agreement. This governmental process was a reflection of their understanding of the fallibility of human kind. Some of their most important observations regarding the necessity of establishing this contract with the people and for its continuance have been noted throughout our investigation. These Founding Visions provided both the rationales for the letter and the spirit of the Constitution and the Bill of Rights. They are relevant insights which can assist us as we evaluate the short and long term public policy recommendations offered by this investigation. Some of their most important observations include the following:

- "It has been said that all government is evil. It would be more proper to say that the necessity of any government is a misfortune. This necessity however exists; and the problem to be solved is, not what form of government is perfect, but which form is least imperfect..." Madison[217]

- Among the numerous advantages promised by a well-constructed Union none deserves to be more accurately developed than its tendency to break and control the violence of factions..." Madison[218]

- "The influence of factious leaders may kindle a flame within their particular States, but will be unable to spread a general conflagration through the other States..." Madison[219]

- "...It is a just observation that the people commonly intend the public good. This often applies to their very errors. But their good sense would despise the adulator who should pretend that they always reason right about the means of promoting it. They know from experience that they sometimes err; and the wonder is that they so seldom err as they do, beset, as they continually are, by the wiles of parasites and the sycophants, by the snares of the ambitious, the avaricious, the desperate, by the artifices of men who possess their confidence more than they deserve it…" Hamilton[220]

- "…But the most common and durable source of factions has been the various and unequal distribution of property. Those who hold and those who are without property have ever formed distinct interests in society…The regulation of these various and interfering interests forms the principle task of modern legislation and involves the spirit of party and faction in the necessary and ordinary operations of the government." Madison[221]

- "…No man will subject himself to the ridicule of pretending that any natural connection subsists between the sun and the seasons and the period within which human virtue can bear the temptations of power…" Madison[222]

- "…The aim of every political constitution is or ought to be, first, to obtain for rulers men who possess most wisdom to discern, and most virtue to pursue, the common good of the society; and in the next place, to take the most effectual precautions for keeping them virtuous whilst they continue to hold the public trust…" Madison[223]

- (Discussing the ultimate check on abuse of power from the "elected") (That they would be) "…compelled to anticipate the moment when their power is to cease, when their exercise of it is to be reviewed, and when they must descend to the level from which they were raised—there forever to remain unless a faithful discharge of their trust shall have established their title to a renewal of it." Madison[224]

- (Arguing that a Bill of Rights would not protect our most fundamental rights and specifically addressing the enumeration of the right to a free press) "…What is liberty of press? Who can give it any definition which would not leave the utmost latitude for evasion? I hold it to be impracticable; and from this I infer that its security, whatever fine declarations may be inserted in any constitution respecting it, must altogether depend on public opinion and on the general spirit of the people and of the government. And here, after all, as is intimated upon another occasion, must we seek for the only solid basis of all our rights." Hamilton[225]

- "An enlightened citizenry is indispensible for the proper functioning of a republic. Self-government is not possible unless the citizens are educated sufficiently to enable them to exercise oversight." Jefferson[226]

- "The most effectual means of preventing the perversion of power into tyranny are to illuminate, as far as practicable, the minds of the people at large, more especially to give them knowledge of those facts which history exhibits that possessed thereby of the experience of other ages and countries, that they may be enabled to know ambition under all its shapes, and prompt to exert their natural powers to defeat its purposes." Jefferson[227]

- (Responding to a question by an interested citizen as to whether the Constitutional Convention had agreed upon a 'monarchy' or a 'republic') "A republic, if you can keep it." Franklin[228]

- (On the importance of political compromise and "joint wisdom") "I confess that there are several parts of this constitution which I do not at present approve, but I am not sure I shall never approve them: for having lived long, I have experienced many instances of being obliged by better information or fuller consideration, to change opinions even on important subjects, which I once thought right, but found otherwise. It is therefore that the older I grow, the more apt I am to doubt my own judgment and to pay more respect to the judgment of others...for when you assemble a number of men to have the advantage of their joint wisdom you inevitably assemble with these men, all their prejudices, their passions, their errors of opinion, their local interests, and their selfish views. From such an assembly can a perfect production be expected? It therefore astonishes me, Sir, to find this system approaching so near perfection as it does...Thus I consent, Sir, to this Constitution because I expect no better, and because I am not sure, that it is not the best..." Franklin[229]

- (On the importance of seeking political compromise) "...the advice of prudence must be to embrace the lesser evil and, instead of indulging a fruitless anticipation of the possible mischiefs which may ensue, to contemplate rather the advantageous consequences which may qualify the sacrifice." Madison[230]

- (While Franklin championed both the virtues and importance of wealth creation, particularly regarding small farmers and shopkeepers, the following language of a proposed Pennsylvania statute regarding the right to acquire private property which he attempted to implant in the state's constitution and his remarks on the extent of the natural right to property are important to note.) (On the proposed state constitutional language) "...That an enormous proportion of property vested in a few individuals is dangerous to the rights, and destructive of the common happiness, of mankind: and therefore every free state hath a right by its laws to discourage the possession of such property."[231]

- (On the natural right to property observation of Franklin.) "All property that is necessary to a man for the conservation of the individual and the propagation of the species, is his natural right which none can justly deprive him of: But all property superfluous to such purposes is the property of the public, who by their laws have created it, and who may therefore by other laws dispose of it, whenever the welfare of the public shall demand such disposition. He that does not like civil society on these terms, let him retire and live among savages. He can have no right to the benefits of society, who will not pay his club towards the support of it." Franklin[232]

Interwoven within these observations on liberty, the role of government, and the obligations of those who hold the public trust is the ever-present responsibility that citizens must play in monitoring the influence of ambition and power at all levels of the governmental process. While the Founders sometimes held differing views regarding where the balance should be struck between liberty and promotion of the public good, they found common ground through the process of open informed debate. They did so by utilizing the institutions of government which they crafted and by respecting the desires of the country determined through an electoral process representative of all Americans. If this country is to step back from the societal dangers created by the "divide and conquer" politics infecting our public policy decision-making, then we must heed the call of the Founders to demand leadership from those who we have selected to "hold the public trust." They must bring into the public forum the unfiltered facts associated with their proposed public policy recommendations. In so doing, they will be obligated to defend their proposals with a demonstration of their commitment to find political compromise within the context of our constitutional First Principles. No longer will superficial one line sound bites crafted by K-Street lobbyists or special interest factions and provided to them or their staffs prior to their scheduled "face time" through our broadcast monopolies be acceptable.

The following public policy objectives are central to any collective effort to confront and overcome the intransience and gridlock paralyzing our body politic. Without resolution of the fundamental issues surrounding these objectives, the Founders' vision of achieving a balance between liberty and promotion of the public good will continue to be held hostage by the "snares of the ambitious." Each of these subjects requires a much more extended analysis and is beyond the scope of this investigation. But particular attention in the following Public Policy Objectives: Comments and Questions section of our investigation has been given to the need to reinvigorate the obligations of citizenship and the equally essential effort to maximize each citizen's right to participation in our electoral processes. It is hoped, that consolidating some of the more specific public policy issues identified below into an initial discussion of the need to address the societal dangers of income inequality, the protection of the nation's economy, and the reduction of the influence of money on our political process, will stimulate future debate and resolution of the more specific public policy objectives enumerated.

- A Reinvigoration of the Importance of Citizenship
- Monitor and Protect the Fundamental Right of "One Person One Vote"
- Reduce the Influence of Money in the Political Process
- Monitor and Regulate the Concentration of Power in the Nation's Communication Industry
- Protect the Nation's Economy from Future "great recessions"
- Reform the Federal Tax Code
- Increase Transparency and Oversight of the "Administrative State"
- Monitor and Protect the Nation's Natural Resources
- Continue the Reformation of the Nation's Healthcare System
- Establish a "Working Wage"
- Reduce the Cost of Educational Opportunities

These public policy objectives, and many others which could be offered, have one important fact in common—They have all received little or no serious attention by the 112th and the 113th Congress of the United States. Regardless, of whether Americans would prefer to place more or less emphasis on the role of government in addressing the issues associated with each of these objectives, our collective disdain for the lack of leadership demonstrated by our "elected" has been reflected in public opinion poll after public opinion poll. At the time of this analysis, only 9% of the American public "approves" of the action or inaction of our "political elite."[233]

For some citizens the task of rebalancing our political process appears to be hopeless. Indeed, they could point to the aforementioned list of public policy objectives, and conclude that they only represent a "wish list" of those who cling to some idealized version of a return of the movie *Mr. Smith Goes to Washington*—a film which captured the hearts of millions of Americans at a time when the country was also gripped with doubt about its future. (The story featured Jimmy Stewart, the actor who most contemporary Americans will remember as their once-a-year-Christmas-movie-featured actor in, *It's A Wonderful Life*, who is again cast as the "everyman," enters politics and discovers the "dark side" of the process. Unwilling to accept the ever-present "snares of the ambitious," he challenges the status quo. In so doing, he finds the personal cost of such an enterprise, yet discovers the power of unyielding positive other—regarding leadership.) Some other critics will point to the absence of what they believe to be equally important public policy issues not identified and conclude that the list is woefully incomplete.

Of course, both observations are, to some degree, correct. There is an element of naiveté associated with a vision of our constitutional republican government which is depended upon the positive action of citizens to shape their own individual and collective destiny. And it is also without question that the list is incomplete and, depending upon unforeseen economic and international events, may require reformulation. But, our collective covenant was hammered out by citizens who refused to be victims of their circumstances. Instead they also held this naïve notion that they could control the forces of self-interest and concentrated power surrounding their lives by demanding a "faithful discharge" of those who they placed in positions of the "public trust." Nevertheless, the naysayers will ask "How do you expect Americans to have an impact on the achievement of the objectives enumerated or any others not listed?" The short answer is to accept your personal responsibility as a citizen.

It should come as no surprise that the first Public Policy Objective noted above is—A Reinvigoration of the Importance of Citizenship. This investigation has noted the present status of our collective understanding of government and its functioning. In so doing, a few suggestions were presented regarding how we might overcome some of the obstacles which have contributed to the problem of what appears to be a growing societal disconnect regarding our personal and collective responsibilities as citizens. Listed below, are some of the suggestions offered throughout our investigation which may assist in the accomplishment of this objective and others. The comments and subsequent questions are offered to reinvigorate a long overdue national discussion on the subjects. Each of these subjects should be evaluated in the context of the overriding first principles of the Founders noted throughout our investigation and consolidated in Chapter Eight. If these first principles are coupled with their observations on the role of government, the dangers of concentrated power, and the nature of humankind, there is every reason to believe that, as Franklin observed, our "joint wisdom" will find through as Madison described our "least imperfect" governmental process the solutions necessary to maintain our "More Perfect Union."

Public Policy Objectives:
Comments and Questions

A Reinvigoration of the Importance of Citizenship

(1) Individual Responsibility—This requires recognition from each citizen of their personal obligation in the process of protecting the importance of liberty and promotion of the public good through their own actions. Essential in the fulfillment of this requirement of citizenship is their insistence on receiving unfiltered information regarding public policy decision-making by their "elected." Each citizen must begin to reject the temptation of unthinking political party loyalty. Regardless of political party, we must challenge any candidate or political interest group that fails to provide nothing more than sloganeering or "fear campaigns" in an effort to glean support from "the party faithful." Additionally, Americans must demand transparency regarding the backgrounds and self-interests of those who seek our support for public policy "solutions." This requirement applies to both our political elite and those who fund special interest organizations which attempt to influence the political process. We must support those among our political representatives who offer public policy "solutions" for the nation, not just their constituents, crafted through compromise and defended through a balancing of constitutional first principles. In so doing, we must respectfully question authority through the process of critical thinking as we evaluate the actions of our "elected" at all levels of the governmental process.[234]

Ultimately, we must reject the arguments of those who would use race, region, religion, gender, or sexual preference, as a method to separate us into marketing "boxes" to seek our support for one public policy position or another. That is, while we can and should applaud our rich and diverse individual, familial, regional and cultural differences, we must be ever vigilant, as Hamilton observed, of the "…artifices of men who (attempt to) possess (our) confidence more than they deserve it." Finally, if we are to keep our republic as Franklin worried, we must take seriously the ultimate obligation of citizenship—*we must vote.*

We must vote in local, state, and national elections. We must vote in primary elections as well as national elections. It is our most solemn responsibility. While both political parties spend billions of dollars in an effort to solicit our support and the mass media reaps the vast majority of the bounty associated with the promotion of one of our political elite or another, at its core this process is the fundamental right and responsibility of citizenship. This right and obligation has come at a devastating cost to individual families, and the country throughout our history. It is a right and obligation that has yet to be realized by billions of individuals across the planet. It is the matrix which binds our "least imperfect" governmental process.

Yet, it is accurate to suggest that our political process is rife with problems which could deter even the most patriotic of citizen from participating in elections which appear to be a *fait accompli*. They could point to the influence of money, of unthinking political party loyalty, or of numerous other reasons to simply "stay home" and accept their perceived powerlessness in shaping their own destiny. After all they could rationalize their decision to not participate by pointing to the glaring inequities which have occurred since the "great recession" and conclude with the maxim that "the rich get richer and poor have children" is a statement of fact. We are at an important crossroad in our history. We can allow the "snares of the ambitious" to divide us or we can begin to take responsibility for our children's future by honoring those who fought and gave the ultimate sacrifice for their country by demanding leadership and "a faithful discharge" of our trust from the "elected" through the power of our vote.

(2) **Institutional Responsibilities**—The primary task of our public and private institutions must be the creation of a nationwide commitment to civic education. The reinvigoration of the importance of civic education can be achieved through the establishment of private/public partnerships which explore innovative techniques to encourage an understanding of the fundamental principles of citizenship and our constitutional republican government. Whether it is the use of social media, institutional incentive driven projects, traditional educational instruction environments, or a combination thereof, institutional recognition of the importance of citizenship and all that it entails will begin to increase the potential of achieving Jefferson's "enlightened citizenry."

The key to success of these efforts must be the encouragement, and in some instances, the requirement of teaching critical thinking. This process of analysis is fundamental to the survival of our constitutional republican democracy. Jefferson understood its importance. We must nurture it as an integral part of civic education. The ability to discern the real from the imagined; to distinguish between honest objective disagreement and manipulative hyperbole; is at the core of self-government. This gift that we must encourage in our private organizations and in our public institutions assists in creating a citizenry capable of treating like cases alike and different cases differently. It is the great equalizer from those who market the "boxes" which divide us in our culture and our government. It allows us to consider not only that which makes us each unique individuals but also those fundamental values which we have in common— which make us Americans. It encourages us to understand that Republicans can be committed to social justice, just as Democrats can be equally supportive of private enterprise.

But, if Jefferson's observations regarding an "enlightened citizenry" are to be reflected in a reinvigorated civic educational process, critical thinking must be taught and encouraged within the context of an unfiltered understanding of our history as a people. Important in the communication of our history must be an examination of our nation's philosophical origins regarding the nature of liberty and its limits, the specific language of our collective covenant—the Constitution—and the Founders' commitment to republican government with protection provided for those not within the political majority. Both the successes and failures need to be identified without collapsing into one-dimensional ideological diatribes. A study of our evolution as a country with a commitment to critical analysis can begin to cleanse the body politic of the demagoguery which has played a significant role in the gridlock of our political process over the last six years. Such a process of examination through our public institutions and private organizations will require us to reach beyond the comfort of the "boxes" we have created for ourselves or have been influenced to believe—a frightening prospect for some and a liberating one for others. Yet, one which as Jefferson noted will "… enable(us) to know ambition under its shapes, and prompt (us) to exert (our) natural powers to defeat its purposes (the perversion of power into tyranny)."[235]

The skill sets necessary to energize students throughout our educational process or Americans who are in the varied workplaces across the nation can and must be incentivized by leaders in our professional and public institutions. That is, depending upon the institutional setting and its private or public sector mission, individuals who have been identified to assist in the process of designing and implementing the process of civic education should receive increased status in the organization. This can be accomplished through various techniques, including but not limited to, such actions as organizational recognition via appointment to highly visible committee assignments or policy making groups; through intra-organizational and external media communications; and or, job promotion or salary incentives. The point is that institutional leadership must demonstrate its commitment to the importance of civic education through both its words and actions.

In Chapter Five, we identified even more specific recommendations which might reinforce the importance of critical thinking throughout our educational process. For example, it was noted that a reexamination of the curricular options available to students in our colleges of education across the country for teacher "certification" should include more substantive course work in a broad range of subject areas in an effort to provide intellectual content to be coupled with the existing emphasis on teaching methodology. Pre-professional education was also addressed regarding the need for more opportunities within their curriculum to participate in classroom discussions which emphasized critical thinking. And, in the case of advanced legal education it was proposed that a reexamination should be instituted regarding entry requirements, the substantive course work required to obtain a Juris Doctor, the evaluative model used to grant licensure to practice law, and the type of subject matter offered for continuing education in the legal profession.

Of course, these recommendations and many others not noted will begin the process which Jefferson understood was necessary to provide citizens with"... knowledge of those facts which history exhibits that possessed thereby of the experiences of other ages and countries..." to recognize abuse of power regardless of its source. But his "enlightened citizenry" must have a mechanism by which to monitor "...ambition under all its shapes...." All the techniques created to revitalize our individual and institutional responsibilities associated with citizenship can be rendered meaningless if the desires of what Madison described as the "great body of the People" are denied expression through manipulation of our electoral processes.

Questions to Consider:

- What other forms of citizen participation should be encouraged or required through our private and public institutions?

- Should we establish a one year commitment of public service for all citizens who reach the age of eighteen? If so, should public service opportunities include not only entry into the armed forces but also participation in not for profit organizations which promote other-regarding citizen participation?

- What reforms, if any, should be instituted throughout our educational system to reinforce the importance of an objective understanding of our history and the intended functioning of our governmental process?

Monitor and Protect the Fundamental Right of "One Person One Vote"

(1) Securing the Consent of the Governed—At the core of the survival of the governmental process crafted by the Founders was a respect for and an allegiance to republican governance. While we must always be vigilant as James Madison observed of the potential of abuse of power and "...the invasion of private rights..." from "...acts in which the government is the mere instrument of the majority...," the alternative of governing through "minority governments"[236] he believed was even more prone to the "...bias of interest or the seduction of power."[237] Therefore, Madison and his colleagues understood that the desires "of the people themselves"[238] must ultimately be determined through a national electoral process. The Framers were careful to craft a selection process which they believed would reflect the wishes of the majority of Americans through their choice of a President, Representatives, and Senators. In Chapter Three of our investigation we discussed the rationales provided by Madison in the design of our bicameral legislative process and his perspectives on the proposed process and the individuals who would be selected to hold positions of the "public trust."[239] While he was always quick to note the potential for abuse of power and therefore designed an electoral process which divided power and required limited periods of tenure in office, he understood that their experiment in republican governance would fail if consent of the governed was not ultimately achieved.

Over the last six years the country has experienced two Presidential elections and numerous primary and mid-term elections. The result of these elections has produced the re-election of Barack Obama for two terms of office as the President of the United States. Our midterm and primary elections have brought to the 112th and now the 113th Congress of the United States a composition of political representatives who have won election or reelection from very disparate state electoral processes. The Popular Vote tally of the 2012 Presidential election was as follows: Obama—65,917,258 votes (51%); Romney—60,932,235 votes (47.15%). The Electoral College vote was: Obama—332 (61.7%); Romney—206 (38.3%) with a total of 538 votes registered. Democrats running for election or reelection to the House of Representatives received 1.4 million more votes than their Republican opponents. But Republicans won control of the House of Representatives by a 234–201 margin.[240] How is such a result possible in an electoral process designed to register the desires of the "great body of the People" through their popular vote for members of the House of Representatives?

The answer is—Gerrymandering of state and local electoral districts.[241] That is, the redrawing or "packing" and "cracking" of groups of voters into electoral districts across a state which will result in a predetermined smaller number of representatives from larger populations of voters in high density regions of each state and correspondingly create more electoral districts from low density state populations producing more representatives. Therefore, even though large swaths of voters in a high density population—name any large metropolitan area of the country—may overwhelmingly support one candidate, if a majority of other typically lower density population districts are created state wide, the influence of the larger number of citizens' vote can be nullified, or reduced in significance. This technique of manipulating voting patterns to maintain political power or to influence the outcome of our electoral process has been with us since the beginning of the republic. In fact, the name "Gerrymandering" was allegedly derived from the actions of Eldridge Gerry, a powerful delegate to the Constitutional Convention, who supposedly used a similar scheme to insure support for ratification of the Constitution.

(2) The Constitutional Requirements for the Protection of "One Person, One Vote"—Article I, Section 2 of the Constitution delegates power to the "People of the several States" to determine who will be selected to represent them in the House of Representatives. Therefore, throughout our history state legislatures have been assigned the constitutional responsibility to shape the electoral process by which members of the House of Representatives of the United States will be selected. As the population of the country has grown and the concentration of citizens has shifted from rural to more metropolitan urban centers the design of electoral districts which reflect the desires of the majority of citizens via their popular vote for both state and national representatives has been a target of manipulation by political party operatives.

Throughout this long period of population shifting, the Supreme Court resisted review of state voting processes for congressional elections until the early 1960's when they were challenged as a form of state sponsored disenfranchisement of African–Americans. The Court struggled with whether they should address the issues involved or whether they should be addressed through Congressional action. One year prior to the enactment of the Civil Rights Act, the Court began to signal its concern with the potential that ill-conceived state electoral districts could have on equal protection considerations for "…all who participate…" in the electoral process. Writing for the Court in Gray v. Sanders,[242] a 1963 case in which the Court invalidated the state of Georgia's method by which to select through primary elections its statewide officials, Mr. Justice Douglas observed "(The) conception of political equality from the Declaration of Independence, to Lincoln's Gettysburg Address, the Fifteenth, Seventeenth, and Nineteenth Amendments can mean only one thing—one person, one vote." One year later and with the enactment of the Civil Rights Act by the Congress of the United States as a legislative backdrop the Court in Wesberry v. Sanders[243] once again reviewed the voting procedures established by the state of Georgia in a congressional districting statute.

The statute created some voting districts which were sometimes twice the population of others—what is now described as electoral "packing." The Supreme Court struck down the state statute. Writing for the majority, Mr. Justice Black wrote "The command of Article I. Section 2, that Representatives be chosen 'by the People of the several States' means that as nearly as is practicable one man's vote in a congressional election is to be worth as much as another's."[244] While the Supreme Court has addressed the subject of reapportionment of voting districts and the associated issues with state created qualification for participation in the electoral process in numerous cases, one case, Reynolds v Sims[245] another 1964 decision, remains instructive regarding the constitutionally legitimate and illegitimate techniques by which state legislatures may shape electoral districts.

While this decision, similar to the cases noted above, did not directly address the practice of "gerrymandering," numerous perspectives were offered by the Court as to how the mandates of Article I, Section 2 and the Equal Protection Clause of the Fourteenth Amendment should be balanced by state legislative bodies in the creation of their electoral processes. Writing for the majority of the Court, Mr. Justice Warren wrote:

> ...the fundamental principle of representative government in this country is one of equal representation for equal numbers of people, without regard to race, sex, economic status, or place of residence within a State. Our problem then, is to ascertain (whether) there are any constitutionally cognizable principles which would justify departures from the basic standard of equality among voters in the apportionment of seats in state legislatures.[246]

The case involved the state of Alabama's failure to establish reapportionment procedures based on population every ten years as mandated by their state constitution. The state legislature had failed to implement such procedures since 1901. Using data collected through the 1960 census, the Court noted that only 25.1% of the State's population "resided in districts represented by a majority of the members of the Senate and only 25.7% lived in counties which could elect a majority of members of the House of Representatives." The Court then determined that "Population-variance ratios of up to about 41–1 existed in the Senate, and up to about 16-to-1 in the House." The question then for the Court was whether such disparities between the population of citizens of Alabama and the actual political representation in both legislative bodies was the result of some constitutionally permissible legislative purpose. If not, the state procedures were a violation of the Fourteenth Amendment's Equal Protection Clause.

The majority of the Court concluded that Alabama's failure to institute a re-apportionment plan based on a decennial census as mandated by their state constitution was a violation of the Equal Protection Clause of the Fourteenth Amendment. There were numerous disagreements among members of the Court eventuating in a majority opinion, a concurring opinion offered by two justices, and a dissenting opinion provided by two others justices. Some of the observations of members of the Court in Reynolds v Sims remain important as we try to determine what mechanisms we can establish to rebalance our contemporary electoral process. Mr. Justice Warren believed that "Diluting the weight of votes because of place of residence impairs basic constitutional rights under the Fourteenth Amendment just as much as invidious discrimination based upon factors such as race, or economic status."[247] He went on to observe that:

> ...A nation once primarily rural in character becomes predominantly urban. Representation schemes once fair and equitable become archaic and outdated. But the basic principle of representative government (remains)— the weight of a citizen's vote cannot be made to depend on where he lives. Population is, of necessity, (the) controlling criterion for judgment in legislative (apportionment)...This is an essential part of the concept of a government of laws not men. This is at the heart of Lincoln's vision of "government of the people, by the people, (and) for the people.[248]

But what weight must be assigned to the concentration of population within a state as it determines how to shape its electoral districts? Accepting that population is a major criteria in determining whether the Equal Protection Clause has been violated by "gerrymandering" electoral districts, what formula for evaluation will reflect the importance of "one person-one vote" and yet also take into consideration other "legitimate governmental interests," not impacting on race or economic status, which may reflect the unique characteristics of each state?

The majority of the Court did not offer anything close to a precise calculation in Sims but Mr. Justice Warren did provide an observation which may assist us as we confront the problem. He wrote:

The Equal Protection Clause requires that a State make an honest and good faith effort to construct districts, both houses of its legislature, as nearly of equal population as is practicable. We realize that it is a practical impossibility to arrange legislative districts so that each has an identical number of residents, or citizens, or voters. Mathematical exactness or precision is hardly a workable constitutional requirement.[249]

It would appear then that, at a minimum, in cases involving a State's blatant failure to reconfigure their electoral districts based on census data gathered every ten years and which demonstrate large population variance ratios in the political selection process, the mandate of the Equal Protection Clause of the Fourteenth Amendment may be violated. The lack of precision regarding how to discern "an honest and good faith effort" and the failure to identify what other considerations could be involved in determining whether there may be a "legitimate governmental interest" which may create unequal populations of voters in State electoral districts was raised by two Justices in their concurring opinion. In fact, while Justice Clark and Justice Stewart agreed with the result in Reynolds v. Sims, they joined the dissent in five other cases decided the same day which invalidated the State apportionment procedures of Colorado, Delaware, Maryland, Virginia, and New York. The various concerns expressed by Justice Clark and Stewart regarding the use of an equal population formula by the majority centered upon their view of representative government.

While agreeing with the majority in Sims that Alabama had violated the demands of the Fourteenth Amendment, they cautioned the majority that their rationale, presumably of "one person one vote," was an unworkable standard as a constitutional mandate. Mr. Justice Stewart expressed his frustration in his dissent in the other five cases and observed "...I could not join in the fabrication of a constitutional mandate which imports and forever freezes one theory of political thought into our Constitution, and forever denies to every State any opportunity for enlightened and progressive innovation."[250] He believed that representative government is a "...process of accommodating group interests through democratic institutional arrangements..." and "... this ideal is approximated in the particular apportionment system of any State by a realistic accommodation of the diverse and often conflicting political forces operating within the State."[251] Ultimately, he wrote that this "realistic accommodation" can best be achieved through what he described as a "strongly held American tradition." That practice he suggested was that "...the public interest is composed of many diverse interests, and that in the long run it can better be expressed by a medley of component voices than by the majority's monolithic command..."[252] He and Justice Stewart offered a different evaluative standard than the population based technique used by the majority. The test to determine if State apportionment plans were constitutional pursuant to the Equal Protection Clause of the Fourteenth Amendment had two requirements: (1) It must "…in light of the State's own characteristics and needs, the plan must be a rational one. … (2) "…the plan must be such as not to permit the systematic frustration of the will of a majority of the electorate of the State."[253]

What we are left with after examining the majority and concurring rationales offered in Reynolds v. Sims are two views of the meaning of constitutional republican government. The majority of the Court understood that the principle required, at a minimum "an honest and good faith effort" to create electoral districts which accounted for population density in the production of political representatives within a state. While other criterion presumably could be used in the shaping of their electoral districts, if "one person one vote" was to be accomplished as demanded by the controlling principle of majoritarian republican government then population density must "of necessity (be)…the controlling criterion…." Thus, apportionment schemes which established electoral districts which provided for regional representation—regardless of population density—and resulted in producing a majority of representatives from low population density regions of the state were presumptively a violation of the majoritarian principle underpinning our system of republican governance.

On the other hand, the concurring justices rejected the use of any one criterion to evaluate state electoral apportionment plans. Instead they believed that republican governance required a "realistic accommodation" of "diverse and often conflicting political forces operating within the State." They believed that using population density as a "controlling criterion" would deny states with the "opportunity for enlightened and progressive innovation." Instead they offered what they believed to be a more open ended constitutional test. As long as the apportionment plan was crafted "in light of the State's own characteristics and needs" and did not result in what they described as "the systematic frustration of the will of the majority of the electorate" the apportionment plan would not violate principles of republican government demanded by the Equal Protection Clause of the Fourteenth Amendment. Both perspectives reflect important considerations for the continuance of our system of rules.

Our constitutional republican government cannot endure if our political process does not culminate in reflecting the desires of the "great body of the People" as Madison and his colleagues understood. The aspirational objective of achieving "one person one vote" as expressed by the majority in Reynolds v. Sims is central to the Founders belief that majoritarian rule surpassed any other government reliant on minority rule. Their understanding of tyranny produced by the minority ruling the majority was noted throughout the ratification process of the Constitution. The observations by Justice Douglas, Justice Black, and Justice Warren in the aforementioned cases correctly noted the overriding importance of monitoring any governmental electoral process which results in a diminishment of the right of each citizen to vote or to have their interests fairly represented in the determination of candidates for political office whether on the local, state, or national level. Therefore, the utilization of evaluative models which provide data regarding voting patterns, the concentration of population, and the outcome of apportionment plans by state legislatures which culminate in the dilution of votes of large numbers of Americans based on their place of residence is central to determining the desires of the "great body of the People."

Justices Steward and Clark correctly noted the importance of accommodation of the diverse interests in the functioning of our republican governmental processes and the need for a reflection of those interests through a state apportionment plan. But unlike the majority, they offered no objective mechanism by which to measure the constitutional legitimacy of the plan other than to require that it be "a rational one" and one which would not "permit the systematic frustration of the will of the majority of the electorate of the State." We are then left with one technique, provided by the Sims majority, which requires statistical calculation to determine "population—variance ratios" in an analysis of whether "one person one vote" has been achieved through state electoral apportionment plans. The other standard, offered by justices Stewart and Clark, requires that the state plan be "rational" and not be a vehicle for denying the will of the majority of its citizens. Unfortunately, their "test" was absent any guidance on how to determine whether the state's plan created a "systematic frustration" of the desires of a majority of its citizens. It may be that a combination of the two perspectives into one evaluative standard and the institution of public policy initiatives to legislatively address the impact of contemporary efforts which dilute the votes of great numbers of Americans would begin to reflect both perspectives.

For example, the federal judiciary could treat all challenges to state re-districting of electoral voting districts which allege dilution of their vote based on population discrimination with a two-step constitutional "test": First, any case which, presents a *prima facie* case of voter dilution based on population density or residency as determined by a calculation of the population variance ratios of the state in question, shall be presumed to be in violation of Article I, Sec. 2 and the Equal Protection Clause of the Fourteenth Amendment of the Constitution. Second, the state in question however, may overcome this presumption of unconstitutional behavior if it can demonstrate that other "rational" objectives (not based on race, or economic status) required the creation of electoral districts which resulted in vote dilution based on voter residence. This "test" would allow for an objective calculation through statistical analysis of the disparities of weight assigned to each citizen's vote throughout the state. But if disparities were demonstrated, the "test" would permit the state to overcome the presumption of unconstitutionality by presenting other state interests which might justify the imbalance in political representation and provide evidence of other "rational" efforts instituted to address the imbalance created. One way by which a state might be able to overcome a showing of vote dilution based on population density and provide evidence of its "good faith" in the design of its electoral districts would be to design electoral processes which provide for increased state-wide voter participation in primary as well as general elections.

(3) Innovative Methods to "Secure the Consent of the Governed"—One potential technique which may assist in reducing vote dilution and demonstrate the state's "good faith" in aspiring toward the constitutional objective of "one person, one vote" may be the creation of "open primaries." Presuming that the vote dilution is not the result of political manipulation via gerrymandering of voting districts but rather the consequence of "natural packing" of citizens through population shifts, the institution of "open primaries" would increase the potential of citizen participation in primary elections in states where up to one third of voters are excluded from voting because they have declared themselves as "independents" and are prohibited by state law from voting in either Republican or Democratic primaries. An "open primary" process then would permit voters, regardless of their political party affiliation, to participate in primary elections held to determine which candidate(s) from whatever political party would stand for general election(s). As of 2012 twenty-one states have some form of an "open primary" electoral process while the remainder of states continue to restrict voter participation in primary elections to those citizens who have declared their political party affiliation. While the establishment of "open primaries" in the remaining twenty-nine states would enable citizens who do not "self-identify" as Republican or Democrat the opportunity to express their support for one candidate or another to stand for general election, the process does possess both positive and negative potential results.[254]

"Open primaries" encourage voter participation and lead to greater turn out at the polls. Additionally, because of the influx of larger numbers of voters the process may reduce the number of ideologically "extreme" candidates. That is, because candidates must appeal to a wider swath of voters they will be encouraged to present more "centrists" views to accommodate the broader electorate. However, "open primaries" do invite what has been described as "party crashing" which allows opposition political parties to vote for who they believe are the most extreme candidate from the other party in an effort to place him or her on the ballot for the general election against who they perceive to be a more "electable" member from their party.[255] Whether this practice, or its eventuality, is enough to discourage the creation of "open primaries" remains to be seen. What is not unclear is that the institution of "open primaries" by state legislatures would be one tangible example of their "good faith" in increasing citizen participation in the electoral process throughout their jurisdictions and provide evidence of their intention to solicit as much voter input into the political representation process regardless of voter residency. This effort by state legislatures to broaden the base for voter participation would be a valuable example of its "rational" effort to prevent the "systematic frustration of a majority of the will of the electorate" as urged by justices Stewart and Clark noted above and would provide support for the majority in Sims' argument that the desires of the "great body of the People" must be solicited. There may be, however, an even more powerful technique for reflecting the will of Americans in our electoral processes—that is, the creation of bi-partisan state citizen redistricting commissions. The largest state in population in the country has begun such a process and has coupled its mandates with another primary process—The Top Two Primary.

The Voters First Act,[256] passed by state referendum in 2008 in California, empowered the California State Auditor to establish the Citizens Redistricting Commission. Created in 2010 through the efforts of an appointed Applicant Review Panel, the Commission is comprised of fourteen members. Pursuant to the Act, the Commission was mandated to "...draw the district lines in conformity with strict, nonpartisan rules designed to create districts of relatively equal population that will provide fair representation for all Californians." The Act permitted state legislative leaders to eliminate twenty four applicants from a pool of sixty. Three members of the Commission are designated as Democrats and three are Republicans with two individuals who "decline" to state their political affiliation or are from another political party with the addition of six other members who were deemed to be the "most qualified" applicants. Three evaluative criteria are used to determine what constitutes "most qualified" for selection to the Commission.[257]

An applicant must possess "relevant analytical skills," "the ability to be impartial," and "a demonstrated appreciation for California's diverse demographics and geography." All three requirements can be criticized as too open-ended and easily subjected to manipulation. But, nevertheless, they can be cited by reviewing courts as a "good faith" effort to find members who are capable of fairly addressing the complexities of drawing electoral districts which reflect the diversity of interests in a large population. In addition to possessing these personal characteristics Commission members are also required to use computer software and to be trained on the "diverse demographics and geography" of the state. Ultimately they then must produce redistricting maps which must receive 9 votes for approval (included within that vote count must be three "yes" votes from members registered with the two largest political parties).[258]

It may be too soon to determine whether California's innovative attempt via the Voters First Act will be successful in fulfilling its objective of providing electoral districts which reflect "fair representation for all Californians." But what is clear is that the desires of the "great body of the People" in the state of California were reflected in the creation of the Voters First Act. This bi-partisan effort to create electoral districts which reflect a commitment to address the concentration of population and also account for the special characteristics of the state bode well for fair representation which is at the core of the concept of "one person one vote." The Top Two Primary electoral system may also assist in the accomplishment of that goal.

California and the state of Washington, with Nebraska and Louisiana using a variation of the electoral system, have utilized this method in their primary elections.[259] This electoral system places all candidates, regardless of political party affiliation, on the same ballot. The top two candidates who receive the most votes in the primary are then placed on the ballot in the general election. The Top Two primary system eliminates party primaries altogether. The elimination of political party primaries, which produce candidates who often shape their campaign platforms in more ideologically strident tones in an effort to engender the support of normally smaller numbers of party loyalist who participate in primary elections, theoretically broadens the electorate to all citizens. That is, similar to some of the "open primary" processes, this primary system opens voting to all citizens regardless of political party affiliation or to self-described Independents. But unlike the "open primary" electoral option, the Top Two system can result in two individuals of the same political party running against one and other in the general election.[260]

Since its creation in 2012 the Top Two Primary process in California has received a wide range of responses regarding its impact on political representation in the state.[261] One election cycle is too narrow a window to evaluate whether the objective of this primary electoral process to increase citizen participation by eliminating the requirement of political party affiliation in the selection of candidates for the general election will be successful. What is clear is that political party operatives are not supporters of the system. Even in electoral districts which have been designed prior to the establishment of the Citizens Redistricting Commission and which are "packed" with voters from one political party, incumbents must compete with other candidates from a much larger group of individuals both within and outside of the incumbent's party to survive a primary election and stand for the general election.

Depending upon the ideological views of the candidates participating in the primary, political party central committees and their chosen candidate must calibrate their campaigns to respond to the positions of their most powerful rival or rivals. While this competition amongst candidates is viewed by some as a way to reduce the "hyper-partisanship" created by "extreme" political party platforms catering to relatively small numbers of ideological true believers on the "right" and "left" in our politics, others have claimed that the process has produced even more partisanship and produced increased polarization of members of Congress. Supporters of the Top Two Primary process, however, point to the fact that very few members of the California delegation to Congress, including Republicans, supported the efforts by Tea Party members to "shut down" the government in the fall of 2013 and appeared to be willing to enter into "bipartisan" negotiations.[262]

The Top Two Primary process may or may not alone resolve the ideological polarization of our political process. But combined with other efforts such as the California Redistricting Commission and nationwide press attention to the negative consequences of state legislative bodies which refuse to reshape their electoral districts, it may be that the "New American Center" has reason to believe that their alleged pessimism regarding our Constitution and its "least imperfect" governmental process was premature. What is, without question, is that the participation of this important segment of our citizenry in the primary electoral process is essential in the rebalancing of our public policies through political compromise.

Questions to Consider:

- What are other factors, in addition to population, which should be identified regarding the establishment of reshaping electoral districts? How can the desires of "the great body of the People" in each state be reflected but also account for the needs of citizens who reside in low population density regions?

- What is meant by the term "bipartisan"? Does it mean ideological neutral? Or, does it infer that our process of public policy creation should seek "political compromise"? Are there any "compromises" which violate mandates of the Constitution and the Bill of Rights?

- How would you balance the demands of majority rule with the Founders' admonition to protect the rights of those not in the political majority"?

Confront the Societal Dangers of Income Inequality, Protect Our Economic System, and Reduce the Influence of Money on Our Political Process

(1) As has been noted throughout our investigation—facts do matter—or, at least they should—Forty six million Americans live in poverty; the wages of American workers, adjusted for inflation, are below the average of workers in 1964; the top 1%—.01% of Americans increased their wealth creation over the last two decades by 200%; most of the income distribution since the "great recession" has flowed to this segment of our population; our political elite—members of Congress—have collectively managed to increase their personal or familial wealth by 5%, if not more, since the last study of their economic status in 2012; the vast majority of American's household wealth has decreased by at least 30% since the beginning of the crash of the financial markets in 2007–2008;[263] studies of wealth creation in America have found that the most important factor in the accumulation of wealth is inheritance.[264] It has been noted that up to 80% of all Americans' ultimate wealth creation is determined by the passing of wealth from one generation to the next;[265] a small number of our so-called "banks"—Goldman Sacks, J P Morgan Chase, Morgan Stanley, etc.,—hold trillions of dollars and continue to participate in proprietary trading without serious domestic or international regulatory oversight increasing the potential of but another public "bailout";[266] our federal tax code continues to allow corporations and select individuals to profit from numerous "exemptions" or tax shelters which result in low or no tax obligations;[267] and, our political campaign processes have become the playground for the highest campaign contributor(s) who argue for public policies which guarantee continued "tax incentives" for their special interests claiming "job creation" regardless of any empirical data to justify the pitch;[268] the American Dream—the aspirational goal of rising through the social class structures of the country through hard work, educational advancement, and sacrifice—is in danger of extinction;[269] and, may be the most disturbing fact of all, the political tactics of gridlock, marketed as a political philosophy by some of our political elite and their oligarchical supporters have kidnapped our political process in the Congress of the United States.[270]

Too strident a commentary? Hardly. Indeed, it may be that we have come to this point in our history because we have been unwilling to collectively enter these dark waters hoping that one of our highly marketed political "leaders" will come to the rescue. But what we have discovered throughout this investigation is that the Founders provided us with a process of governance which requires our participation. While each of the following subjects obviously requires a much more in-depth analysis than can be provided here, hopefully, the following comments and recommendations will begin a discussion regarding the necessary remedies to these and other issues facing the country and encourage us to once again become more than just observers in fulfilling the Founders aspirational objectives for America.

(2) Rebalancing the Nation's Tax Code—Locke's, Madison's and Franklin's perspectives on the relationship between the individual and civil society are important in any discussion of this subject. As we enter this always controversial subject a brief restatement of their commentary may help us place the following recommendations in context with their observations.

It will be remembered that while Locke was unyielding regarding the importance of each individual possessing the "natural right" to reap the "fruits of his labor," he qualified that fundamental given with the observation that it was "… useless, as well as dishonest, to carve himself too much, or take more than he needed."[271]

Contrary to the bond trader's bombastic commentary which allegedly triggered the "Tea Party" movement and who confidently suggested that Benjamin Franklin would be "rolling over in his grave" regarding the federal government's attempt at providing mortgage refinancing for the "losers" at the beginning of the crash of the markets,[272] Franklin's actual statements and actions reflect a completely different view of the relationship between the individual and the community. He observed that "… an enormous proportion of property vested in a few individuals is dangerous to the rights, and destructive to the common happiness, of mankind: and, therefore every free state hath a right by its laws to discourage the possession of such property."[273] He, like Locke, believed that every citizen possessed the "natural right" to acquire all the property "necessary… for the conservation of the individual and the propagation of the species…," but he went on to conclude that "…all property superfluous to such purposes is the property of the public, who by their laws have created it, and who may therefore by other laws dispose of it, whenever the welfare of the public shall demand such disposition…"[274] With the stinging clarity which rendered him one of the most respected members of the Founders and widely popular author and observer of early American life, Franklin concluded that "…He that does not like civil society on these terms, let him retire and live among savages. He can have no right to the benefits of society, who will not pay his club towards the support of it."[275]

Madison also recognized that if their experiment in government was to succeed, then the "…most durable source of factions" which were derived from the "various and unequal distribution of property" must be regulated. In fact, he observed that,"…the regulation of these various and interfering interests (those who hold and those without property) forms the principle task of modern legislation…" He understood that the regulation of these interests must be the result of balancing the "…spirit of party and faction in the necessary and ordinary operations of the government."[276]

Our collective efforts across time in finding some accommodation between the numerous interests noted by Madison have resulted in the multi-level governmental system of local, state, and federal taxation which we are experiencing in 2014. That the overwhelming majority of Americans comply with our tax laws is a fact. That we collectively fail to understand the complexity of our tax laws and are often outraged by what appears to be an intentional manipulation of its design and implementation by powerful factions is also a fact. Indeed, as was pointed out in Chapter Two of our investigation, our federal tax code has become a fertile ground for "divide and conquer" politics, spurred on by K-Street lobbyists and their oligarchical supporters. That being noted, other special interest groups who claim to represent citizens who are recipients of social security or healthcare benefits also bring their power to combat "those who hold" property.

But recognition of both the Founders understanding of the absolute necessity and fundamental legitimacy of our individual responsibilities to as Franklin put it to "pay (our) club" toward the support of the collective community, has not resulted in any leadership from our political elite to provide an honest discussion of how to accomplish the goal of encouraging wealth creation and yet begin to reverse the widening economic divide between classes of our citizenry. It would appear that fear, by those who we have earlier described as "political survivalists" within our political class, of retaliation by the campaign contributors often hidden from public view behind the protected walls of so-called non-for-profit tax exempt funding organizations, has played a significant role in making the subject of tax reform in the halls of Congress a public policy issue for another day.

But a national dialogue regarding how best to balance our quest for the security that wealth creation brings with our innate understanding that as Locke observed that it was,"…useless, as well as dishonest, to carve himself too much, or take more than he needed" is exactly what must be done. Just what do we believe is "too much"? Or, put another way, "How much is enough"? What shared responsibilities must be instituted to assist in the Herculean efforts necessary to reduce our national deficit to manageable levels, to incentivize job creation, reduce the income inequality gap, to continue to honor our commitments to and protect our growing aging population, and to revitalize the American Dream for our children? Some of the answers to these questions begin with a reformation of our federal tax code, the institution of actual regulation of our "financial industry," and a bipartisan effort to reduce the impact of money in our political process.

One needs only to remember the significant gaps in wealth acquisition in England and the aspirations of individuals who fled to the "New World" in hope for a more secure future or of the literally billions of citizens of the planet Earth in the twenty-first century who possess similar aspirations but are mired in seemingly endless violent conflicts, to understand both the legitimacy and urgency associated with establishing transparent and balanced methods for taxation across our social classes. It simply is disingenuous—if not downright dangerous—to describe Americans to be either "makers" or "takers."[277] Just as it is equally destructive to claim that personal accomplishment which some-times brings with it financial reward is always a reflection of greed.[278] These are the arguments of the political marketers—the box makers—who profit from the one line sound bites which divide us. What is accurate is that one segment of our citizenry which has secured wealth has been asked to "pay their club," while those who have been unsuccessful in obtaining wealth or are hampered because of age or disability contribute to a lesser degree. What is also important to understand is that to achieve a rebalancing of our system of taxation we must distinguish between income generation and wealth creation. That is, while a variety of modifications can be designed within our federal income taxation process to repair imbalances in tax rates across the income spectrums of Amer-icans, our focus must also be on the major contributor to the vast disparities in wealth creation—inheritance.[279]

Depending upon which "study" of our taxation process one identifies for one reform or no reform of our present federal tax code there are a few generally accepted facts. The first is that a relatively small percentage of Americans con-tribute the most to our collective effort to fund the functioning of our federal government through the income tax process. Using the data presented in 2010 regarding 2007 tax revenue creation, the top 1% of Americans earned 22% of the national income and paid 40% of the federal taxes; the top 5% of Americans earned 37% of the national income and contributed 61% of the federal taxes; the top 10% of Americans earned 48% of the national income and paid 71% of the federal taxes; the top 25% of Americans earned 68% of the national income and contributed 85% of the federal taxes; the bottom 50% of Americans earned 12%

of the national income and contributed 3% through federal income taxation.[280]

Regardless of how one "spins" the aforementioned data it is true that, for the most part, only a quarter of our citizenry is making a significant contribution to our collective goals determined by our political representatives via our federal income taxation process. That being said the top 25% to 1% of our population produced/received/earned 88% of the national income while the bottom 50% of Americans produced/received/earned only 12%. It is also a fact that the bottom 50% of Americans, while contributing significantly less than the top 1% of income tax payers, did "pay their club" to the community via payroll taxes and numerous excise taxes.[281] Another important fact to note is that this data is from 2007—right before the so-called "great recession" in 2008. Since this time it has been reported that 93% of the "distributional effect" (increase in wealth creation) has gone to the top 1%.[282] It is also true that modest increases in tax rates on the top 1% of Americans were instituted as part of so-called budget "compromises" by the Congress in an effort to avoid a politically manufactured "fiscal cliff" emergency. One result of this "compromise" was the reformation of estate taxes.

Tax free limits (exclusions) on estate taxes were established in the American Taxpayer Relief Act of 2012 and passed into law in January of 2013.[283] That legislation, which received little comparative media attention, made permanent as part of the tax code exemptions, from federal taxation, amounts up to $5.34 million dollars for each individual's estate. In addition to automatically indexing the figure to inflation for future years, a surviving spouse may add any amount not used in the decedent's estate to their total estate tax exemption totaling up to $10,680,000 dollars beginning in 2014. The estate tax rate after the aforementioned exemptions are exhausted is 40%. Therefore, 60% of the decedent's estate, after potentially $10,680,000 is excluded from estate taxation is also capable of being distributed without taxation.[284] Of course, if one chooses, he or she may distribute portions or all of their wealth creation prior to their death to their children or other beneficiaries reducing or eliminating estate tax obligations. A variety of so-called "tax shelters" are available to the beneficiaries of such transfers which may eliminate, reduce or postpone their tax obligations.

As of 2014 there are more than 6.1 million American households—5.1% of our population—who have accumulated one million dollars in wealth. That figure does not include whatever capital (equity) each household has in their home. Approximately one million households have accumulated five million dollars or more.[285] The United States is the home of (depending upon which source is used) 515 to 442 billionaires and it remains the place of residence for the most billionaires on the planet. The top seven wealthiest Americans in 2013 include Bill Gates and Warren Buffet at the number one and two positions with $72 billion and $58.5 billion respectively, and tied for the sixth and seventh positions are Charles and David Koch at $36 billion a piece or $72 billion in the aggregate.[286] The largest segment of Americans—12.7 million—who have been described as the "Broader Affluent Population" has accumulated $500,000 to $1,000.000 in household wealth.[287]

It may be misleading to include this segment of our population in any discussion of our country's billionaires. Depending upon each citizen's place of residence, the cost of living, purchasing a home, etc., is significantly different. The fact that one lives in the cities of New York, Washington, San Francisco, for example, which have some of the most expensive housing in the country along with high cost of living requirements may distort their actual "wealth creation" compared with citizens who reside in other geographical regions of the country. That being noted, these citizens annual "income" taken collectively creates an easily identifiable group of Americans for income tax collection. But the tendency of grouping citizens into classifications based on their "income" or percentage of income tax contribution without examining the multitude of "exemptions" offered to a relatively small percentage of our wealthiest citizens through our income taxation process, our estate tax structure, and our "corporate tax" system is a serious problem if we are to fairly rebalance our 74,000 page tax code. However, once the mind numbing requirements and exemptions implanted into our taxation process through the efforts of 17,500 registered lobbyists in cooperation with our political elite are parsed, a few facts must be put before the American people and debated.

The first is that "income" is taxed—not wealth creation.[288] That being noted, our income tax code provides numerous methods by which to redefine the meaning of "income" and thereby create different techniques by which to avoid taxation. For example, if one does not declare "income" or a very small "income" then one is not required to pay income tax. Obviously this must apply to the poorest amongst us? It would only be logical. But there is more to the story. With the advice of excellent legal counsel some of our very wealthiest citizens also have declared little or no "income" in the process of reaping the "fruits of their labor." They have done so legally and pursuant to our tax code. Here is how the income tax avoidance process works. Instead of taking a salary for their efforts in managing a private equity fund (hedge fund), or a real estate partnership, for example, they are compensated by taking a share of the fund or project they "manage." They then become "owners" of the entity and in so doing their "ownership" under the present income tax rules allows their compensation to be defined as a "carried interest" not "income." The result is that "interest" is taxed as a "capital gain" at 20%—not at the 39.6% rate that most American's contribute when they declare their salary as "ordinary income."[289]

This "carried interest" definition also applies to ownership in stocks, real estate, and other assets. As these assets continue to appreciate (increase in value) no income tax is required until or if they are sold and the owner receives a financial benefit. But if these assets are not sold and the "owner" borrows against what may be a significant increase in value of the assets no income tax is required. Regardless of the potential wealth creation over time—if the assets are not sold—no tax. Upon the citizen's death he or she may pass the interest via the estate tax process which provides for up to $10,680,000 tax free to a decedent's surviving spouse, or distribute some or all of the wealth creation prior to death through another perfectly legal device called a "charitable contribution."

While this method of wealth transference is often believed to be, and often is, a societal benefit, it too can be legally manipulated for tax avoidance purposes.[290] How can such "charitable contributions," created to enhance the "public good," be used to shelter the transfer of wealth and power from generation to generation of our American oligarchy? Presume for a moment that one of the aforementioned billionaires or other multi-millionaires not mentioned establishes a "charitable trust." Also presume that the trust identifies the billionaire's or multi-millionaire's child or children as executors or salaried administrators of the trust. Pursuant to our current taxation rules such "charitable trusts" are not required to spend the wealth transferred into the trust. Instead IRS rules only require these "charities" to spend 5% of their assets annually (using the most "conservative" portfolio management "investments" available in the current stock market and through purchase of differing bonds this amount would probably represent the "interest" received on the trust's initial contribution or "principal").

Because the rules permit this amount to include "salaries" and "expenses," not only the finances necessary to fulfill the alleged "charitable purpose" behind the tax exempt trust, the children of the trust contributor may receive a "salary" for the life of the trust and are permitted to use part of the transferred wealth of the trust for whatever "expenses" are determined to be necessary in the functioning of their "administrative" duties. Remember, there is a requirement that at least 5% of the contribution for the trust must be spent. Hypothetically, if a contribution was made to establish a "charitable trust" which was designed to provide controlling interests for the contributor's children as described above and the trust amount was 1 billion dollars—you enter whatever amount you want—depending upon the number of children identified, their "salaries" plus "expenses" could be legally drawn from the "assets" of the trust totaling to a minimum of 50 million dollars annually and potentially more depending upon the success of the trust's investment portfolio. Even if the children's "salaries" are within reach of federal taxation the "expenses" claimed as necessary for the functioning of the trust may be sheltered from taxation. Such activities as social gatherings on behalf of the trust, travel costs, or real estate used in the administration of the "charitable" activities of the trust may be exempt from taxation and a "fringe benefit" to the children.[291]

It is important to remember that not one dime is taxed on the money transferred by members of our oligarchy into the "charitable trust" even if the wealth was created through the "appreciation" of their "assets" (their "ownership" or "management" in their hedge fund, stocks, real estate holdings, etc.) over time. Additionally, no estate tax is due on this "donation." Another interesting legal consequence of this transfer of wealth is that the individual who creates a charitable trust is insulated from creditors or from any proceeding via a divorce which attempt to "invade" the trust for compensation. The reason is that the donor to the "charity" no longer "owns" the proceeds—even if the donor's children control the trust.

The aforementioned analysis is intended as but one of literally hundreds of examples of how well intended rule creation established presumably to incentivize contributions for the "public good" may have unintended consequences. Contrary to what some may argue is an attack on individual liberty and the essence of the American Dream—wealth creation—recognition of the potential manipulation of our taxation process is at the core of what millions of Americans believe to be an out of control process which is unnecessarily complex and benefits only those few who can "game the system." The issue is not whether we should all "pay our club" as Franklin argued, but rather than in so doing the methods by which that debt to our fellow citizens is executed is deemed "fair." Central to the continuance of our constitutional republican democracy is trust in the institutions of government and in our system of rules. Providing a process by which citizens from all walks of life can contribute to the multitude of organizations created to provide a positive impact on the quality of life for our diverse communities is something to which we can proudly identify as part of the American character. And by carefully dissecting the rules which are in need of reformation we can rebalance the process whereby, regardless of social class, we all are asked to "play by the same rules."

That is, most Americans more than likely would support providing incentives to individuals and corporations who can demonstrate how their particular contributions to society advances the public good and thereby deserves special recognition pursuant to our tax code. But it strikes against any concept of fundamental fairness to shape and apply rules which in their application benefit a small fraction of our society and diminishes or eliminates their tax obligations and maintains or increases the wealth gap in the country. As has been noted pursuant to our present estate tax laws an individual can avoid taxation, protect up to almost six million dollars from any taxation on their death, or pass all their accumulated wealth to a surviving spouse totaling approximately to ten million, and still have whatever is remaining in the estate be taxed at 40% leaving 60% of their wealth to be passed without taxation. One does not have to be a solider in the class warfare conflicts created by the wealth creation gaps in the country and exacerbated since the so-called "great recession" to ask: "How much is enough?"

But as has been suggested, our tax code is replete with provisions which were created to incentivize or encourage a multitude of behaviors which, similar to "charitable contributions," reflect generally accepted American values. One such example is the code's mortgage deduction provision. It was designed to encourage home ownership in the country by permitting each homeowner to reduce their income tax contribution by "deducting" the interest paid annually on whatever loan amount secured from their lender for the purchase of their home. Used by millions of Americans this "deduction" has traditionally stimulated the broader economy through new home construction and all of the "spin off industries" associated with the purchase of commodities necessary for home ownership.[292]

This "deduction" is, however, a technique for tax avoidance. If we are to begin the process of rebalancing our tax code it is only fair to note that billions of dollars are exempted from taxation because of the "mortgage interest deduction." It is also important to remember that this perfectly legal technique of reducing one's taxable income is not available to millions of other Americans who are not homeowners. And, similar to our discussion of "charitable trusts," this theoretically defensible provision of our tax code does not significantly benefit the vast majority of "middle class" Americans with its present design and implementation. Instead only those households with incomes of $250,000 or above begin to see significant deductions averaging around $5,459. Households who declare annual incomes of $40,000—$75,000 have an average deduction of $523—10 times less.[293] Indeed, one of the most important considerations for a fair rebalancing of our tax code may be how to better target the "exemptions" and "deductions" to the segments of our population which would most benefit from these and other forms of tax relief. Presently, our tax code disproportionately benefits only a very small percentage of Americans.

For example, it has been estimated that taxpayers who claim an annual income of $1,000,000 or more (.03% of all taxpayers) receive 70% of the "capital gains" tax calculations[294]—that is, having one's "assets" taxed at a rate of 20% rather than 39.6%. Another area of the code which is ripe for rebalancing is the so-called "step-up in basis" rule that was briefly mentioned in relation to some of our wealthiest practices of legally avoiding taxation and transferring wealth to their heirs. This rule permits the beneficiaries of an estate to pay taxes on the value of an asset at the time they received the bequest. What that means is that even though the value of the asset may have significantly increased in value from the time it was purchased/created, the required tax on the asset is the difference between its value when the heirs receive it and when they sell it. Presume the decedent held stocks which grew in value from their original purchase price of $100,000 to $400,000 over an extended period of time; she then dies and passes the assets on to her heirs; if the heirs choose to sell the stocks and receive $500,000 only the difference between $400,000 and $500,000 ($100,000) would be capable of being taxed. While the assets increased in actual value from $100,000 to $500,000—an increase of $400,000—only $100,000 is taxable. It has been reported that the cost to the country via the implementation of the "capital gains" tax rate and "step-up in basis" rule was approximately 38.5 and 61.5 billion for fiscal year 2012.[295]

The question before the country then is whether these and the literally hundreds of other provisions of our tax code which benefit a relatively small segment of our population should be rebalanced.[296] By recognizing the present disproportionate impact that some of our rules have produced and by retargeting the original tax incentives for Americans with household incomes which have been most devastated by the "great recession," we would begin to repair some of the distrust of our taxation process. But this rebalancing should not end with an examination of our estate and income tax codes. Shining a bright light on our corporate tax structures, as well as our estate tax and income tax rules, will provide a necessary public debate regarding where we believe the necessary balance should be struck, in the case of corporate America, between tax policies intended to incentivize business practices which generate profit for its shareholders and those which permit the transference of billions of dollars off shore in an effort to avoid taxation or oversight by the American people.

One public policy discussion, led through a bi-partisan effort of our political elite, which may engender support from the American public, would be the reduction of the overall corporate tax rate coupled with requirements for a return of capital held offshore and then used for private/public infrastructure development across the United States.[297] Targeting incentives to our domestic and multinational corporations to become partners with government in the revitalization of our nation's roads, bridges and communication networks would once again demonstrate the positive interconnectivity between our business and public sectors. While such a discussion will once again see the forces of "divide and conquer" politics driven by one faction or another enter the fray with arguments of "government intervention" into the functioning of their distorted view of free enterprise and/or claims that proposed corporate tax incentives are an overly generous reward to corporations who should simply "do the right thing" for their country, it may be that Americans will follow James Madison's guidance—"…the advice of prudence must be to embrace the lesser evil and, instead of indulging a fruitless anticipation of the possible mischiefs which may ensue, to contemplate rather the advantageous consequences which may qualify the sacrifice." One can surmise also that Madison would couple his recommendation with a reminder of the necessary transparency and oversight of our "elected" in constructing the process of implementation of such a venture.

Following the observations of Madison we must demand that our political elite begin to rebalance our system of taxation as one of their most important responsibilities. In so doing, they must be emboldened by Franklin's demand that we must all "pay our club" as part of our individual responsibilities to "civil society" if we want the "benefits" we have collectively created. Finally, our political elite who hold the "public trust" must be reminded by an engaged and "enlightened citizenry" of Locke's insistence that as we continue to reward personal accomplishment in wealth creation that no individual has the right to "… carve himself too much, or more than he needed." Where the balance is to be struck must be determined through the process of open and transparent debate in the public forum with the "free press" fulfilling its responsibility of assisting Americans, as Alexis de Tocqueville noted, in its obligation "…to detect the secret springs of political designs, and summon the leaders of all parties in turn to the bar of public opinion."

Questions to Consider:

- Should the Taxpayer Relief Act of 2012 be amended to reduce the amount exempted from estate taxation? If so, what modifications should be established?

- Should the definition of "income" pursuant to the Internal Revenue code regarding who qualifies for "capital gains" taxation rates be modified? Should the "capital gains" taxation rate be changed? Too what? Why?

- What rule modifications would you recommend, if any, regarding the "sheltering" of wealth transfers through the use of "charitable trusts"?

Should the "step up in basis rule" be changed"? If so, what modifications would you recommend?

- Should the "mortgage deduction rule" be rebalanced to target increased
benefits to a redefined "middle class"? What, if any, other tax benefits
can be implemented to assist Americans who rent?

- Should our tax code be rebalanced to incentivize the recapitalization
of small businesses? If so, should "lending institutions" be rewarded by
the continuance of low interest loans from our Federal Reserve? Should
the issuance of such loans be contingent on a clear demonstration of
the issuance of loans to small businesses?

Protect Our Economic System From Future Financial "Crashes"—The Regulation of "Too Big To Fail Banks"

(1) As Madison noted the task of "modern legislation" is "…the regulation"
of the source of the "…interfering interests" of factions which originate from
the "…various and unequal distribution of property."[298] It should be remembered that he believed that it was our collective responsibility through our governmental process which must control the deleterious consequences of these
factions through political compromise. The key word is "regulation" not "eradication." If our new experiment in government was to accomplish this goal
Madison understood that "curing the mischiefs of faction" could be accomplished through two methods. The first was to "remove its causes." The second
was "by controlling its effects." Once again he and the Founders called upon
their understanding of the human condition—that the "latent causes of faction
are … sown in the nature of man…" and that any attempt to eradicate the reasons for the creation of factions would destroy liberty.[299] They therefore rejected
any arguments for the prohibition of factious groups. Instead Madison and his
colleagues believed that the role of government was to establish mechanisms by
which to control the "…schemes of injustice" which can be produced by "…any
one party being able to outnumber and oppress the rest."[300]

The impact of the failure to regulate our "financial industry" prior to—let us
call it what it was and remains to be for millions of Americans—the depression
of our economy beginning in 2007-2008—has been documented by countless
economists, journalists and political commentators. Depending upon whatever
ideological "box" to which the analyst subscribes the reason(s) for the collapse,
is (are) attributed to the failure of governmental oversight of the "financial industry," the greed and hubris of the financial wizards of Wall Street, the lack

of international monetary standards which encourage the "flow of capital" to the most unregulated foreign casino (financial institution) in an effort to grab short-term profits, and the failure of the American public to restrain its debt accumulation via easily attainable mortgages or their "easy money" credit card addiction. Regardless if one selects one or a combination of these perspectives or others not identified as the cause(s) of the "crash," the continuing devastating economic and psychological impact on the vast majority of the American people is without debate. Yet, the legislative responses enacted to prevent future collapses continue to be tepid at best. Therefore, a brief but necessary chronology of the legislative efforts of our political elite which both opened the door to the manipulation of our "financial industry" and the contemporary "solutions" which have been instituted to protect the country from future similar debacles is in order.

As with the creation and implementation of rules regarding our tax code the regulation of our financial system also depends upon a definition of certain key terms. Narrow the definition of "income" for taxation purposes and create categories of wealth generation such as "ownership," "asset management," etc. and permit lower taxation calculations—if any. Redefine the meaning of a "bank" from the fundamentally essential role of providing capital for the functioning of our commercial economy, which is overwhelmingly composed of small and mid-size businesses, to also include what is now termed—"investment banking" and the country if not the world is put at risk. It should be noted that some of the same players in the creation and initial marketing of the Tea Party, Freedom Works, and Americans For Tax Reform were also involved in the effort to free the American economy from the scourge of governmental interference with the "free markets" and voted or lobbied heavily for the new legislation in this area of the American economy. They were indeed successful.

With the assistance of key Republican leaders in both the House of Representatives and Senate during the Clinton Administration, a majority of our "elected"—Democrats and Republicans alike—passed legislation which was heralded as the beginning of a new era of "free enterprise" spurred on by the "deregulation" of the "financial industry." The term "bank" after the passage of the Gramm-Leach-Bliley Act of 1999[301] now included proprietary trading houses, brokers, and other entities in the "financial community."[302] With this legislative rejection of the Glass-Steagall Act of 1933 enacted after the market crash of the late 1920's which prohibited banking institutions from participating in proprietary trading,[303] brokerage houses and insurance companies were now permitted to either merge with traditional banking institutions or to create their own "holding banking" companies to complement their already existing financial operations.[304] Happy days were here again. But after almost eight years after the passage of the Gramm-Leach-Bliley Act the "financial" system began to unravel.[305]

The collapse of one of the country's largest provider of mortgages, Countrywide Financial, and its purchase by Bank of America, began a whirlwind of negotiations between the Bush Administration through the Secretary of Treasury, Hank Paulson—once CEO of Goldman Sachs—and industry "insiders" regarding other potential "bank" failures. With the encouragement of the Secretary of Treasury and other government actors, JPMorgan Chase was encouraged to purchase the next potential "investment bank" failure—Bear Stearns. As the financial house of cards began to collapse Lehman Brothers, one of New York's oldest "investment banks" failed to receive financial "cover" from other members of the "financial" community and declared bankruptcy. The British "bank" Barclays subsequently purchased select divisions of Lehman Brothers. Throughout this period of time Fanny Mae and Freddie Mac, the country's largest holders of residential mortgages, was for all extents and purposes "nationalized." The next "investment bank" to fall was Merrill-Lynch. It was subsequently acquired by Bank of America. Additionally, insurance companies which were permitted after the passage of the Gramm-Leach-Bliley Act of 1999 to participate in proprietary trading as an "investment bank" were also "bailed out" with the assistance of the United States Treasury. One of the world's largest insurance companies—American International Group (AIG)—received billions of dollars in an effort to keep it from being the next "financial institution" to fold. Throughout this period and unknown to the American people, the United States Federal Reserve Bank shuffled billions of dollars to foreign "financial institutions" in an effort to stabilize their under-capitalized "banking" operations.[306]

But the collapse and mergers of these so-called "investment banks"—otherwise known as trading houses which created, negotiated, sold and/or purchased financial instruments—were not the only victims to an under-capitalized and unregulated financial system dependent upon investor confidence and trust. Millions of Americans who either through their associational groups or government were encouraged to establish stock market dependent IRA's (Individual Retirement Accounts) were seriously impacted by its collapse as were so-called private "financial management" funds (Hedge Funds) who regularly borrowed millions of dollars from the "investment banks" to finance their trading activities. What once was a relatively simple task of raising capital support for their betting activities, now actually required a demonstration of equity in their balance sheets and the sale of assets.[307] The result of all this was the restriction of capital to some of the most important players in our economy—small businesses, regional and community banks, and Americans who were attempting to secure mortgage loans to purchase a home, a car, or other consumer goods. Companies began to "downsize" and the unemployment rate in the country began to spiral.

With the assistance of billions upon billions of dollars initially injected into the "financial community" through Congressional legislation, the actions of the Federal Reserve, and seven years of political debate and societal frustration, it would appear that our economy has "stabilized" into what has become a "new normal." That is, protracted relatively high unemployment, underemployment of the nation's college graduates, unsustainable income/wealth inequality gaps amongst our citizenry, and the continuance of lobbying of our "elected" by the same oracles of unregulated "free enterprise" that sold the country on the wisdom of the Gramm-Leach-Bliley Act of 1999 and the need to continue its objectives. But before we examine the remedial legislative enactments which were created in response to the "deregulatory" policies instituted in 1999 and now are under attack, it is important to recall the reason why the barriers established by the Glass-Steagall Act after the market crash of 1929 allegedly needed to be abolished in the first place.

The "pitch" sold to Congress and the American people during the Clinton Administration from the podiums, and backrooms, of the House of Representatives, and the Senate was that American banks were being strangled by antiquated regulatory restrictions and they must be freed to allow them to compete in the world markets. Our international competitors like, UBS, Credit Suisse, or Deutsche Bank, so the argument went, were not chained to outdated prohibitions on proprietary trading as were American banks. If we were to successfully compete, particularly in the "emerging markets," our banks needed the same opportunities to secure trading partners and fund our multinational corporations "doing business" around the planet. Passage of the bill, it was argued, would insure America's dominance in the world marketplace and provide jobs. The legislation would create an environment of "fair" competition in international trade.[308] After fifteen years since its passage and six years of economic "recession"/"depression" in the country and across much of the world, even the most strident supporter(s) of "free markets" and their potential of "self-regulation" through market forces, could question the one-dimensional thinking associated with the aforementioned rationales justifying the need for "deregulation."

Most Americans, regardless of which political ideological "box" they have been encouraged to join, have experienced competition in their lives. Indeed, the idea of competition which can stimulate innovation and personal growth is at the core of the American character. What we have come to understand, however, is that regardless of what definition one places on the word "fair," competition requires rules—rules which must be agreed to by all participants. It is also been our experience that unless there is a "referee" assigned the task of providing some level of consistent application of the rules established, the "competition" can result in nothing more than a charade too often reflecting the "dark side" of cronyism and raw concentrated power. Without constant oversight of agreed upon rules and their consistent application and enforcement too often the result is the concentration of power—both in economic markets and our politics.

With the crashing of the "house of cards" of our "investment banks" and the subsequent merging of some of these entities within just a few of what once were either proprietary trading firms such as Goldman Sachs now treated as a "bank," or traditional banking institutions such as JPMorgan Chase now permitted to engage in proprietary trading, the country had become the ultimate unprotected lender to unregulated traders in a world of "casino capitalism." Americans were beginning to understand the meaning of the now oft repeated phrase "Too Big to Fail Banks." Literally trillions of dollars were now being consolidated into the coffers of a few "banks" which control the stability of the American economy and portions of the world economy.[309]

While there were efforts during the so-called "bailout" process to create legislation which would either provide protections to the American people from the actions of the new "banks," or reinstitute provisions of the Glass-Steagall Act of 1933, they failed to receive support from the Congress of the United States.[310] But by 2010 some legislative action began to emerge. With the passage of what has now become to be known as the Dodd-Frank legislation some Congressional efforts began to address the potential of another "great recession."[311] The legislation created two administrative agencies whose primary task would be to monitor the "financial stability" of the "banking" community and provide a process by which "failing banks" would be "liquidated." The Financial Stability Oversight Council[312] and the Orderly Liquidation Authority[313] were delegated the power through the legislation to promulgate rules to achieve these broad legislative objectives. Other Congressional responses which were established to protect the country from another implosion of the "financial community" was the creation of the Consumer Fraud Protection Bureau, the Office of Credit Ratings (placed under the auspices of the Securities and Exchange Commission),[314] and what was touted as the ultimate check on "Too Big to Fail Banks"— the Volcker Rule.[315] Each of the aforementioned legislative responses to some of the causes of the collapse of our economy may be important first steps in monitoring the functioning of our so-called "investment banks" created by the

Gramm-Leach-Bliley Act of 1999. But there is reason to believe that much remains to be accomplished. After four years since the passage of Dodd-Frank many of its "intended" purposes have still to be implemented. And some important legislative "loop holes" need to be reexamined.

For example, almost five years after the creation of the various administrative agencies noted above many of their proposed rules to provide oversight of these "banks" are yet to be implemented.[316] Because the design and implementation of administrative rules requires good-faith input from all sectors of our community which may be impacted from the enforcement of proposed rules "notice and comment" proceedings are instituted. Not surprisingly, with the assistance of legal counsel, publicly contrite "Too Big to Fail Banks" corporate leaders who allegedly support the promulgation of rules by these oversight agencies, challenge rule after rule within the rulemaking process as unreasonable. To be clear, the "bankers" have every right to offer their insight on what they believe will be the impact of any rule as does any citizen or advocacy group. But the question must be asked whether their good-faith input is simply a tactic to stall or defeat the will of the American public as reflected in the creation of these oversight agencies.

Another lingering cause for concern as to whether the country remains on the precipice of yet another devastating economic calamity is the failure to actually curb the high risk proprietary trading once abolished by Glass-Steagall but actually encouraged with the Gramm-Leach-Bliley Act of 1999. The so-called Volcker rule was promoted to the American public as the panacea to the high risk trading by our so-called "banks." But the present design of many provisions of the rule has produced serious criticism from a wide variety of "market" observers and even some of the initial legislators who argued for inclusion of such a rule within the original Dodd-Frank legislation. It is suggested that the current provisions of the rule are too vague and provide enumerable exceptions to the prohibition against high risk proprietary trading by the few "Too Big to Fail Banks" left standing after the collapse of the markets beginning in 2007–2008.[317]

Among the many criticisms of the rule is its reliance on the "self-regulation" of the "banks" trading activities through their mandated "compliance programs" which must be "appropriate to the size, scope, and risk of its activities and investments." Supporters of the present configuration of the Volcker rule suggest that the establishment of such "compliance programs" will allow regulators to more readily assess the "liquidity" of the "banks" capital and detect prohibitive "short term" and "high risk" trading. They argue that so-called "risk mitigation" determined by the "banks" through the utilization of such in house compliance programs which are enforced and documented by occasional individual testing of the investments (trading) will provide the necessary oversight to prevent a recurrence of the "trading" activities which created the shell games that eventually collapsed taking our economy with them.[318] Yet, for these mechanisms to function as the protections they are presented to be two presumptions must be accepted as fact. The first is that the behemoth "banks" which hold trillions of dollars will resist the greed and hubris associated with the "trading" which occurred prior to the collapse of the markets and actually "self-regulate." The second is that our administrative agencies assigned the task of oversight will receive the political and legal support to identify and successfully enforce the general prohibitions within the Volcker rule against "high risk" proprietary trading. The critics of the present configuration of the Volcker rule believe there is reason to believe that there are simply too many provisions of the rule which permit such activity and that its effectiveness is doom to failure.

For example, the "loop holes" within the adopted rule include but are not limited to the following permissible "trading" activities or the creation of "investment management" services or products: A security, including an option on a security; A derivative, including an option on a derivative; and a contract of sale of a commodity for future delivery or an option on a contract of sale of a future commodity. Additional permitted "investment" activities include proprietary trading "…provided the trading occurs solely outside of the United States and the "banking entity" is not controlled by a banking entity organized under the laws of the United States."[319] Most Americans would asked "But I thought that Dodd-Frank and its intention in establishing the Volcker Rule was to prevent proprietary trading and to restrict the "instruments" which played such an important role in the "high risk" trading—derivatives?"

As was noted in our commentary regarding the need for the rebalancing of our tax code, the legal shell game of wealth creation and transference is often protected by carefully drafted exceptions within our system of rules. Such is the case with the status of the Volcker rule. Regulatory oversight as well as judicial review requires adherence to the rules initially designed by the administrative agency or agencies assigned the task to implement the broad objectives of any legislation—in our case, Dodd-Frank. If the initial legislation failed to address certain issues associated with the implementation of its overall objective, then it is the task of the administrative agency to "fill in the blanks" through its rulemaking and enforcement process. However, if the rules created are so riddled with exceptions to the general legislative intent, reviewing courts may reluctantly be required to intercede into the sanctity of administrative rulemaking and prevent their enforcement. But judicial review of administrative rulemaking is a comparably rare eventuality.[320] If the numerous "loop holes" identified by "financial industry" observers are in direct conflict with the publically promoted "intention" for the Dodd-Frank legislation, then further legislative oversight is in order. The likelihood that this will occur also remains highly doubtful in the present environment of political gridlock fed by the millions of dollars of lobbying of our "political elite" by those who would once again profit the most from keeping the "gaming tables" open under the guise of "doing business" in the world markets.

Of course, much of the critical analysis of one vaguely described "permitted activity" within one section or another of the present Volcker rule, while worthwhile in the effort to bring the potential deleterious impact that they may produce into the public forum, may have overlooked the real "elephant in the room"—that the rationale for justifying the Gramm-Leach-Bliley Act of 1999 was simply wrong. Whether the lobbying behind the Act was motivated by an honest belief that it was the only way to "fairly" compete in the world markets or a deceitful effort to wrench more concentrated power into the hands of a few "players," is the subject of another investigation. What is important is that a renewed public dialogue initiated by our "political elite" in fulfillment of their "faithful discharge" of the public trust be instituted. At the center of such a national discussion must be a balanced examination of whether the Dodd-Frank legislation is an inadequate response to the underlying issues associated with permitting a few unregulated "bankers"—with the support of their "investors"—to control the world markets.

Remember the argument. It has been reported that Jamie Dimon the present Chairman, President and Chief Executive Officer of JPMorgan Chase, one of our four "Too Big to Fail Banks" holding trillions of dollars in their corporate coffers, declared during the relatively recent process to reexamine Gramm-Leach-Bliley that,

> The fact is that some businesses require size in order to make necessary investments, take extraordinary risks, and provide vital support globally… America's largest companies operate around the world and employ millions. This includes companies that can make huge investments-as much as $10 billion to $20 billion a year-and compete in as many as fifty to one hundred countries to assure America's long-term success.[321]

This commentary offered as justification for the abolition of the Glass-Steagall prohibitions against proprietary trading by American banks sealed the deal to ensure that "America's largest companies" could "operate around the world and employ millions" and "assure America's long-term success." There are, of course, some very important questions which must be asked. Presuming that "some" American multinational corporations require massive loans of capital to "compete" and "operate around the world," why should the source of that capital formation be consolidated into the hands of a few unregulated traders or brokers? Were (are) there no other alternatives which could (can) provide the "necessary" capital support to "compete"? Had the world markets in which our corporations, prior to Gramm-Leach-Bliley, participated now so dramatically changed that the destruction of the American economy would ensue if traders from Goldman-Sachs or JPMorgan Chase could not negotiate a deal on behalf of "some" of our multinational corporations? What was and is the evidence that such activity actually benefits our economy or creates jobs for American workers not employed in our "financial" industry? What rules, if any, would be (have been) instituted to oversee this dramatically different global marketplace? What role, if any, should American government play in our participation through international financial organizations, the negotiation of multilateral trade agreements and foreign policy action to help shape the rules of competition?

Raising these questions and the multitude of others relating to both the underlying presumption(s) of Mr. Dimon's observation should not be understood to be a rejection of the need for this country to participate in world markets or to provide assistance to American corporations in the global marketplace. With the ascendency of the other competitors from "emerging" economies who receive government funded support directly or indirectly in their search for "trading partners" across the planet, it would be a fundamental mistake to retreat into some form of economic isolationism. That being noted, our participation in world markets does not require a rejection of the values which have served us well over the last two hundred plus years. Mr. Dimon was correct when he concluded that our long-term economic success should be at the center of any decision to compete in the global marketplace. But his faith in "deregulation" and by implication the ability of the "players" in the market to establish through "self-regulation" rules by which the competition would take place was (is) misplaced. The discovery of manipulation of the "libor rates" upon which proprietary trading relies, the loss of eight billion dollars through the alleged trading practices of the so-called London Whale and his associates, and the continuing hubris exhibited by traders now called "bankers" who once again construct highly leveraged "loans" (bets) only reinforce the need for a serious reexamination of the limits of self-regulation both within the borders of this country and internationally. Similar to the failure to institute important portions of the Dodd-Frank legislation so too is the failure of the international financial community to establish oversight rules. No better example of this continuing problem is the failure of the international "financial" community to actually provide leadership in the creation of enforceable regulatory oversight of so-called international "banking."

One of the most widely recognized gatherings of world "financial" leaders occurs on a yearly basis in Davos, Switzerland. Some the most powerful corporate "banking," private equity, and political figures in the world attend what is touted as the World Economic Forum. During this forum these representatives provide their perspectives on the state of the world economy and offer recommendations regarding what they believe are the most pressing issues facing the planet. This event provides each organization or individual the opportunity to provide their particular perspective on the varied issues surrounding the functioning of the world economies and in so doing grants the public the rare occasion to listen to the individuals whose decision-making impacts the economic stability of the planet. The recent forum discussed a wide range of issues from the potentiality of continuing the injection of billions of dollars into national and international monetary efforts to support lower interest rates, proposals to establish infrastructure development through private investment, the status of "emerging economies," the impact of new technologies on the world's workforce and even the importance of "stress reduction" in the world's corporate boardrooms through meditation. The nature of such gatherings, make it very difficult to determine whether any of the speeches, recommendations, or predictions will produce any positive results in "...improving the state of the world..." which is the objective of the forum. But one thing can be said with confidence—little discussion and no recommendations were presented to establish international regulatory oversight of so-called "investment" schemes or "trading" which have the potential of devastating economies and the widening wealth inequality that it produces across the planet.[322] However, at least one or two participants at the forum did provide some insight on what may be the current thinking on the subject from the "banking" community.

The Chairman of the Swiss Bank, Credit Suisse, Urs Rohner, is reported as saying that letting "banks" fail is essential in "rebuilding trust" for future "investment." He said that "...people have to be convinced that there may be banks that fail. If they fail, they have to be taken out of the system..." He then suggested that a "number of countries" have eliminated the need to "designate" banks as "Too Big to Fail." Instead the problem he believes is that regulators "...around the world haven't agreed to take a "universal approach, or how to approach the next global crisis, or even if they will honor the other's solutions." On the same forum panel was David Rubenstein, the co-founder of the Carlyle Group, a private equity fund (hedge fund) who offered a familiar "industry" response on the topic of regulation. He argued that there was a tendency to "overregulate" the "financial industry" in response to what he described as a "financial turndown." The result of this action is to restrict "business." He went on to suggest that regulators have to understand that they can't eliminate "financial cycles."[323]

Apparently, Mr. Rohner is convinced that a "number of countries"—otherwise interpreted to mean, the United States via the Dodd-Frank legislation—have (has) successfully "eliminated" the need for further worry regarding the functioning of our "banks." While it is a hopeful sign that the Chairman of one of the world's "Too Big to Fail Banks" is willing to support the process of legislative oversight that was begun by Dodd-Frank, the task of strengthening the legislation may be incomplete. But his observation regarding the need for international regulatory standards is an even more hopeful indication that additional action must be instituted to repair the "trust" lost in the world "financial markets."

Mr. Rubenstein's commentary also is important. In fact the role that his "fund" and that of a relatively small number of "private equity" groups play in the functioning of the "markets" across the world should not be underestimated. Trillions of "investor" dollars are not only accumulating in the balance sheets of "banks" both in and outside the United States but also are held by "private equity" managers—traders, brokers—whose day to day objective is to find profit for their investors and themselves. Hedge funds can provide a counter-balance, an alternative for the "players" in the "market" to bet against "trades" or other "high risk" "investment packages." In fact, the interrelationship between our "Too Big to Fail Banks" and some of the extraordinarily powerful "private equity" funds in the formation of capital has an enormous impact on both private and public sector functioning.

There should be no question that "private equity" investment is essential to the stability and growth of both our economy and the world markets. That being the case, is there really a tendency to "over regulate"? It would be helpful if we knew what is meant by "over regulation." There is a difference between stifling the rewards which comes from "investment" risk taking through good-faith negotiation established through transparent trading based on accepted business practices and manipulation of unregulated world markets in an effort to glean short-term profits. The world community continues to experience the result of the later and one can conjecture that even some of the "players" at the casino would be willing to sacrifice some of their winnings for more assurances that the game is not rigged. The world community continues to feel the devastating results which have been produced in no small measure by the financial packages (loans) created by some "banks" and private equity funds and sold to municipalities or even countries without domestic or international oversight.

As has been pointed out in our discussion of the need for reform of our tax code "definitions" matter. What is simply a "financial turndown" for those who manage/trade enormous amounts of money on a daily basis, may be a devastating loss of another's home or result in his/her inability to fund their child's education. It is also true that regulatory oversight will not always produce absolute protection from what some have described as "financial cycles." But if the "trust" that Mr. Rohner believes needs to be established through regulatory oversight and a willingness to provide a process for failed "banks" to be forced from the system, then international agreements with strong enforcement procedures need to be established. The old and often repeated truisms justifying no action to curb the excesses of the human condition or diminish any effort to limit the impact of greed and hubris were noted by the Founders as they hammered out our "least imperfect" political process. Their observations are equally relevant in their application to the preservation of our economy which is so interconnected with the functioning of world "markets."

We must demand from our "political elite" an objective reexamination of the Gramm-Leach-Bliley Act of 1999 and the subsequent functioning of the Dodd-Frank legislation with particular attention placed on the rulemaking process for its implementation in addition to the need to amend portions of the Volcker rule. In so doing, we must determine whether there are alternative mechanisms which can be created to assist our multinational corporations "doing business" across the planet by providing the capital necessary to "compete" and yet establish the regulatory oversight and transparency necessary to minimize the potential of corrupt business practices. We must also require meaningful governmental policy making which can encourage, through international agreements, co-ordinated regulatory oversight of the casino capitalism which continues to threaten the world markets. There simply is no escaping the interconnectivity of our economy and that of our trading partners and those who we want to solicit throughout the world "emerging economies." But "fair" competition requires rules which must be agreed to by all participants and consistently applied and enforced.

Once again the insight of the Founders regarding the dangers of unregulated concentrated power and its origins should guide us as we seek through our "joint wisdom" the "least imperfect" techniques by which to control its deleterious impact on the country and the lives of the American people. It will be remembered that James Madison observed:

> ...No man will subject himself to the ridicule of pretending that any
> natural connection subsists between the sun and the seasons and the period

within which human virtue can bear the temptations of power. Happily for mankind, liberty is not, in this respect, confined to any single point in time, but lies within extremes which afford sufficient latitude for all variations which may be required by the various situations and circumstances of civil society.[324]

It was a matter of fact for Madison and the Founders that the "temptations of power" constantly challenge the process of establishing a balance between liberty and the promotion of the public welfare. They did not recoil from the task of creating methods by which to control (regulate) the potential excesses produced by concentrated power. Neither should we.

Questions to Consider:

- Should the Gramm-Leach-Bliley Act of 1999 be repealed? If so, should the prohibitions instituted in the Glass-Steagall Act of 1933 against proprietary trading be revisited? If so, should provisions of the Dodd-Frank mandated Volcker rule be strengthened to better reflect the mandates of Glass-Steagall? If not, why not?

- If you believe that more restrictions on the functioning of our "Too Big to Fail Banks" and other foreign "Too Big to Fail Banks" doing business in the United States is required, would you support a reexamination of the "self-compliance" requirements of the Volcker rule? If so, do you believe that increased funding of the administrative agencies delegated the responsibility to monitor/regulate these "banks" in an effort to solicit, train, and retain more regulators is required?

- If you agree with the presumption that "some" of our multinational corporations require access to large (billions of dollars) of capital to successfully "compete" in world markets, would you support the creation by the Congress of the United States of a national bank whose sole function would be to provide liquidity (loans) to these corporations? If so, what incentives should be incorporated into the design of the bank which would encourage private sector participation? What oversight and transparency requirements should be mandated? Should access to capital from the bank also be contingent on the creation of jobs for American workers? If so, if over a relatively short time horizon the multinational corporation cannot demonstrate such job creation, should the bank withhold further support and institute "claw back" proceedings which require return of capital, suspension of tax "exemptions," or institute other legal remedies?

- Should an "enlightened citizenry" demand from their "elected"—both the Congress and the Executive Branch—the creation of international agreements which establish enforceable regulatory standards for the functioning of foreign "banks"? If so, through the negotiation of trade agreements, international treaties, future participation in international monetary organizations, and our continued involvement in international security agreements, should we require enforcement procedures which are transparent and "verifiable"?

Reducing The Influence of Money on the Political Process: Campaign Financing Reform

(1) Similar to all the public policy objectives which have been identified and discussed, the subject of campaign financing is fundamentally important to any enterprise which is in search for solutions to the political gridlock which has gripped the country for over six years. It is also true, as with the other subjects which have been addressed, that competing principles and arguments which support either the status quo or the need for change are in no short supply. But unlike some of our other subjects the topic of campaign financing reform has an additional element which must be addressed—that is, its relationship to the constitutional prohibition against restriction of "political speech." While much has been, and one suspects, will continue to be written regarding this subject, there is no debating the significance that one Supreme Court decision continues to have on any effort to legislatively address the subject. The seminal decision is Citizens United v. Federal Election Commission.[325]

This 5–4 decision of the Court decided in 2010 has generated a litany of commentaries both within and outside the legal community. The case has raised some of the questions which this investigation has discussed regarding the Founders' arguments for an independent judiciary, the special function that the Supreme Court must play in American governance, and the obligation of individual justices to the institution of the Court beyond their particular ideological preferences in judicial decision-making. It is beyond the scope of this investigation to critique each issue/argument identified by either the majority or dissenting opinions in Citizens United. But because this case continues to present an important consideration to any legislative attempts to address the impact of money on our electoral process, a few of the most important arguments presented in the decision must be confronted and debated.

The case involved a "non-for-profit" corporation, Citizens United, which produced and released a "documentary" in 2008 critical of Hillary Clinton, a candidate seeking the endorsement of the Democratic Party for President of the

United States. The "documentary" was to be presented on both cable and broadcast television. Concerned that Federal Election Commission rules promulgated pursuant to the Bipartisan Campaign Reform Act of 2002 would prohibit them from airing the "documentary," Citizens United sought a decision (declaratory judgment) from a lower federal district trial court which would find that such provisions in the FEC rules as applied to them were unconstitutional. The lower court rejected that argument and found that their claim was without merit. Citizens United appealed the district court's decision and the Supreme Court accepted jurisdiction of the case, heard oral arguments and reviewed the written "briefs" from the "parties" in the case (Citizens United and the Attorney General of the United States) and other "interested" parties (through the use of "amicus curiae"—friend of the court—briefs). The Supreme Court reversed the lower court decision and determined that the Federal Election Commission's rule(s) were a violation of the First Amendment's "political speech" protections.

Among the numerous issues involved in this case was the question of whether section 203 of the Bipartisan Campaign Reform Act of 2002 which prohibited corporations and unions from using their "general treasury" funds to make independent expenditures for speech that is an "electioneering communication" or for speech that expressly advocates the election or defeat of a candidate was a violation of the First Amendment. In one of the most lengthy and wide ranging Supreme Court decisions in recent memory, five justices of the Court in both a majority opinion and separate concurring opinions overruled two previous precedents (decisions) which provided for limited governmental regulation of corporate speech and concluded that "...the government may not render a ban on political speech constitutional by carving out a limited exception through an amorphous regulatory interpretation..."[326] Justices Kennedy, Alito, Thomas, Roberts, and Scalia all agreed that the Federal Election Commission rule which restricts corporate "electioneering communication" would unconstitutionally prohibit Citizens United from airing their "documentary" in violation of their "corporate speech" right under the First Amendment. Rejecting the opportunity to address what Justice Kennedy determined would be the "defining" of "preferred" types of "communication" he and the four other members of the Court concluded that "...the drawing of fine distinctions" would create the "serious risk of chilling protected speech"[327] and most importantly, citing New York Times v. Sullivan—a cornerstone case involving the importance of a free press in its reporting of the actions of public officials "...First Amendment standards must give the benefit of doubt to protecting rather than stifling speech."[328]

What is of particular importance to our discussion of how to reduce the impact of money on our electoral process is the majority's "analysis" and justi-

254 Confronting the Politics of Gridlock

fication for equating "corporations" as "individuals" and their belief that the protections for political speech of the First Amendment which attached to individual citizens also apply to "corporate speech." Even presuming that one agrees with the majority's concern with the proliferation of rules produced by the Federal Election Commission in implementing Congress' mandate pursuant to the Bipartisan Campaign Reform Act and their concern that their rules create the potential "...for a regime that allows it to select what political speech is safe for public consumption...,"[329] they fail to provide a convincing constitutional analysis of why "corporate speech" should receive the same protections as those traditionally provided to individual citizens. In fact, the Congress operating under the previous decisions of the Supreme Court regarding the constitutionality of creating reasonable restrictions on the differing entities created by corporations and unions—Political Action Committees—(PACs) in their efforts to persuade Americans to support one candidate or political cause, relied on their past precedents to shape limitations on the influence of corporations and unions as to their "electioneering communication."

Certainly one of the most important functions of the Court in American government is to carefully monitor visa via "cases and controversies" the actions of the other co-ordinate branches in an effort to detect breaches of our Constitution and the Bill of Rights. Using their judicial review power they are obligated to overrule past decisions which incorrectly interpreted past precedents or actions of the other coordinate branches which reach beyond their delegated power or fail to reflect the protections of the Bill of Rights. That being noted, justification for their action, if it is to receive compliance from the American people, must reflect ultimately both the desires of the country determined by the actions of their representatives and must be grounded in sound constitutional theory and precedent. The majority's rationale(s) in Citizens United v. Federal Election Commission, while providing powerful arguments for the protection of political speech, is less than convincing that the "free marketplace of ideas" is damaged by "governmental intervention".

It is one thing to suggest that administrative rules such as those under question by the FEC can create the unintended consequence of restricting access to the American people of the opinions of some "non-for-profit" political organizations prior to elections, but it is another thing to conclude that Congress' attempt via the FEC to establish reasonable restrictions on who, when, and how much involvement for profit corporations and groups such as Citizens United and other PAC's can have on our electoral process is an unconstitutional violation of the fundamental right to political speech. The majority's reliance on the case law and theories which provide constitutional support for the protection of political speech for individual citizens and then interpreting them to be equally compelling for the non-regulation of so-called "corporate speech" needs to be examined within the context of the meaning of a "corporation" and its status in our electoral process. Justice Kennedy's reading of the Founders' understanding of "corporations" generally and their protected status under the First Amendment is questionable at best.

Justice Kennedy's vigorous defense of the importance of freedom of political speech and its overwhelming support by colonial Americans is powerful and accurately portrays its essentiality in the creation of the Republic. He is correct in observing that during the founding of the nation "...speech was open, comprehensive, and vital to society's definition of itself;"[330] And, similar to our analysis of James Madison's observations regarding factions, Mr. Justice Kennedy accurately quotes a portion of his arguments in *Federalist* no. 10 about the subject. Madison wrote:

> ...Factions will necessarily form in our Republic, but the remedy of "destroying the liberty" of some factions is worse than the disease...[331]

Madison did argue vigorously that to eliminate factions would be to destroy liberty. But he also was adamant that the "violence of factions" must be controlled. While the ultimate check on factions was to be the formation of a legislative body which would bring all factions together thus requiring political compromise, he was clear in *Federalist* no. 10 and his other writings that the "...most common and durable source of factions has been the various and unequal distribution of property...The regulation of these various and interfering interests forms the principal task of modern legislation..."[332] Therefore, while Madison would wholeheartedly have agreed with Justice Kennedy's conclusion that we must ultimately "entrust the people to judge what is true and what is false,"[333] there is also reason to believe Madison would support the essential legislative function of "regulating" the actions of for profit corporations/unions and the "non-for-profit" PACs in our electoral process.

While the majority opinion of Mr. Justice Kennedy cites very briefly the works of two of the most respected researchers of early American history regarding the publication of diverse political opinions throughout our founding,[334] he fails to mention the dramatically different environment in which the "free marketplace of ideas" was generated in colonial America versus the functioning of the contemporary mass communication behemoths of today. As we noted in our investigation, the intellectual and revolutionary fervor which sparked and ultimately sustained the Revolution and creation of our Constitution was energized by as de Tocqueville would later describe it as "...the power of the periodical press" which "...causes political life to circulate throughout all the parts of that vast territory..." and whose attention was "...constantly open to detect the secret springs of political design..."[335] Indeed, it was the proliferation of newspapers and polemical political pamphlets distributed across the nation, and published by fiercely opinionated owners, which as de Tocqueville noted "...summon(ed) the leaders of all parties in turn to the bar of public opinion..."[336] Unfortunately, such is not status of our mass communication industry today. Mr. Justice Kennedy failed or refused to address the concentrated power that now exists in our contemporary "free press." And, with all the eloquent arguments for the importance of political speech provided by the majority, very little analysis was provided that would justify, either theoretically or historically, equating our collective support for a proliferation of political speech and that of "corporate speech." The dissent in Citizens United v. Federal Election Commission, however, did address the distinction.

Mr. Justice Stevens, writing for his dissenting colleagues—Justices Ginsburg, Breyer, and Sotomayor—argued that the rationales provided by Kennedy, Alito, Roberts, Scalia, and Thomas were wrong on almost every issue presented in Citizens United. By accepting review of the lower court decision and then overruling the two important past precedents(decisions) which generally supported the cautious shaping of administrative rules regarding the impact of PACs on our electoral process, the dissenters believed that the majority had seriously threatened the integrity of the Court. Stevens argued that even if the majority believed that judicial review of the case was necessary, the issues in Citizens United should have been more narrowly examined and determined. Instead he wrote:

> ...Essentially five justices were unhappy with the limited nature of the case before us, so they changed the case to give themselves an opportunity to change the law.[337]

He was quick to note that those members of the Court who had been always consistent in past decision-making regarding the importance of judicial restraint and the dangers of "judicial legislating" were now more than willing to overlook those principles. But what is of particular importance to our investigation of reducing the impact of money on our political process is the dissent's historical analysis of the distinction between a "corporation" and an "individual" citizen under the Constitution. Are "corporations people too" as Presidential candidate Mitt Romney was so fond of saying throughout the 2012 campaign? Do all of the important protections of the First Amendment regarding "political speech" also apply to "corporate speech"? To answer the question Mr. Justice Stevens reached back into colonial history and called upon numerous academic resources.

Noting that the Founders and colonial Americans held a more narrow understanding of "speech" than do contemporary citizens (citing the work of Robert Bork, in his provocative law review article, Neutral Principles and Some First Amendment Problems, published in 1971, by the Indiana Law Journal), Justice Stevens argued that they "...held very different views about the nature of the First Amendment and the role of corporations."[338] He went on to observe that "Those few corporations that existed at the Founding were authorized by grant of a special legislative charter. Corporate sponsors would petition the legislature, and the legislature, if amenable, would issue a charter that specified the corporation's powers and purposes."[339] Referencing noted scholars of the evolution of "business corporations," Stevens reminded his colleagues that corporations were "created, supervised, and conceptualized as quasi-public entities,"[340] designed to serve a social function of the state. It was beyond debate that corporations were legislatively created entities which one business historian concluded,"...had to be closely scrutinized by the legislature because their purposes had to be made consistent with the public welfare."[341] The most compelling reference regarding the status of "corporations" in early American constitutional history to which Mr. Justice Stevens turned was the 1819 case of Trustees of Dartmouth College v. Woodward. Mr. Chief Justice John Marshall wrote in this decision:

> A corporation is an artificial being, invisible, intangible, and existing only in contemplation of law. Being the mere creature of law, it possesses only those properties which the charter of its creation confers upon it.[342]

Using both a historical overview of the development of corporations and past precedent which defined the meaning of corporate entities under our system of rules, Mr. Justice Stevens concluded,

> The Framers thus took it as a given that corporations would be comprehensively regulated in the service of the public welfare. Unlike our colleagues, they had little trouble distinguishing corporations from human beings, and when they constitutionalized the right to free speech in the First Amendment, it was the free speech of individual Americans that they had in mind...In light of those background practices and understandings, it seems to me implausible that the Framers believed "the freedom of speech" would extend equally to all corporate speakers, much less that it would preclude legislatures from taking limited measures to guard against corporate capture of elections[343]

But regardless of Mr. Justice Stevens' well-reasoned and historically grounded defense of governmental regulation of "corporate speech" and the legal status of "corporations" as compared with individual citizens under the Constitution, Citizens United and the rationales presented by the majority remain the law of the land. While we have discussed throughout our investigation numerous other factors in the seemingly endless political gridlock in the Congress of the United States, the impact of this decision on the body's willingness to once again address the potential deleterious consequences that money plays on our electoral process appears to be significant. It would seem that the rationales provided by the five Justices of the majority in Citizens United which failed to distinguished time honored case law and constitutional theory for the protection of each citizen's "political speech" with that of, as Justice John Marshall noted in Woodward "...an artificial being, invisible, intangible, and existing only in contemplation of the law...,"[344] are now but one more excuse to continue the status quo. In fact, the "chilling effect" on political speech that Mr. Justice Kennedy argued was created by previous decisions which upheld reasonable restrictions on corporate and union funding of our electoral process, has instead been used as justification for little or no public policy action regarding future negotiation of campaign financing.

There are other important issues associated with the Court's analyses in Citizens United which were left undeveloped but require a transparent airing in the public forum. Indeed, the question of just who constitute the "majority shareholders" in our nation's corporations and the influence that they wield in our electoral process ought to receive a robust national debate. The majority's seeming assumption that "corporate democracy"[345] will adjust any, let us call them, imbalances in the utilization of the corporation's treasury to defeat or support particular political candidates by "majority shareholders" contrary to the desires of "minority shareholders" and that governmental oversight is unnecessary or potentially unconstitutional requires a response.

The fact is that an extraordinarily wealthy individual or small number of investors can acquire "majority shareholder" status in any corporation leaving other shareholders relatively impotent in corporate decision-making including decisions as to whether to create "spin-off" PACs or to use their corporate status in other ways by which to influence the electoral process. All of this is perfectly legal. But to equate the acquisition of majority ownership with the majoritarian principles of our governmental process as the five justices in Citizens United seem to infer is questionable at best. It is a strange twist of logic for the majority in Citizens United to rely on the principles of so-called "corporate democracy" to reject any governmental oversight of this corporate acquisition potentiality, particularly when "foreign investors" may hold majority status or control powerful swaths of shares in the corporation. But, Mr. Justice Kennedy and his colleagues in the majority in Citizens United believed that the issue of "foreign investors" was not raised in the case brought before them and therefore left the issue for another "case and controversy."

The American public deserves an open and far reaching reexamination of the impact of both corporate and union funding either directly or through the use of PAC's on our electoral process. At a minimum, such a discussion should involve a reconsideration of the need for public disclosure of the sources of funding beyond the identification of the marketing names of the PACs created by well compensated public relations firms. If these "non-for-profit" corporate entities are to receive even limited constitutional protections regarding their "corporate speech" shouldn't Americans have the opportunity to evaluate the legitimacy of their advocacy by coupling the content of their speech with knowledge of who is actually funding the "ideas"? Do we really evaluate the legitimacy of one political position or another based solely on the content of the speech? Or, do we incorporate the speech with the speaker? Mr. Justice Kennedy wrote eloquently about the Founders' commitment to a robust "free marketplace of ideas" in support of protecting "corporate speech." But the environment in which political advocacy was communicated and evaluated by their countrymen was open and transparent compared with the "communication" techniques of contemporary America.

If one truly believes that a "free marketplace of ideas" should provide our political process with a multiplicity of perspectives to be evaluated by an "enlightened citizenry" does not such a process require transparency? In fact, the present status of our law permits, even encourages, individuals to hide behind the protective walls of for profit and non-for-profit corporate and associational groups such as unions in their "electioneering communication" campaigns. No personal responsibility for the claims, distortions, or fabrications required. Simply write the check and the snake oil salesmen/women of our twenty-first century (political marketers) will sell the claim(s) and our publicly licensed mass communication industry will run to the nearest bank to deposit the check(s)— All under the cover of "political speech" and "freedom of the press."

At a time in our history when there is an enormous concentration of power in our communication industry, a significant accumulation of wealth into a very small segment of our population, and the funneling of billions of dollars of campaign financing by corporate sponsored PACs, is now not the moment to demand a transparent accounting of the individuals who fund the "ideas" marketed during our electoral process? Is it too much to ask of those Americans who presumably fund one political marketing campaign or another based upon their fervent belief that the country needs to go in one direction or another, to step out from behind the walls of anonymity provided by the artificial entities we call corporations or the insulation provided by membership in our nation's unions, and take responsibility for their public policy "solutions"?

What is being suggested is that we actually demand a "free marketplace of ideas." One that is open and transparent. One which will provide the American public with not only the ideological "one-liners" so often marketed in campaign advertising but also the speakers (those who fund) the political product (candidate(s)) or public policy "solutions." Public disclosure of individual contributors in our electoral process has been the subject of review by the Supreme Court. As with all issues which involve a balancing of competing constitutional protections, cases which have involved disclosure of individual citizens participating in some form of our electoral process have resulted in the Court authorizing limited disclosure requirements.

That the subject of disclosure has created strange bedfellows amongst members of the Court and some political advocacy groups would be an understatement.[346] Often described "conservative" justices have joined in support with some "liberal" justices to argue for no disclosure requirements claiming such mandates would "chill speech" and violate "associational" rights of citizens. Other justices, who some court observers would predict, would be hesitant to support governmental regulation of any species, have defended state public disclosure requirements. What is clear from the cases which have involved some state or federal governmental disclosure requirements in elections is that some form of campaign disclosure has overcome constitutional challenge. But the status of requiring disclosure from those who fund corporate PACs is still in doubt.

The list of suggestions regarding campaign financing reform ranges from requiring absolute disclosure of contributions, to only those which reach a significant contribution threshold, to prohibition of any disclosure requirements. An objective analysis of this important public policy issue challenges all the imaginable ideological "boxes" in American politics. It asks the "progressive/liberals" to reach beyond their fear of governmental intrusion on "associational" rights of privacy, it requires "conservatives" to accept the argument that reasonable governmental regulation is not synonymous with censorship, and asks all citizens to address whether the "harm" that is inflicted on the community by the continuance of the anonymous flooding of our electoral process with billions of dollars under the guise of "corporate speech" is justification for disclosure requirements. Without conjecturing about Mr. Justice Scalia's motivation(s) in his support for a state disclosure law in Doe v. Reed,[347] a case which involved a requirement of disclosure of those citizens requesting a referendum regarding same sex marriage in the state of Washington, his observation is powerful. He wrote:

> Requiring people to stand up in public for their political acts fosters civic courage, without which democracy is doomed.[348]

Questions to Consider:

- Despite the Supreme Court's decision in Citizens United v. Federal Election Commission, should the Congress reinstitute new campaign reform legislation? What reason(s) can you provide for your support or non-support of the legislation?

- If you support a renewed effort by Congress to address the influence of money on our electoral process, would you support mandated limits on contributions by for profit, non-for-profit corporations, or associational groups such as unions? Why? Why not?

- If you do not support monetary campaign limitations on these entities, would you support disclosure requirements of contributors? If you support disclosure requirements, should disclosure be triggered by the amount of contribution?

- What responsibility, if any, do you believe the mass communication industry has to provide low cost campaign advertising as part of their licensure requirements?

- Why was Justice Scalia's observation correct or incorrect?

Acknowledgments

I OWE A DEBT OF GRATITUDE to many individuals who have made positive contributions to the writing of this book.

To Kitty Werner who patiently has directed the editing, design, and publication process of the book, I will be forever indebted. Her gentle but firm advice regarding its structure and emphasis provided the support necessary to complete the project in a timely manner. Her constant encouragement and professionalism injected a positive energy always essential in the research and writing process. To my fellow Vermonter, thank you.

To Paul Krupin who has applied his incalculable skills in an effort to bring the message of the book to the public for their consideration, thank you. Without his guidance the potential to begin a national discussion regarding the causes and solutions to our political gridlock would not be possible. That he was willing to assist me in this effort is a source of support which is genuinely appreciated.

To the hundreds of students I have had the privilege to teach across thirty years of undergraduate and graduate education, thank you. To have had the opportunity to discuss and analyze the Constitution with you is something I will treasure always.

To my friend Henry (Hank) Liebling who attempted, sometimes unsuccessfully, to transport me back to the twenty-first century after living too long in the Eighteenth with the Founders, thank you. If anyone could understand my commitment to the importance of citizen participation in government, it would be another fellow progeny from the Maxwell School of Citizenship and Public Affairs at Syracuse University. Thank you for asking "How is the book coming?"

To my son, Ian Sheldon Ludd who patiently listened to excerpts of the book, provided invaluable observations about its contents and structure, and most importantly provided unconditional support, thank you. His insights on the subjects within the book as one of this country's bright and newly minted college graduates served to reinforce the central theme of the book—the protection of our children's future.

To my wife, Oksana M. Ludd who more than anyone contributed to the completion of this book, thank you. Her willingness on innumerable occasions to listen to a subject, review the structure or discuss an analysis from the book, to understand the frustration that comes from too many hours in front of a blank computer screen, and to support the project because of a shared commitment to the values expressed within it, provided the intellectual and emotional support to "run through the tape." I will be forever grateful.

Lastly, to the memory of my loving parents, Edward S. Ludd and Elizabeth A. Ludd, thank you. May the world that you and your generation of Americans provided for us, be preserved through our efforts for our children.

Suggested Reading

Attenborough, Richard, ed., *The Words of Gandi.*

Bailyn, Bernard, *The Ideological Origins of the American Revolution.*

Barber, James David, *The Presidential Character.*

Barbera, Robert, *The Cost of Capitalism.*

Bradley, Bill, *We Can All Do Better.*

Burke, Edmund, *Reflections on the Revolution in France.*

Burns, James MacGregor, *The Vineyard of Liberty: The American Experiment, Vol. I.*

--------, ----------------------, *The Workshop of Democracy: The American Experiment, Vol. II.*

--------, ----------------------, *Crossroads of Freedom: the American Experiment, Vol. III.*

Cardozo, Benjamin, *The Nature of the Judicial Process.*

Carroll, Lewis, *Alice's Adventures in Wonderland.*

Cox, Archibald, *The Role of the Supreme Court in American Government.*

Crawford, Susan, *Captive Audience: The Telecom Industry and Monopoly Power in the New Gilded Age.*

De Tocqueville, Alexis, *Democracy In America.*

Dalai Lama, (His Holiness), *Ethics for the New Millenium.*

Ellis, Joseph, *Founding Brothers.*

Emerson, Ralph Waldo, *Self-Reliance.*

Franklin, Benjamin, *The Way to Wealth.*

Friedman, Milton, *Capitalism and Freedom.*

Friedman, Thomas L., *Hot, Flat, and Crowded.*

Hamilton, Alexander, *The Federalist Papers.*

Hochshild, Jennifer, *Facing Up to the American Dream: Race, Class, and the Soul of the Nation.*

Holmes, Oliver Wendall, *The Common Law.*

Hunt, Galliard, ed., *The Writings of James Madison.*

Jacobson, David, *The English Libertarian Heritage.*

Ketcham, Ralph, *The Anti-Federalist Papers and the Constitutional Convention Debates.*

------------, -------, *James Madison: A Biography.*

King, Martin Luther, *Where Do We Go From Here: Chaos or Community.*

Lao Tzu, *Tao Te Ching.*

Levi, Edward, *An Introduction to Legal Reasoning.*

Lippman, Walter, *The Public Philosophy.*

Locke, John, *The Second Treatise of Civil Government.*

Lusky, Louis, *Democracy and Distrust.*

Madison, James, *The Federalist Papers.*

Pangle, Lorraine, *The Political Philosophy of Benjamin Franklin.*

Paton, Alan, *Cry, The Beloved Country.*

Sandburg, Carl, *Abraham Lincoln: The War Years.*

Schlesinger, Arthur, T*he Age of Jackson.*

--------------, --------, "*The Crisis of the Old Order, 1919-1933, Vol. I, The Age of Roosevelt.*"

--------------, --------, "*The Coming of the New Deal: Vol. II, of The Age of Roosevelt.*"

--------------, --------, "*The Politics of Upheaval: Vol. III, The Age of Roosevelt.*"

--------------, --------, The *Imperial Presidency.*

Shammas, Carole, *Inheritance in America: From Colonial Times to the Present.*

Sorkin, Andrew Ross, *Too Big To Fail.*

Soros, George, *The New Paradigm For Financial Markets.*

Wood, Gordon, *The Creation of the American Republic.*

Notes

Chapter 1. The Origins of the American Experiment in Governance

1 John Locke, *Two Treatises of Government*, Peter Laslett, ed., (Cambridge: Cambridge University Press, 2012), 271.

2 Ibid., 302.

3 Bernard Bailyn, *The Ideological Origins of the American Revolution*, (Cambridge: Belknap Press of Harvard University Press, 1967), 36; Gordon Wood, (Chapel Hill: University of North Carolina Press, 1969); see also, Bernard Bailyn, *Pamphlets of the American Revolution*, (Cambridge: Belknap Press of Harvard University, 1965).

4 David Louis Jacobson, *The English Libertarian Heritage*, (Indianapolis: Bobbs-Merrill, 1965), 127, 129.

5 Ibid.

6 Ibid., 131.

7 Charles Frances Adams, *The Works of John Adams*, (Boston: Little Brown and Company, 1850–1856).

8 Gaillard Hunt, *The Writings of James Madison*, (New York: G. Putnam's Sons, 1900).

9 Ibid., 22.

10 Ibid., 527.

11 U.S. Constitution, Preamble.

12 Ralph Ketcham, *The Anti-Federalist Papers and the Constitutional Convention Debates*, (New York: Penquin Books, 1986), 5.

13 Ibid.

14 Ibid.

15 James Madison, Alexander Hamilton, John Jay, the *Federalist Papers*, No. 10, Ralph Gabriel, ed., (New York: The Liberal Arts Press, 1954), 10-11.

16 Ibid., 12, 13.

17 Ibid., 12.

18 Ibid., 18.

19 Ibid., 19.

20 Ibid.

21 Ketcham, 173.

22 Ibid.

23 Ibid., 199.

24 Hamilton, the *Federalist Papers*, No. 67, 141

25 Hamilton, the *Federalist Papers*, No. 71, 154.

26 Ibid.

27 Ibid., the *Federalist Papers*, No. 78, 169.

Chapter 2. Curing the Mischiefs of Factions

28 Madison, the *Federalist Papers*, No. 10, 12.

29 Ibid., 13.

30 Ibid., 10, 11.

31 Ibid., 19.

32 Ibid., 12.

33 Ibid., 11.

34 Ibid., 13.

35 Watch the Rick Santelli, "Rant of the Year," on YouTube, uploaded on February 19, (2009), as part of CNBC's business programming.

36 Jim Geraghty, "A Short History of the Tea Parties," National Review Online, nationalreview.com, June 28, (2011). See Also: David E. Campbell and Robert D. Putnam, "Crashing the Tea Party," the *New York Times*, opinion page, Nytimes.com, August 16, (2011) and Alan J. Abramowitz, "Partisan Polarization and the Rise of the Tea Party Movement,"Faculty.washington.edu, (a paper presented at the conference of the American Political Science Association), (2011).

37 For a brief overview of the origins of FreedomWorks see: FreedomWorks-Ballotpedia, ballotpedia.org; See Also: Brendan DeMelle, "Study Confirms Tea Party was Created by Big Tobacco and Billionaire Koch Brothers," www.huffingtonpost.com/study, February 11, (2013). and David Corn, "Dick Armey: 'This kind of secrecy is why I left FreedomWorks, *Mother Jones*, motherjones.com, December 7, (2012).

38 The supporting rationales for the Tea Party Patriot's "core principles" have been modified since the initial investigation was instituted. Depending upon which separate group is established under the umbrella of Tea Party Patriots, various perspectives have been offered to support their functioning. However, the central organization, under the heading of "Core Values," continues to claim three principles: Free market economics, constitutionally limited government and fiscal responsibility. The analysis provided by this investigation of their previous "principles" and rationales remains relevant regarding their contemporaneous understanding of the founding vision and our Constitution. For a general snapshot of the "interpretations" of our constitutional history articulated by the fragmented groups using the umbrella name of Tea Party Patriots see: The Mission Statement of the Lanier Tea Party Patriots. Note their understanding of Fiscal Responsibility; Personal Responsibility; National Sovereignty; State Sovereignty; and Philosophy, Lanier Tea Party Patriots, laniertea-partypatriots.org.

39 Madison, the *Federalist Papers*, No. 39, 45.

40 Ibid., 50.

41 His views on government were expressed clearly in an interview with Stephen Kroft on CBS News, uploaded by CBS News to YouTube, www.cbsnews.com/.../the-pledge-grover-norquists, November 29, (2011).

42 For additional information regarding the membership and activities of the American Legislative Exchange Council, see: Molly Jackman, Fellow, Brookings Institute, "ALEC's Influence over Lawmaking in State Legislatures,"www.brookings.edu/.../06, December 6, (2013).

43 Zeke Miller, "The Keeper of the Tax Pledge,"the *Atlantic*, theatlantic.com, November 21, (2011).

44 Jerry Taylor and Peter Van Doren, "Why Grover Norquist Is Wrong about Taxes," *Forbes*, www.forbes.com/sites.../2011, August 25, (2011).

45 Paul Bedard, "Grover Norquist gets his wish—both of them," Washington Secrets, the *Washington Examiner*, August 16, (2012).

46 Madison, the *Federalist Papers*, No. 10, 13.

Chapter 3 The People's Representatives—The Founding Vision and Contemporary Political Demographisc

47 James Madison, the *Federalist Papers*, No. 52, 102.

48 Ibid.

49 Ibid.

50 Ibid.

51 Ibid., 104.

52 Madison, the *Federalist Papers*, No. 53, 104.

53 Ibid.

54 Ibid., 106.

55 Ibid., 107.

56 Ibid., 108, 109.

57 Ibid., No. 57, 111.

58 Ibid., 112.

59 Ibid., 113.

60 Ibid., 114.

61 Ibid., No. 62, 116.

62 Ibid., 117.

63 Ibid., 118, 119.

64 Ibid., 119.

65 For an excellent review of wealth creation and income inequality in America, see: John Cassidy, "American Inequality In Six Charts," the *New Yorker*, newyorker.com, November 18, (2013). See also: Stone, Trisi, Sherman and Chew, "A Guide to Statistics on Historical Trends in Income Inequality," Center on Budget and Policy Priorities, cbpp.org, December 5, (2013).

66 Adriel Bettelheim and Jay Hunter, "50 Richest Members of Congress: The Wealth Keeps Growing," *Roll Call*, rollcall.com, September 13, (2013).

67 For an overview of the demographic composition of the 113th Congress see: "Congress Diversity Peaks as 113th Class Members are Sworn In," *Huffington Post*, huffingtonpost.com, January 1, (2010).

68 Tarini Parti, "7 Billion Spent on 2012 campaign, FEC says," Politico, politico.com, January 31, (2013).

69 Alexander Hamilton, the *Federalist Papers*, No. 71, 152.

Chapter 4. Freedom of the Press and the Shaping of an Enlightened Citizenry

70 70 Alexander Hamilton, the *Federalist Papers*, No. 84, 194.

71 Ibid.

72 Ibid.

73 Ibid., 195.

74 Alexis De Tocqueville, *Democracy In America*, ed. Richard D. Heffner, (New York: Mentor Books, 1956), 94, 95.

75 Ibid.

76 250 U. S. 616 (1919)(Dissenting opinion of Justice Oliver W. Holmes), 631.

77 See generally: 47 U. S. Code sec. 154.

78 For a wide ranging examination of NewsCorp and its activities, ownership, and lobbying of politicians see: OpenSecrets.org, Center for Responsive Politics, "Profile for 2014 Election Cycle."

79 For a description of Comcast and its ownership and holdings see: "Who Owns the Media," *Free Press*, freepress.net, 2014. See also: "The FCC's Big Move to Curb Media Consolidation," Free Press, freepress.net/blog/2014.

80 Ibid.

81 Susan Crawford, *Captive Audience: The Telecom Industry and Monopoly Power In the New Gilded Age*, (New Haven: Yale University Press, 2012).

82 Steven R. Weisman, ed., *Daniel Patrick Moynihan: A Portrait in Letters of an American Visionary*, (New York: Public Affairs, 2010).

83 Courtney Coren, "PPP Poll: Fox News Most Trusted TV New Source Five Years in a Row," *News Max*, newsmax.com, (January 31, 2014). An analysis of the data from the survey provides a different understanding of the survey participants opinions than the title of this report indicates. 57% of the Americans polled say that they "trust" PBS, while only 24% did not.

Chapter 5. We the People—A Reinvigoration of Citizenship in America

84 This commentary is attributed to Dr. James McHenry, one of Maryland's delegates to the Constitutional Convention of 1787. His notes of the convention were included in the Records of the Federal Convention of 1787. The date of the quotation remains "uncertain." See: McHenry's notes first published in the *American Historical Review*, vol. II, 1906.

85 Benjamin Franklin, Speech in Defense of the Constitution at the Constitutional Convention of 1787, as quoted in, *Benjamin Franklin: An American Life*, (New York: Simon and Schuster, 2004).

86 See generally, Thomas Jefferson writing about "Educating the People," collected by Reid Cornwell, The Center for Internet Research, (TCFIR), http://tcfir.org.

87 Thomas Jefferson writing in support of the Diffusion of Knowledge Bill, 1779, FE 2:221, Papers, 2:526, Jefferson on *Politics and Government: Educating the People*, famguardian.org/subjects/politics/thomasjefferson/jeff1350.htm.

88 "83 Percent of U.S. Adults Fail Test on Nation's Founding," PRNewswire, prnewswire.com, (December 2, 2009).

89 For a detailed report of the findings of the survey see: *The Guardian of Democracy : The Civic Mission of Schools*, Annenberg Public Policy Center, www.civicyouth.org/wp-content/uploads/2011.

90 Andrew Romano, "How Ignorant Are Americans?" *Newsweek*, newsweek.com, (March 20, 2011).

91 See generally: James Fishkin, *Democracy and Deliberations: New Directions for Democratic Reform*, (New Haven: Yale University Press, 1991).

92 Madison, the *Federalist Papers*, No. 576, 113.

93 Colin Moynihan, "In Occupy; Well-educated Professionals Far Outweighed Jobless, Study Finds," *New York Times*, (January 28, 2013).

94 Ibid. (Discussing why she and her co-authors, Professor Stephanie Luce and Professor Penny Lewis, began their study looking at the "backgrounds and motivations" of Occupy Supporters.) The study was produced by the Joseph A. Murphy Institute For Worker Education and Labor Studies. For a detailed analysis of the research see: Changing the Subjective Bottom-up Account of Occupy Wall Street New York City.

95 Ralph Waldo Emerson, *Essays: First Series Essay II*, Self-Reliance, (1841).

96 See: Law School Admission Council, Test Format, What the Test Measures, LSAC.org (2014).

97 Adam Robinson, Kevin Blemel, (updated by Mindy Eve Myers, Bob Sproill and Andrew Brody), Cracking the LSAT, *The Princeton Review*, (New York: Random House, 2013).

98 See: National Conference of Bar Examiners, The Multi State Bar Examination (overview of the MBE), ncbex.org, (2014).

99 Ibid.

Chapter 6. In Search of Political Compromise In An Environment of Gridlock: A Return to the Founding First Principles

100 James Madison, the *Federalist Papers*, No. 62, 117.

101 For an excellent historical description of the interpersonal relationships of John Adams, Benjamin Franklin, Alexander Hamilton, Thomas Jefferson, James Madison, and George Washington, see: Joseph J. Ellis, *Founding Brothers: the Revolutionary Generation*, (New York: Alfred A. Knopf, 2001).

102 Schenck v U. S., 249 U.S. 47 (1919), Debs v U.S., 249 U.S. 211 (1919), and Abrams v U.S., 250 U.S. 616 (1919), Gitlow v New York, 268 U.S. 652 (1925), Dennis v U.S., 341 U.S., 341 U.S. 494 (1951), and Brandenburg v Ohio, 395 U.S. 444 (1969).

103 Chaplinsky v New Hampshire, 315 U.S. 568 (1942), Terminiello v Chicago, 337 U.S. 1 (1949), Feiner v New York, 340 U.S. 315 (1951), and a case which involved "offensive words," Cohen v. California, 403 U.S. 15 (1971).

104 Near v. Minnesota, 283 U.S. 697 (1931).

105 New York Times Co. v Sullivan, 376 U.S. 255 (1964).

106 Reynolds v. U.S., 98 U.S. 145 (1879).

107 Cantwell v. Connecticut, 310 U.S. 296 (1940).

108 554 U.S. 570 (2008).

109 Ibid., Scalia, majority opinion., 22.

110 Ibid.

111 Ibid., Stevens, dissenting opinion., 12, 13.

112 Ibid., 46.

113 Bruce Drake, "A Year After Newtown, Little Change in Public Opinion on Guns," Fact-Tank: New in the Numbers, pewresearch.org, (December 12, 2013). This article cites numerous surveys which found support ranging from 49% to 90% from the public on differing proposals to regulate gun safety.

114 The Public Safety and Second Amendment Rights Protection Act, Senate Bill 649, (2013).

115 Drake, note 14.

116 James Madison, the *Federalist Papers*, No. 62, 117.

117 See also Grassley's prepared statement on the motion to proceed in "debate" on gun safety bill, www.grassley.senate.gov, (April 11, 2013) and Jonathan Weisman, "Senate Blocks Drive for Gun Control," www.nytimes.com/2013/04/18/us, (April 17, 2013).

118 Ibid.

119 Alexis De Tocqueville, Democracy in America, 94, 95.

Chapter 7. That the Public Good is Disregarded in the Conflicts of Rival Parties

120 For the organization's general objectives see: www.freedomworks.org/; for another view of the organization see: FreedomWorks, Source Watch.org/index.php/freedomworks and, FreedomWorks for America, FactCheck.org/2014/02.

121 For a report on Romney's observation and its impact, see: Ezra Klein, "Romney's Theory of the 'takers class', and Why it Matters," WashingtonPost.com, (September 17, 2012).

122 Lewis Carroll, *Alice's Adventures in Wonderland*, (New York: The Dial Press, 1935).

123 Ibid., 8.

124 See: "Estimates of Federal Tax Expenditures for Fiscal Year 2007–2011," prepared for the House Committee on Ways and Means and the Senate Committee on Finance, by the Staff of the Joint Committee on Taxation, (2007); for an analysis see: Daniel Weiss, "Big Oil, Big Profits, Big Tax Breaks,"realpolitics.com, (January 17, 2014).

125 Elaine Magilaro, "Wealthy "Faux Farmers" Get Huge Agricultural Tax Breaks on Their Properties," submitted to jonathanturley.org, (April 17, 2011).

126 Ibid.

127 Carroll, *Alice's Adventures in Wonderland*, 105.

128 See generally: FreedomWorks, www.freedomworks.org.

129 James Hammerton, "The Hidden Cost of Regulation," www.freedonworks.org, (June 10, 2011).

130 Ibid.

131 Discussing "regulation," www.freedomworks.org.

132 Logan, Albright, "Why So Many Regulations Make So Little Sense," www.freedonworks.org, (April 24, 2013).

133 5 U.S.C.A. section 501, et. Seq.

134 Pendleton Civil Service Reform Act of 1883 (Ch. 27, 22 Stat. 403).

135 Enacted into law October 13, 1978, Pub. L. 95-454, 92 Stat. 1111.

136 Clyde Wayne Crews and Ryan Young, "America's Soaring Regulations Cost $1.8 Trillion A Year," news.investors.com, (May 29, 2013). See also: Clyde Wayne Crews, "Ten Thousand Commandments 2013," Competitive Enterprise Institute, cei.org/studies/ten-thousand-commandments. (May 21, 2013).

137 Albert Kleine, "What the Media Should Know About the Competitive Enterprise Institute's Regulation Report," Media Matters for America, mediamatters.org/blog/2013/05/20/.

138 Ibid.

139 Ibid. Bureau of Labor Statistics, the National Federation of Independent Business (EPI analysis of NIF113 small business survey data through 2011, quarter 2.).

140 Office of Management and Budget Annual Report on Costs and Benefits of Major Rules Implemented 2011.

141 R. L. Revesz and Michael A. Livermore, "Who Benefits from Regulation?" huffingtonpost.com (February 23, 2011.

142 Ibid.

143 Carroll, *Alice's Adventures in Wonderland*, 104.

Chapter 8. Designing the "Least Imperfect" Government: Eighteenth Century Insight for the Twenty First Century

144 Benjamin Franklin, Speech at the Constitutional Convention, III. Dangers of a Salaried Bureaucracy, bartleby.com (Philadelphia: June 28, 1787).

145 For an excellent overview of the impact of the "great recession" and its so-called "recovery" see: Richard Fry and Paul Taylor, "A Rise in Wealth for the Wealthy; Declines for the lower 93%," Pew Research Center's Social and Demographic Trends Project, www.pewsocialtrends/org/files/2013/04. See also: United States Census, U.S. Department of Commerce, highlights, (2012).

146 See Chapter 1, endnotes 1-7.

147 Ibid.

148 David Jacobson, ed., *The English Libertarian Heritage: From the Writings of John Trenchard and Thomas Gordon in the Independent Whig and Cato's Letters*, (Indianapolis: Bobbs-Merrill Co., 1965), 127, 128.

149 Omitted from Locke's observations in his writings on "the State of Nature," sec. 6 in our

Declaration of Independence are the following words, "...take away, or impair the life, or what tends to the presentation of life, the liberty, health, limb, or goods of an other."

150 James Madison, the *Federalist Papers*, No. 10, 19.

151 Joann S. Lubin, "CEO Pay in 2010 Jumped 11%," *Wall Street Journal*, onlline.wsj.com, (May 9, 2011).

152 Marylynn Salmon, Michel Dahlin, and Carole Shammas, *Inheritance in America: From Colonial Times to the Present*, (New Brunswick: Rutgers University Press, 1987).

153 Anthony Carnevale and Stephen Rose, "Socioeconomic Status, Race/Ethnicity, and Selective College Admissions: A Century Foundation Paper," www.tcf.org/Publications/Education/carnevalerose.pdf, (March, 2003). See also: Alexander W. Astin and Leticia Oseguera, "The Declining 'Equity' of American Higher Education," *The Review of Higher Education*, Volume 27, Number 3, Spring 2004, 321-341, muse.jhu.edu.

Chapter 9. Marketing a Twenty First Century Anti-Federalist Vision for America: An Examination of the Claims and Solutions

154 Mark R. Levin, *The Liberty Amendments: Restoring the American Republic*, (New York: Simon and Schuster, 2013).

155 Cal Thomas, "A Constitutional Cure for What Ails Us," Townhall, townhall.com, (August 15, 2013).

156 Levin, *The Liberty Amendments: Restoring the American Republic*, (New York: Simon and Schuster, 2013).

157 Ibid., 1.

158 Ibid.

159 Ibid., 2.

160 Ibid., 17.

161 Ibid., 18.

162 Ibid.

163 James Madison, the *Federalist Papers*, No. 10 (New York: Liberal Arts Press, 1954), 19.

164 Levin, *The Liberty Amendments: Restoring the American Republic*, 10.

165 Ibid.

166 Ibid.

167 Madison, the *Federalist Papers*, No. 14, "Objections to the Proposed Constitution from Extent of Territory Answered," http://www.constitution.org/fed/federal14 htm, (November 30, 1787).

168 Madison, the *Federalist Papers*, No. 44, (New York: Liberal Arts Press, 1954), 65.

169 Ibid.

170 Levin, *The Liberty Amendments: Restoring the American Republic*, 11.

171 Ibid.

172 Patrick Henry, Speech Delivered at the Virginia Ratifying Convention 1788, (New York: Penguin Books, 1986), 199.

173 Mr. Levin's view of the alleged role of "progressives" can be noted throughout the book. While he does not provide much clarity regarding what he believes to be the influence of "progressive" thinking regarding Supreme Court decision-making, one can deduce that he believes that "progressive" inspired rationales of the Court which balance competing societal, cultural and economic perspectives are indications of a conspiratorial "judicial oligarchy" bent on usurping his view of "liberty."

174 Levin, *The Liberty Amendments: Restoring the American Republic*, 34.

175 Ibid., 35.

176 Madison, the *Federalist Papers*, No. 39, 45.

177 Ibid., 48.

178 Ibid.

179 Ibid.

180 Madison, the *Federalist Papers*, No. 57, 113.

181 Levin, *The Liberty Amendments: Restoring the American Republic*, 30.

182 Ibid., 27.

183 Madison, the *Federalist Papers*, No. 62, 117.

184 Galliard Hunt, ed., *Writings of James Madison, In Letter to Jefferson*, (New York: J Putnam's Sons, 1900).

185 Kurt T. Lash, "The Lost Original Meaning of the Ninth Amendment," Texas Law Review, Vol. 83, No. 2 (2004). For Professor Lash's recent publications regarding this subject see: *The Lost History of the Ninth Amendment*, (Oxford: Oxford University Press, 2009). "The Original Meaning of an Omission: The Tenth Amendment, Popular Sovereignty, and "Expressly" Delegated Power," *Notre Dame Law Review*, Vol. 83, 5, (2008). For another analysis of the subject see: Randy Barnett, *The Rights Retained by the People: The History and Meaning of the Ninth Amendment*, (Washington D.C.: George Mason University Press, 1989). For Professor Barnett's more recent work see: *Restoring the Lost Constitution: The Presumption of Liberty*, (Amazon.com: Books, 2005).

186 Levin, *The Liberty Amendments: Restoring the American Republic*, 30.

187 Lash, "The Lost Original Meaning of the Ninth Amendment," 337.

188 Ibid., 336.

189 Ibid., 338.

190 Ibid., 337.

191 Levin, *The Liberty Amendments: Restoring the American Republic,* 5.

192 Ibid., 66.

193 60 U.S. 393 (1856).

194 163 U.S.537 (1896).

195 323 U.S. 214 (1944).

196 See: Brown v Board of Education, 347 U.S. 483 (1954). For a discussion of the impact of the Korematsu case and the Court's subsequent decision-making on the subject generally see: Fritz Snyder, "Overreaction Then(Korematsu) and Now (the Detainee Cases)," *University of Montana School of Law Journal*, Vol. 2, Issue I, (Winter, 2009).

197 Levin, *The Liberty Amendments: Restoring the American Republic*, 7.

198 379 U.S. 241 (1964), 379 U.S. 294 (1964).

199 379 U.S. 241, 259 (1964).

200 Ibid., 262.

201 317 U.S. 111 (1942).

202 Levin, *The Liberty Amendments: Restoring the American Republic*, 64.

203 Public Law, 73-10, Stat. 48 Stat.31 (1933).

204 317 U.S. 111, 128.

205 Ibid.

206 For a list of Mr. Levin's "solutions," see: *The Liberty Amendments: Restoring the American Republic*, 209–219.

207 330 U.S. 1 (1947).

208 381 U.S. 479 (1965).

209 457 U.S. 202 (1982).

210 539 U.S. 558 (2003).

211 132 S. Ct. 2566 (2012).

212 Levin, *The Liberty Amendments: Restoring the American Republic*, 64.

213 U.S. Constitution, A III.

214 See generally, Levin, *The Liberty Amendments: Restoring the American Republic*, 49-71.

215 Ibid., 69.

Conclusion

216 Mark Warren, "The New American Center," *Esquire*, www.esquire.com, (October 15, 2013), 138-150.

217 Gailliard Hunt, *The Writings of James Madison*, (New York: G Putnam's Sons, 1900), 523.

218 James Madison, the *Federalist Papers*, No. 10, (New York: Liberal Arts Press, 1954), 10,11.

219 Ibid., 19.

220 Alexander Hamilton, the *Federalist Papers*, No 71, (New York: Liberal Arts Press, 1954) 152.

221 Madison, the *Federalist Papers*, No. 10, 13.

222 Ibid., No 53, 104.

223 Ibid., No. 75, 111.

224 Ibid., 113.

225 Alexander Hamilton, the *Federalist Papers*, No. 84, 195.

226 Thomas Jefferson, On Politics and Government, Educating the People, famguardian.org: See also: www.uni.edu/icss/352/sp11/top2.html.

227 Thomas Jefferson, *A Bill for the More General Diffusion of Knowledge 1779*, people.cehd. tamu.edu.

228 Benjamin Franklin, www.ourrepubliconline.com/author/21.

229 Benjamin Franklin, *Speaking in Favor of the Proposed Constitution at Constitutional Convention of 1787*, www.pbs.org/benfranklin/pop-finalspeech.html.

230 Madison, the *Federalist Papers*, No. 62, 117.

231 Benjamin Franklin, Vol. 111, Wealth, Corruption, Debt and Taxes, www.foundersvbush. com/wealth-corruption-debt-taxes.html. See also: Lorraine Smith Pangle, *The Political Philosophy of Benjamin Franklin*, (Baltimore: the John Hopkins University Press, 2007).

232 Benjamin Franklin, in a letter to Robert Morris, 25 December, 1793, press-pubs.uchicago. edu/founders/documents/v1ch16512.html.

233 This figure has vacilated over the past two years. As of January 14, 2014, the approval rating "climbed" to 13%, www.gallup.com/pol/166838.congress-pub-appeal-starts-2014.aspx.

Public Policy Objectives: Comments and Questions

234 Benjamin Franklin is often quoted as saying that, "It is the first responsibility of every citizen to question authority." Whether this attribution is historically accurate or not, the observation certainly reflects his and the other Founders' vision of concentrated power and the need for its constant monitoring by the people.

235 Thomas Jefferson, writing in support of the Diffusion of Knowledge Bill, (FE 2:221, papers 2:526, 1779). For more of Jefferson's observations on the importance of an educated citizenry, see: *Thomas Jefferson, On Politics and Government, Educating the People*, famquardian. org. See also: www.univ.edu/icss/352/sp11/top2.html.

236 Galliard Hunt, *The Writings of James Madison*, (New York: G. Putnam's Sons, 1900), 272.

237 Ibid., 523.

238 James Madison, the *Federalist Papers*, No. 39, (New York: Liberal Arts Press, 1954), 48.

239 Ibid., No. 57, 111.

240 David Leip, 2012 Presidential General Election Results, uselectionatlas.org/2012.php.

241 See: Sam Wang, "The Great Gerrymander of 2012," www.nytimes.com/2013/02/03. For a different analysis see: John Sides and Eric McGhee, "Redistricting Didn't Win Republicans the House," washingtonpost.com, (February 17, 2013); electionlawblog.org/?p=47401.

242 372 U.S. 368 (1963).

243 Ibid., 381.

244 376 U.S. 1 (1964).

245 Ibid., 8.

246 377 U.S. 533 (1964).

247 Ibid., (Justice Warren, majority opinion), 533.

248 Ibid., 566.

249 Ibid., 568.

250 Ibid., 578.

251 Lucas v Forty-Forth Government Assembly of Colorado, 377 U.S. 749 (1964).

252 Ibid., 750.

253 Ibid., 752, 754.

254 For an interesting analysis of "open primaries" see: Tom Murse, "Open Primary—Definition," uspolitics.about.com; see also: "Congressional and Presidential Primaries: Open, Closed, Semi-Closed, and "Top Two," the Center for Voting and Democracy, fairvote.org.

255 Ibid.

256 Article XX of California Constitution, Redistricting of Senate, Assembly, Congressional and Board of Equalization istricts.

257 Ibid., Sections 1-4.1; for Citizens Redistricting Commission Selection Process see: section 8252, California Voter Information Guide, wedrawthelines.ca.gov.

258 Ibid.

259 Murse, "Open Primary—Definition."

260 Ibid.

261 For a discussion of the differing viewpoints regarding the impact of the "Top Two" primary process, see: Jean Meri, 'Top Two' Shakes it Up, Los Angles Times, (February 15, 2014). articles.latimes.com; and, Logan Brown, "Analysts Say Top Two Primary Right for Independent Shift in California Electorate," ivn.us, (February 24, 2014).

262 Ibid.

263 John Cassidy, "Piketty's Inequality Story in Six Charts," newyorker.com, (March 26, 2014); see also: Chad Stone, Danilo Trisi, Arloc Sherman and William Chen, A Guide to Statistics on Historical Trends in Income Inequality, Center on Budget and Policy Priorities, chpp.org, (December 5, 2013).

264 Carole Shammas, Marylynn Salmon, and Michael Dahlin, Inheritance in America: From Colonial Times to the Present, (New Brunswick: Rutgers University Press, 1987).

265 Ibid.

266 Gary H. Stern and Ron J. Feldman, Too Big To Fail: The Hazards of Bank Bailouts, (Washington, D.C.: Brookings Institution Press, 2004). See also: Mike Konczal, "Dodd-Frank is Finally Being Implemented. Will that be enough?" washingtonpost.com, (May 6, 2013).

267 Alexander Arapoglou and Jerri-Lynn Scofield, "10 Tax Dodges That Help the Rich Get Richer," alternet.org, (April 11, 2013).

268 For differing analyses which come to similar conclusions regarding the impact of "tax cuts" on job creation, see: Bill Harris, "Tax Cuts Don't Create Jobs," forbes.com, (November 5, 2012); Olivia Sandbothe, "New Study Shows that Corporate Tax Cuts Won't Create Jobs,"

afscme.org, (December 18, 2013), citing a report from the Center for Effective Government, Scott Klinger and Katherine McFate, "The Corporate Tax Rate Debate: Lower Taxes on Corporate Profits Not Linked to Job Creation,"foreffectivegov.org, (December 3, 2013). For in yet another analysis see: Timothy J. Bartik, "Not All Job Creation Tax Credits Are Created Equal," Economic Policy Institute, epi.org, (February 12, 2012).

269 Steve Hargreaves, "The Myth of the American Dream," CNNMoney, money.cnn.com, (December 18, 2013), see also: Heather Wyatt-Nichol, "The Enduring Myth of the American Dream: Mobility, Marginalization, and Hope," *International Journal of Organization Theory and Behavior*, Vol. 14, issue 2, (January 6, 2011), 258-279.

270 For an excellent overview of the billions of dollars injected into the process of lobbying the Congress of the United States see: Lobbying Database, Center for Responsive Politics, opensecrets.org; See also: Ashley Portero, " 30 Major U S Corporations Paid More to Lobby Congress Than Income Taxes, 2008–2010," *International Business Times*, ibtimes.com, (December 9, 2011); Tyler Durden, "Who Spends the Most Dollars Lobbying Washington, D. C.?" ZeroHedge, zerohedge.com, (March 11, 2013), citing data extracted from the database collected and reported by the Center for Responsive Politics; and Tiffany Kaiser, "Comcast Paying Millions to Congress to Solidify Time Warner Cable," *DailyTech*, dailytech.com, (March 10, 2014).

271 John Locke, *The Second Treatise of Civil Government*, Chap V, "On Property," sec. 51, (Cambridge: Cambridge University Press, 1960), 302.

272 The entire commentary of Rick Santelli described as the "Rant of the Year" can be viewed at www.you.tube.com/wathc?v=bezb4taSE.A, (February 19, 2009).

273 Lorraine Smith Pangle, *The Political Philosophy of Benjamin Franklin*, quoting Franklin letter to Robert Morris, December 25, 1783 (Baltimore: John Hopkins University Press, 2007), 27.

274 Ibid.

275 Ibid.

276 Madison, the *Federalist Papers*, No. 10, 13.

277 Ezra Klein, "Romney's Theory of the "takers class," and Why it Matters," *Washington Post*, washingtonpost.com, (September 17, 2012). For a video of Republican Presidential candidate Mitt Romney's commentary to campaign funders see: David Corn, "Secret video: Romney Tells Millionaire Donors What he Really Thinks of Obama Voters," *Mother Jones*, motherjones.com, (September 17, 2012).

278 Jonathan Wells, "7 Ways to Look at Money Differently," Advanced Life Skills—Recreating Your Reality, advancelifeskills.com ; See also: Desmond Berghofer and Geraldine Schwartz, "Ethical Leadership: Right Relationships and the Emotional Bottom Line—The Gold Standard for Success, Institute for Ethical Leadership, ien.arch.virginia.edu, http://www.ethical leadership.com/BusinessArticle.htm, (March 22, 2013); For a completely different perspective on the subject of greed see: Milton Freidman, *Capitalism Freedom*, (Chicago: University of Chicago Press, 1962).

279 Carole Shammas, Marylynn Salmon, and Michael Dahlin, *Inheritance in America: From Colonial Times to Present*, (New Brunswick: Rutgers University Press, 1987).

280 These figures, initially reported in 2007, continue to be debated: For an analysis of these and other statistics presented regarding taxation and public policy proposals see: Chuck Marr and Chye-Ching Huang, "Misconceptions and Realities About Who Pays Taxes," Center on Budget and Policy Priorities, cbpp.org, (September 17, 2012). See also: Josh Barro, "Is It True That Only 85 Million Americans Pay Federal Tax? No." *Forbes*, forbes.com, (April 17, 2012).

281 Ibid.

282 See generally: Stone, Trisi, Sherman, and Chen, "A Guide to Statistics on Historical Trends in Income Inequality," Center on Budget and Policy Priorities, cbpp.org, (December 5, 2013).

283 H.R. 8 (112th): American Taxpayer Relief Act of 2012.

284 For an analysis of the potential impact of this legislation on Americans see: Shari A. Levitan, Edward F. Koren, and Abigail B. O'Connor, "The American Taxpayer Relief Act of 2012: What it Means for You," www.hklaw.com/abc.aspx?xpST=abc&url=http%2F%2Fwww, (January 4, 2013).

285 For a snapshot of the "wealth distribution" of Americans as compared with other citizens of the "developed world" see: Drew DeSilver, "5 Facts About Economic Inequality," Pew Research Center, www.pewresearch.org/fact-tank/2014, (January 7, 2014).

286 Luisa Kroll and Kerry A. Dolan, "Inside the 2013 Forbes 400: Facts and Figures on America's Richest," *Forbes*, forbes.com, (September 16, 2013).

287 Emmanuel Saez, "Striking it Richer: The Evolution of Top Incomes in the United States (Updated with 2012 preliminary estimates), elsa.berkeley.edu/-saez/saez-UStopincomes-2012.pdf, (September 3, 2013).

288 G. William Domhoff, "Wealth, Income, and Power," Who Rules America, www2.uscsc.edu/whorulesamerica/power/wealth.html, (update February, 2013).

289 There are "variations" on a theme when it comes to the amount of capital gains tax each citizen is required to pay. Depending upon whether the "gain" is short-term or "long-term" and depending upon the "income bracket" each person falls within different rates apply. For an excellent discussion of the subject see: Motely Fool, "5 Myths about Capital Gains Tax in 2014," nasdaq.com, (February 22, 2014).

290 Alexander Arapoglou and Jerri-Lynn Scofield, "10 Tax Dodges That Help the Rich Get Richer," alternet.org, (April 11, 2013).

291 Ibid.

292 Ibid.

293 For differing perspectives on the benefits and detriments of this provision with the tax code, see: Richard Morrison, "Eliminating Mortgage Interest Deduction a Risky Move," the Tax Foundation, taxfoundation org/, (July 29, 2013). For a different analysis see: Jeremy Horpedahl and Harrison Searles. "The Home Mortgage Interest Deduction," Mercatus Center George Mason University, mercatus.org/publication/home-mortgage-interest-deduction, (January 8, 2013).

294 Ibid.

295 Report from the Peterson-Pew Commission, "The Tax break-down: Preferential Rates on Capital Gains, Committee for a Responsible Federal Budget, crfb.org, (August 27, 2013).

296 Alexander Arapoglou and Jerri-Lynn Scofield, "10 Tax Dodges That Help the Rich Get Richer," alternet.org, (April 11, 2013).

297 Some tax experts point out that trillions of dollars are not "off-shore." They argue that they are simply not taxed through the use of a provision in the tax code known as "deferral" used for "accounting" purposes. For an extended analysis of the subject of corporate off-shore profits see: Kitty Richards and John Craig, "Offshore Corporate Profits: The Only Thing 'Trapped' is Tax Revenue, Center for American Progress, americanprogress.org, TrappedRevenue-brief1.pdf, (January 9, 2014). And for but another perspective see: Joseph F. Kovar, "Overseas Profits And the U.S. Tax Rate: Why IT Vendors Say Their Hands Are Tied," CRN, crn.com, (January 13, 2014).

298 Madison, the *Federalist Papers*, No. 10, 13.

299 Ibid.

300 Ibid., 19.

301 113 Stat. 1338, Public Law 100-102, November 12, 1999.

302 Ibid., See sections, Title 1-3.

303 Ibid.

304 Section 101 repeals Glass-Steagall.

305 For an excellent account of the collapse of the "financial industry" and the interaction of its "players" with each other and government officials see: Andrew Ross Sorkin, *Too Big To Fail: The Inside Story of How Wall Street and Washington Fought to Save the Financial System—And Themselves*, (New York: Penguin Books, 2009, 2010).

306 Ibid.

307 Ibid., 396, 397.

308 For an analysis of the efforts to repeal Glass-Steagall since its inception see: Corinne Crawford, "The Repeal of the Glass-Steagall Act and the Current Financial Crisis," *Journal of Business and Economics Research*, Vol. 9, Number I, 949-3747-1-PB-1.pdf, (January, 2011).

309 Stephen Gandel, "By Every Measure, the Big Banks Are Bigger," CNNMoney, finance.fortune.cnn.com, (September 13, 2013). At the time of this article/blog, the assets of the six largest American banks totaled to $1.4 trillion dollars.

310 Sorkin, *Too Big To Fail*, 554. Efforts by Senator Bernie Sanders of Vermont and Senators John McCain of Arizona and Maria Cantwell of Washington failed to receive support.

311 Public Law No. 111-203, 124 Stat. 1376 (2010)(codified in numerous sections of the United States Code).

312 Ibid.

313 4.2 Title II.

314 4.1 Title X.

315 Title VI, see:"The Volcker Rule," skadden.com FSR-The-Volcker-Rule-pdf.

316 Agence France-Presse, "Five Years After Lehman: Bank Regulation Incomplete," globalpost.com, (September 11, 2013). See also: Kevin McCoy, *USA Today*, "Dodd-Frank Act: After 3 Years, A Long To Do List," usatoday.com, www.usatoday.com/story/money/business/2013.../dodd-frank.../2377603, (September 12, 2013).

317 Tyler Durden, "How Goldman Found the Volcker Rule Loopholes," ZeroHedge, www.zerohedge.com/...how-goldman-found-volcker-rule-loopholes, (December 23, 2013). See also: Bonnie Kavoussi, "Volcker Rule To Restrict Banks' Proprietary Trading Contains Loopholes, Experts Say," *Huffington Post*, huffingtonpost.com, (April 3, 2014).

318 Ibid.

319 For differing views as to the future success of the multi-agency produced "Volcker Rule" in restricting proprietary trading among other high risk activities see: Charles Horn, Melissa hall and Julie A. Marcacci, "Community Bank TruPS CDOs Exempted From the Volcker Rule," Morgan Lewis, Mondaq, mondaq.com, www.mondaq.com/...Community+Bank+TruPS+CDOs+Exempted+from+t..., (January 23, 2014). Donna Borak, "Toughest Challenge is Still Ahead for the Volcker Rule," American Banker, americanbanker.com, www.americanbanker.com/...toughest-challenge-is-still-ahead-for-the-volc...,(December 10, 2013).

320 Steven O. Ludd, "Judicial Review of Administrative Discretion: Friend or Foe of the Administrative Process," *Administrative Theory and Praxis*, 16(2): 263-272, 1994.

321 Sorkin, *Too Big To Fail*, 554.

322 C. W., "The World Economic Forum: Speaking Louder Than Words," *The Economist*, economist.com, www.economist.com/blogs/freeexchange/2014/01/world-economic-forum, (January 22, 2014).

323 Watch the youTube video of Mr. Rohner and Mr. Rubenstein and others on the panel discussing the "Rebuilding of Trust in Finance," noted by J. Manning, internationalbanker.com, (January 21-24, 2014).

324 Madison, the *Federalist Papers*, No. 53, 104.

325 558 U.S. 310 (2010). Another recent decision of the Court has further expanded the rationales provided by the majority in Citizens United and struck down so-called "aggregate

contribution" limitations on campaign donations. See: McCutcheon v. FEC, No. 12-536, 2014 BL 89958 (U.S. Apr. 02, 2014, Court Opinion, www.2.bloomberglaw.com. It is important to note that this decision while allowing massive amounts of contributions to be given by individual donors, does not overturn FEC requirements for disclosure. To remain anonymous individuals would still need to secret themselves within corporate or union PACs. Thus, Citizens United remains an important obstacle for future legislation attempting to confront the problem of the influence of money on our political process.

326 Ibid., Justice Kennedy, majority opinion, 9.

327 Ibid., 10.

328 Ibid.

329 Ibid., 37.

330 Ibid., 39.

331 Madison, the *Federalist Papers,* No. 10, 12.

332 Ibid., 13.

333 558 U.S. 310 (2010), 39.

334 Bernard Bailyn, *Ideological Origins of the American Revolution,* (Cambridge: Harvard University Press, 1992), 5. Gordon Wood, Creation of the American Republic, 1776—1787, (Chapel Hill: University of North Carolina Press, 1969), 6.

335 Alex De Tocqueville, *Democracy in America,* (New York: Mentor Books, 1956), 94, 95.

336 Ibid.

337 558 U.S. 310 (2010), Justice Stevens, dissenting opinion, 6.

338 Ibid., 34.

339 Ibid., 35.

340 Ibid. Justice Stevens cited numerous sources see his footnote: Edwin Merrick Dodd, *American Business Corporations Until 1860,* (Cambridge: Harvard University Press, 1954), 197; Lawrence M. Friedman, *A History of American Law,* (New York: Simon and Schuster, 1973), 188, 189; Simeon Eben Baldwin, "American Business Corporations Before 1789," (*The American Historical Review: 1903*), 449,450—459.

341 Ibid., 36.

342 Ibid.

343 Ibid., 37, 38. (Citing Chief Justice John Marshall in Trustees of Dartmouth College v Woodward, 4 Wheat. 518 (1819), 636.

344 Ibid., 38.

345 558 U.S. 310, Justice Kennedy, majority opinion, argued that, "…there is, furthermore, little evidence of abuse that cannot be corrected by shareholders, 'through the procedures of corporate democracy'," citing First National Bank of Boston v Bellotti, 435 U.S. 765 (1978), 794.

346 In fact, one of the few points of agreement between the majority and the dissenters in Citizens United v FEC was their seeming unanimity that non-disclosure requirements of PACs should be maintained.

347 130 S. Ct.2811 (2010).

348 Ibid., 10.

Index

About the Author,
Steven O. Ludd

STEVEN O. LUDD IS A PROFESSOR Emeritus at Bowling Green State University. Dr. Ludd, a professor of Political Science, taught undergraduate and graduate students in classes of Constitutional Law, Administrative Law, and the Judicial Process. He is the recipient of numerous university honors for teaching and service including the Master Teacher award. With the collaboration of student organizations, he designed BGSU's Student Legal Services — the first pre-paid legal service program for students in Ohio. The co-editor of *Outlook On Ohio: Prospects and Priorities*, he has published numerous professional and academic articles on the constitutional right to privacy and the use of administrative discretion in public administrative agencies. As a member of the Ohio bar and Federal District Court, he was selected by the Court to be an Alternative Dispute Resolution Mediator and a Federal Court Monitor. He has worked with a variety of non-for-profit and local government entities on issues of dispute resolution. He received his law degree from Syracuse University College of Law and his Ph.D. from the Maxwell School of Citizenship and Public Affairs at Syracuse University.

www.ingramcontent.com/pod-product-compliance
Lightning Source LLC
Chambersburg PA
CBHW031502270326
41930CB00006B/210